PRAISE FOR *MI MARÍA*

"A crucial oral history by Puerto Ricar ___ Hurricane María and colonialism." — ___ *Drawing Blood* and *Brothers of the Gun* (___

"For a disaster born at the intersection of colonization and the climate crisis, only a first-person plural account can truly do justice in a post-tragedy landscape where there has been no justice. *Mi María: Surviving the Storm* is a triumph of eyewitness accounts that centers survivors and tells a three-dimensional truth that can only be pieced together from multiple perspectives." —AYA DE LEÓN, author, *Side Chick Nation*

"Through first-person narratives and biographical profiles *Mi María* offers a kaleidoscope of experiences and personal stories that take readers behind the headlines of Hurricane María. The book offers an important archive of experiences, challenges, and stories that are otherwise absent from mainstream coverage of Puerto Rico and is sure to be of interest to both current audiences and future generations of readers interested in the lived experience of one of the largest political and environmental disasters in US history. The chance to hear directly from those left out of national headlines is at once moving, unsettling, and eye-opening." —YARIMAR BONILLA, coeditor, *Aftershocks of Disaster: Puerto Rico Before and After the Storm*

"Passionate and urgent; heart-wrenching and deeply infuriating. *Mi María* holds space for us to process the multiple and ongoing traumas of Hurricane María—the violence and devastation of the storm itself, yes, but also the deep-seated traumas of state failure, colonial neglect, and capitalist corruption Puerto Ricans found themselves forced to find solutions to while rebuilding their communities in the aftermath of the storm. These are stories not just of resilience. They are stories of resistance, solidarity, and the ethos of mutual aid—the daring to radically reimagine our world in new ways when confronted with our own survival." —SARA AWARTANI, Committee on Ethnicity, Migration, and Rights at Harvard University

"Though the narrators in *Mi María* endure great hardship, their stories soar with strength and resolve and love of their fellow humans. Anyone who loves Puerto Rico must read this book." —DAVE EGGERS, writer, cofounder of Voice of Witness

Editorial Consultant and Project Collaborator
Jocelyn A. Géliga Vargas

Student Interviewers, Transcribers, and Translators
Marco A. Acosta León, Julianna M. Canabal Rodríguez, Alexandra Thaís Colón Rodríguez, Brenda Y. Flores Santiago, José A. Fuentes Bonilla, Daniela Isabel Mulero Morales, Andrea Isabel Ramírez Figueroa, Bryan Ramos Romero

Additional Transcribers
Barbara Beroza, Charles Bowles, Rachel Carle, Julie Chinitz, Willa Rae Culpepper, Molly Hawkins, Kaye Herranen, Ari Kim, Hannah Kramm, Josh Manson, Brenna Miller, Margaret O'Hare, Mai Serhan, Barbara Sheffels, Phoebe Ying Lok Stallabrass, Eliana Swerdlow, Marcella Villaça, Madison Wright, Amber Yearwood

Additional Research
Rebecca McCarthy, Carmen Merport

Curriculum Specialist
Zaira Arvelo Alicea

Fact-Checking
Reading List Editorial, readinglisteditorial.com

Copyeditor
Brian Baughan

*In honor of the thousands who lost their lives
in the long aftermath of Hurricane María*

INTRODUCTION

Telling Stories after the Storm

The first interview for this book was conducted in the spring of 2018, just seven months after Hurricane María decimated Puerto Rico. Zaira Arvelo Alicea and I met at an outdoor café on the plaza of Rincón, a town on the west coast of the main island. She had been staying at a tiny Airbnb since the hurricane destroyed her home in the nearby town of Aguadilla and was happy to have any excuse to escape for a little while and sit in the sunshine. We were worried about the noise on the plaza as supply trucks frequently rumbled past, people walked by loudly discussing the hurricane, and the reverberations of tools being used to rebuild nearby homes and shops echoed through the air. Eventually, though, we agreed that there had been too much silence after María, so we let the recording of our discussion capture the background sounds of the activity all around us. The commotion underscored the fact that we—and our communities—were still alive.

Although it was the first time we met, we talked for hours that day, eating big, sloppy burgers with piles of crispy fries as if everything were normal, even finding small reasons to laugh together. As the conversation went on, though, I think that we were both grateful to have the framework of an interview to fall back on. It gave us a kind of permission to speak, to let go of some of what we were holding on to, even though it was hard for Zaira to talk about what had happened to her and difficult for me to listen to her story.

1

Zaira and her husband, Juan Carlos, had survived the hurricane by floating for sixteen hours on a patched air mattress. They were eventually rescued and brought to a small apartment where they stayed with twenty-two other evacuees for two nights before walking miles from their ruined home in Aguadilla to a family member's house in Aguada. As Zaira was recounting their slow trek toward family, describing cars that had been caught up in a storm surge of ocean water and balanced upside down along the highway, she paused to ask, "How do you describe the smell of decaying bodies?" Our conversation for the day ended there as I turned off the recorder and reached for Zaira's hand across the table. We held onto each other as a warm afternoon rain started to fall all around the café umbrella that sheltered us.

Zaira's narrative opens this collection, which is fitting for many reasons, perhaps the most important being that this interview significantly shaped the project while it was still in its infancy. We ultimately decided not to include the details of Zaira's long walk down Highway PR-2 out of respect for the dead who were unknown to us and the grief that their families must feel in knowing that their loved ones laid on the roadside unattended for days after the hurricane. Hurricane María was—and is—a site of trauma for all who have survived; that trauma entailed not only the violent storm that battered the archipelago for over thirty hours, but also the long months, now years, of inadequate relief and aid from governmental systems that exist to help those in crisis.

Our deep sense of respect for our narrators and their experiences has cultivated an obligation to recognize these survivors not as victims, but as heroes. This book is populated by stories of people who meet tragedy and loss with strength and hope. As Zaira and Juan Carlos worked to find resources for themselves, they simultaneously returned to their flooded community to help others fill out and file necessary FEMA paperwork and liaise with government officials. Even as they grappled with the loss of every one of their possessions, they turned their efforts toward aiding those around them. This is the ethos that infused the nascent beginnings of our project, one that works to underscore the widespread injustice of insufficient governmental disaster response while highlighting the fortitude of the individuals who survived Hurricane María and its aftermaths in Puerto Rico.

Even though Zaira's was the first interview formally conducted for this book, the seeds of this project were planted months earlier in classrooms at the University of Puerto Rico at Mayagüez, where the editors of this volume teach in the English department. Hurricane María made landfall in the Puerto Rican archipelago on September 20, 2017, leaving no part of Puerto Rico unscathed.[1] The hurricane triggered floods and mudslides, washed out roads, destroyed tens of thousands of homes, farms, and businesses, caused the largest blackout in US history (the second largest in the world), knocked out communications, led to widespread shortages in food, drinking water, and gasoline, and was ultimately responsible for thousands of deaths. When classes at the university resumed just over a month later, we returned to campus knowing that it was one of the only places on the west coast of Puerto Rico that had somewhat stable electricity and running water. The university became a haven for our students and our community, but we learned quickly that many students who had restarted their semesters were in precarious positions because of what they had lost in the storm.

University administrators encouraged faculty to ask about the post-hurricane material conditions of our students so that we could direct them to whatever relief services were available, and we hurriedly reshaped our classrooms to meet students' new needs. I added a voluntary, ungraded hurricane memoir assignment to the official questionnaire, asking students to share in writing anything they wanted about their experiences in the storm. The intent was to give

---

1. Puerto Rico is an archipelago, consisting of the main island, the island municipalities of Vieques and Culebra, and numerous other uninhabited islands and cays.

them a way to voice their recollections and lighten their loads while transitioning back into the work of the classroom. Every student filled notebook pages with handwritten accounts of the hurricane and its aftermath, and, as I read their words by candlelight—it would still be months before electricity was restored to our homes— the desire grew to begin a project that would amplify stories of the hurricane in the hopes of generating immediate relief and building long-term change.[2]

Students wrote about the doors and windows of their family homes bursting open, watching helplessly as wind and rain destroyed their possessions. One student, Gabriel, wrote about how he and his grandmother held onto each other for hours—rocking back and forth and weeping together—as the storm peeled off their roof, and their belongings whirled around them. There were stories about rivers overflowing their banks and storm surges of ocean water pouring through houses with three, nine, and even eleven feet of floodwaters and stinking mud filling homes. Others wrote about seeing the animals on their farms drowned and crops ruined, businesses destroyed, empty grocery stores and the search for drinking water, and towns that looked like postapocalyptic movie sets "after the bomb went off." The words "screaming" and "crying" appeared over and over again.

Eventually, I came to Alejandra's memoir, in which she described sitting helplessly on her porch as she watched her neighbors bury two of their family members in their backyard. "The saddest thing," she wrote, was "to see our neighbors digging graves in their backyards because relatives had passed away due to the lack of medical attention in Aguadilla, since the only hospital [there] had to be

---

2. UPRM does not have dormitories. Students typically live in small, shared apartments in Mayagüez during the week and return home on the weekends. Prior to Hurricane María making landfall, the campus closed, and the majority of students returned to their family homes. Many of the apartments in Mayagüez were not reconnected to the power grid at the same time as the university.

shut down" and the electricity remained off. Her neighbors had been unable to receive their routine medical care and died because of it. Reading this narrative, catching a glimpse of what Alejandra carried with her every day, made me want to do more to alleviate that burden. This was the moment of commitment to a project that would gather stories of surviving Hurricane María in Puerto Rico, one that would assemble individual voices as part of a polyphonic narration of disaster, with the intent of making real change for us and others who have survived natural and human-made disasters.

In August 2018, less than a year after the hurricane made landfall, we met this objective with the inception of the Mi María project, in collaboration with Voice of Witness.[3] I was quickly joined by two colleagues, Marci Denesiuk and Jocelyn Géliga Vargas, both of whom are longtime collaborators and friends who had developed their own exemplary in-class projects about the hurricane. Together, Jocelyn and I offered four courses in which we trained approximately one hundred undergraduate students from all majors and disciplines at the university in the ethical collection, transcription, translation, and initial stages of editing oral histories.[4] All of these students are survivors of Hurricane María—each with their own story to tell— who went into their home communities to collect unheard stories of the hurricane and its aftermaths. Many of the narratives collected in this volume began as oral histories recorded, transcribed, and translated by our students.

At the same time, Marci and I were also doing fieldwork, traveling through a Puerto Rico scarred by the hurricane and marred by insufficient relief efforts, in order to collect additional interviews.

---

3. Zaira's narrative was collected in the Story Lab, or pilot phase, of our collaboration with Voice of Witness during the spring and summer of 2018, and our formal development phase began when we returned to campus for the autumn 2018 semester in August of that year.

4. We were glad to have both resources and guest lectures provided by Voice of Witness in support of these courses.

Our work brought us from a farm nestled in the peaks of the Cordillera Central mountain range in Adjuntas to a community arts center in the underserved neighborhood of La Perla in San Juan to a health clinic being rebuilt on the island of Culebra off the easternmost coast of the main island. We have edited these raw recordings into readable narratives, labor that has been exacting and, at times, daunting. Always, though, we have kept sight of the fact that this project is rooted in the work of our students and the communities that we participate in together.

The stories collected in this volume illuminate some of the obstacles to surviving Hurricane María in Puerto Rico. In the middle of the hurricane, Emmanuel Rodríguez frantically tries to drive his pregnant wife to the hospital, only to be forced to return home when they find the road has collapsed because of a mudslide. Carlos Bonilla Rodríguez watches from a neighbor's home as the hurricane peels the roof off his house and throws it into the wind, with his possessions following close behind. Nilda Rodríguez Collazo describes her adrenaline "rising to a million" when her neighbor bursts into her home to warn of a rising storm surge at his heels. Other narrators tell of desperately holding doors shut against the wind and barricading windows as best they could, all while frantically mopping the water that relentlessly poured into their homes. Still others describe being forced into hastily organized government shelters, where the sick lay crying in the night and the disabled were left to fend for themselves.

The aftermaths of María are equally fraught, and these stories bring attention to the precarity of surviving in the weeks and months that followed the hurricane. Neysha Irizarry Ortiz's premature son is brought into the world in a makeshift clinic with no electricity. For days, Luis G. Flores López watches his father get sicker and sicker as they desperately pray for the dialysis clinic to reopen so that he can receive lifesaving treatment. A month passes before any nonprofit or government agency comes to check on Windy Díaz Díaz, leaving her trapped in her own home because of the debris blocking her wheelchair ramp. Miliana Ivelisse Montañez León's mother is sent home from the hospital—with her condition undiagnosed—only to die in her own bedroom.

The immediate losses in these stories are obvious, but other ongoing issues also come into focus in the aftermaths of Hurricane María. This natural disaster was compounded by repeated government-level failures. In reading these accounts, we learn of a perpetually underfunded electric utility that was unable to rise to the challenges of a hurricane that caused the largest blackout in US history. Again and again we are told that FEMA fell far short of its objectives—instead appropriating gasoline and moving it from local stations to the sites it deemed essential, leaving none for privately owned cars or generators; redirecting shipments of food to locations that did not reach rural communities or urban neighborhoods; and failing to provide shelter to those who had lost their homes.

President Donald Trump arrived in Puerto Rico on October 3, two weeks after the hurricane, only to taunt Puerto Ricans by joking that they'd thrown the federal budget "out of whack" and suggest that María was not a "real catastrophe" in comparison to Hurricane Katrina. The US Navy hospital ship *Comfort* arrived in San Juan with 250 beds, but the bureaucratic process for admittance was so convoluted that nearly two weeks after its arrival only thirty-three of those beds were occupied. An early $300 million no-bid contract to oversee restoration of the electric grid was awarded to Whitefish Energy Holdings—a company with just two employees—only to be canceled: actions that significantly delayed work on the grid. Organization of relief supplies was so chaotic that stores of potable water and warehouses of goods are still being discovered, the most recent being an abandoned 43,000-square-foot government warehouse found in Ponce in January 2020.[5]

---

5. An investigation into possible government wrongdoing regarding these undistributed emergency supplies was referred to the Department of Justice. See Karma Allen, Joshua Hoyos, and Ella Torres, "Puerto Rico Refers Investigation into Unused Emer-

Yet, despite the widespread government-level failures, we repeatedly see communities rising together to take care of each other. Grassroots organizations—most often without telecommunications or internet—brought people together to cook community meals, care for children and elders, rebuild shelters, provide first aid, and pool funds. Neighbors sharing with each other—and even with strangers—became friends through small acts of kindness.

In addition to government-level failures, the complex colonial roots of Puerto Rico have also shaped the aftermaths of the hurricane and stalled recovery. In the twenty-first century, the US Congress allowed laws that had been enacted to stimulate the economy to lapse, and in 2016 the PROMESA law established an external Financial Oversight and Management Board to oversee all aspects of governing Puerto Rico related to finances.[6] Detrimental austerity measures enacted by this board create an ongoing humanitarian crisis, accelerate mass migration from Puerto Rico to the continental United States, and place medical care, education, and infrastructure in the archipelago in jeopardy. These are the conditions from which we were already suffering when first Hurricane Irma and then, two weeks later, Hurricane María struck.

In this book, we have incorporated *testimonios*—shorter, issue-driven narratives that bear witness to specific events—alongside the longer, birth-to-now oral histories for which Voice of Witness is known. We use these spaces to underscore concerns related to disability, community-driven relief work, the gasoline shortage, work on the electrical grid, hurricane-related deaths, and failures in conducting autopsies and filing reports within the Institute of Forensic Sciences: all problematic elements of the post-hurricane landscape that our narrators witnessed and that we believe are essential to

---

gency Supplies to DOJ," ABC News, January 21, 2020, https://abcnews.go.com/US/puerto-rico-distributes-supplies-left-rot-warehouse/story?id=68409678.

6. PROMESA is an anacronym for the Puerto Rico Oversight Management and Economic Stability Act, which was signed into law by President Obama.

understanding Hurricane María and its ongoing aftermaths in Puerto Rico.

Each of the stories included in this collection—even the shorter testimonios—spans to some degree three aspects of experiencing the hurricane in Puerto Rico: surviving the storm, building community responses to disaster, and the long aftermaths of the hurricane. We have, therefore, made an effort to order the pieces of this collection in a progression that—when read together—tells the breadth of the disaster and its aftermaths as a multivocal people's history of Hurricane María. It is our intent that, while engaging with our individual narrators, the connections between their stories will emerge, fostering a greater understanding of the failures of governmental disaster response across the archipelago and the correlating strength of the people impacted by these failures. Ultimately, we have crafted this volume with attention to the way that these stories speak to each other and the belief that the voices in them are louder together.

These stories are unique to the individual narrators in Puerto Rico, but the insights gleaned from them have larger implications that supersede geographic boundaries. The treatment Puerto Rico received from the federal government that is an aspect of many of these narratives was on display once again during the COVID-19 pandemic, during which the Trump administration refused to aid US citizens. Furthermore, we in Puerto Rico are on the forefront of the global climate emergency, and this crisis is one that impacts the entire world. The ways in which these collected oral histories demonstrate community response to disaster are pertinent to other places in the world that are likewise being impacted by climate change.

While we are proud to be able to share these stories of Puerto Rico after the hurricane, we recognize that this collection is a beginning and not an end, and that there are countless other stories left to be told. As I write this introduction, my chair dances underneath me, a tangible reminder that we are in the midst of an ongoing earthquake swarm in Puerto Rico that began on December 28,

2019. To date, there have been over fifteen hundred earthquakes, the largest of which was a 6.4 and the most recent occurred just as I was about to save this document. It is a stark signifier that in a place not yet recovered from the 2017 hurricanes, people are again being forced out of their homes, electricity is often unstable, and a shared communal trauma rears its head again and again. Simultaneously, the governor has declared a state of emergency because of drought and water shortages. These situations also cause us to rethink what sheltering in place during the global pandemic of COVID-19 means when many people do not have a stable home in which to shelter or the running water necessary to wash their hands.

Resilient is a word that has often been used to describe the people of Puerto Rico in the aftermaths of Hurricane María. This label is problematic, though, as it sidesteps the reality that this resiliency is born of repeated abandonment by the federal government during the almost 125 years that Puerto Rico has been a part of the United States. What is named "resilience" is in actuality what occurs when a people are taught not to expect equitable treatment from their own government, developing a necessary understanding that they must be largely self-reliant in order to survive. While the stories included in this volume demonstrate the laudable tenacity and generosity of the people of Puerto Rico, it is important to remember that government-level assistance was not forthcoming, and this "resilience" manifests from generations of neglect. Rethinking this term does not take away from the remarkable accomplishments of the people of Puerto Rico; instead, it moves toward holding government officials accountable for their shortcomings. Reading the stories collected in this volume, then, is one way to support the people of Puerto Rico as they resist these attempts at forcing them into second-class citizenship.

Our title, *Mi María*, accentuates the need to resituate ownership over the public narrative from the government or media to the people who experienced this disaster, emphasizing that who tells the story matters. We believe that listening to these witnesses—thinking through what it means to tell one's own story—can inspire a wider inquiry of what work remains to be completed throughout our nation to guarantee equality and dignity for all.

   ¡Pa'lante!

Ricia Anne Chansky
January 2021
Rincón, Puerto Rico

EXECUTIVE EDITOR'S NOTE

The seventeen narratives in this book are the result of oral history interviews conducted over a two-and-a-half-year period between spring 2018 and fall 2020. With every Voice of Witness narrative, we aim for a novelistic level of detail and (whenever possible) a birth-to-now, chronologized scope in order to portray narrators as individuals in all their complexity, rather than as case studies. We do not set out to create comprehensive histories of human rights issues. Rather, our goal is to compile a collection of voices that (1) offers accessible, thought-provoking, and ultimately humanizing perspectives on what can often seem like impenetrable topics; and (2) can meaningfully contribute to the efforts of social justice and human rights movements.

In order to honor our narrators' experiences, Voice of Witness oral histories are crafted with the utmost care. For this project, editors and interviewers were trained in VOW's oral history methodology by education director Cliff Mayotte and managing editor Dao X. Tran. Recorded interviews were transcribed, translated, and organized chronologically. Then, under the guidance of our managing editor, narrative drafts were subject to multiple rounds of editorial revision and follow-up interviews, to ensure depth and accuracy. The stories themselves remain faithful to the speakers' words (we seek final narrator approval before publishing their narratives) and have been edited for clarity, coherence, and length. In some cases, names and details have been changed to protect the identities of our narrators and the identities of family and acquaintances. All narratives have been carefully fact-checked and are supported by various appendixes and a glossary included in the back of the book that provide context for, and some explanation of, the history of Puerto Rico.

We thank all the individuals who courageously, generously, and patiently shared their experiences with us, including those whom we were unable to include in this book. We also thank all the frontline human rights and social justice advocates working to promote and protect the rights and dignity of Puerto Ricans.

Finally, we thank our national community of educators and students who inspire our education program. With each Voice of Witness book, we create a Common Core–aligned curriculum that connects high school students and educators with the stories and issues presented in the book, with particular emphasis on serving marginalized communities. As we continue to amplify a diversity of voices in our book series, we are also committed to developing a curriculum that directly supports students in English Language Learner (ELL) communities. At the time of writing, about one out of every ten public school students is learning to speak English. In California alone, ELLs account for 19.3 percent of the total public school student population, and this number continues to grow. In response to this need in our education networks and beyond, in 2018 we launched our first oral history resource for ELLs, and we continue to expand our offerings in this area.

Our education program also provides curriculum support, training in ethics-driven storytelling, and site visits to educators in schools and impacted communities. I invite you to visit the Voice of Witness website for free, downloadable educational resources, behind-the-scenes features on this book and other projects, and to find out how you can be part of our work: voiceofwitness.org.

In solidarity,
Mimi Lok
Cofounder and Executive Director
Voice of Witness

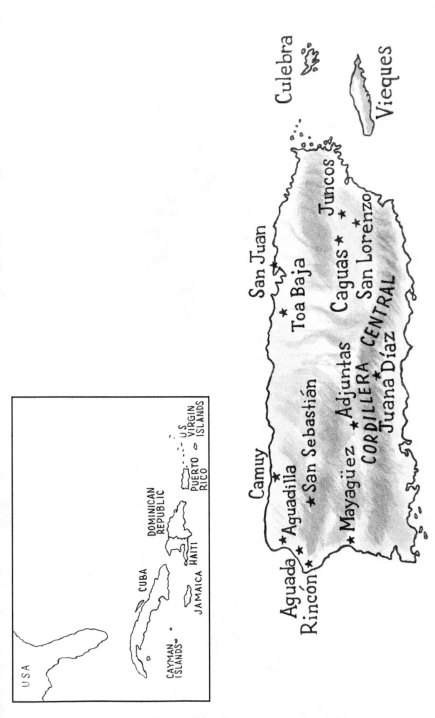

Culebra

Vieques

San Juan

Juncos

Caguas

San Lorenzo

Toa Baja

CORDILLERA CENTRAL

Adjuntas

Juana Díaz

San Sebastián

Camuy

Mayagüez

Aguadilla

Aguada

Rincón

USA

CUBA

DOMINICAN REPUBLIC

HAITI

JAMAICA

CAYMAN ISLANDS

PUERTO RICO

US VIRGIN ISLANDS

ZAIRA ARVELO ALICEA

BORN IN: 1984
LIVES IN: Aguadilla
Educator

We meet Zaira only in lively places: on the plaza of Rincón, where trucks are loading and unloading all around us; at a new breakfast place that is hosting a big birthday party with lots of singing and clapping; in a small bar where an impromptu dance party starts up in the middle of our conversation. Each time, we worry about all this noise—that it is too loud for us to talk or that the recordings will not be clear—but we always change our minds and decide that we are starving for these sounds. Maybe it is the many hours Zaira and her husband, Juan Carlos, spent trapped in their own home as they waited for rescue after the hurricane or the months that have dragged on since then without any government assistance after their house was destroyed, but Zaira tells

17

*us that she wants to be surrounded by these signs of life. As she shares
her story, several failures in the federal disaster-response systems become
apparent, ones that have led to her and Juan Carlos remaining homeless
for well over a year after the hurricane.*

"WE'RE WITH THE PEOPLE NOW!"

I couldn't speak about myself today without going back to Lares.[1] I
was born and raised in Lares. Well, actually born in Arecibo.[2] Lares
stopped having a birth unit at the hospital years ago. Everything was
moved to Arecibo, which is probably a forty-minute drive from Lares.
And when you're in a rush because someone is coming into this world,
it's difficult, but the people got used to it. So, in other times, in another decade, I might have been born in Lares. Generations were born
there, and then, suddenly, everyone else was born in Arecibo.

People know Lares because of the Independentista movement
and the Revolución del Grito de Lares.[3] It's known as the mecca
where the largest uprising took place in Puerto Rico in 1868 against
our Spanish oppressors. And it's still a place where everyone gathers
on September 23 to speak about Puerto Rican independence, nationalism, and other political movements against colonialism and
for the people.

---

1. Lares is a municipality in the central-western mountains with a population of
approximately 24,000.

2. Arecibo is on the northern coast of Puerto Rico, approximately eighteen miles
from Lares. The roads between the two are mountainous and winding, and the
driving is slow.

3. El Grito de Lares was a collective of landowners, agricultural workers, and enslaved individuals who rose up in opposition to Spanish colonialism in Puerto Rico.
For more on the rebellion, see "El Grito de Lares" in the "Contexts" essay.

If you drive through town on that day, it's almost like the *cara-vanas* that we have on the island right before any big election event.[4] You start seeing green everywhere: the color of the Independentista political party. Their green flag with the white cross is everywhere. Then you start seeing the flag of Lares: red, blue, one white star in the upper corner. And you just know, "Okay, we're in Lares! We're with the people now!" It's a special group. And when you make it up to the plaza, everyone's congregated there. And it doesn't matter if you're from any of the other nonaffiliated or independence parties; you're all together, all there for the common cause.

No matter how hot it is, someone always takes that mic to speak. And you forget about the heat, you forget about the sun, forget about that huge raincloud that's forming in the Cordillera Central, the mountain range. You know it's going to pour, and you know you're going to be sunburned, but you want to listen to what they have to say anyway. There's always the talk about nationalism and the independence movement in Puerto Rico—about pride— that doesn't feel like it has to be hush-hush.

I remember being told in the second grade that we were going to sing the anthem of Puerto Rico, "La Borinqueña," every morning, but that we would sing the more revolutionary version, "El Himno del Grito de Lares."[5] This unofficial part was written against Spanish imperialism in 1868 by the poet Lola Rodríguez de Tió. "*Ya no quer-emos déspotas, caiga el tirano ya. . . . Vámonos, borinqueños, vámonos ya, que nos espera ansiosa, ansiosa la libertad. La libertad!*" We no longer want dictators, let the tyrants fall. . . . Come, Puerto Ricans,

---

4. *Caravanas* are popular mini-parades in which people drive their cars through the streets honking, singing, and shouting. Sometimes these are informally organized around a graduation or wedding, other times they are more formalized with set speakers and routes.

5. *Borinqueña* and *borinqueños* are forms of the Taíno word for the people of Puerto Rico. For more on the Indigenous peoples of Puerto Rico, see "Spanish Coloniza-tion" and "Transatlantic Slave Trade" in the "Contexts" essay.

come now, we are anxiously awaiting freedom. Freedom![6] From then on—and still today—I have those lyrics in my brain. It's always the twenty-third of September somewhere in my mind.

THE LITTLE GLIMPSE OF READING

When I was a child, people would go house to house selling books, encyclopedias. At that time, if people had books in their house, they had a Christian Bible and they had an encyclopedia set—Britannica or Encyclopedia Cumbre—and that was it. And if you had one of those encyclopedia sets, you could count on all the kids in your neighborhood coming in the afternoon to use it. Because you couldn't find information anywhere. These were the times before the internet.

One day when I was around eight, when the vendors came to sell the Encyclopedia Cumbre, they also brought a set of Dr. Seuss books. When I got home and saw those books, I went crazy! I remember just looking at the images because I couldn't understand everything I was reading as the books were in English. But I was so excited because it was the whole set. They had a tiny red plastic case that held the books together and I could look at them every day when I came home from school. They were on *el multimueble*, the shelf next to the TV that held all of our family fishing trophies, little figurines from quinceañeras, and all of those things.[7] That's where my books were. And I say it in past tense because I went to school a

---

6. Rodríguez de Tió (1843–1924) was a feminist, poet, intellectual, and revolutionary. She wrote a poem inspired by El Grito de Lares that was then set to the tune of the popular piece of music known as "La Borinqueña." Manuel Fernández Juncos (1846–1928), a founding member of the Orthodox Autonomist Party, rewrote Rodríguez de Tió's poem in 1903. His version was adopted as the official Puerto Rican anthem in 1952, when the Commonwealth of Puerto Rico, or Estado Libre Asociado, was established.

7. Quinceañeras are a celebration of a girl's fifteenth birthday and are widely celebrated throughout Latin America and in Latinx families.

couple of weeks later and when I came back home, the books were gone. When I asked my parents what happened, they said the salesperson came back and told them that the books weren't free. We couldn't afford them, so we had to give them back. And that was the little glimpse of reading outside of school that I got.

ENGLISH WITH "EL CUCO"

In high school, I started to understand that when people said they hated a teacher or that a teacher was horrible, I needed to find out who that person was. Some teachers were called "el Cuco." El Cuco is a boogeyman in Puerto Rico passed down to us from our Spanish heritage who kidnaps and eats naughty children. I heard about this English teacher, Mr. Ortiz, who the other students said was "el Cuco." And I said, "I'm going to take a class with Mr. Ortiz." I figured he'd actually teach me something, that I would really learn English, and I was tired of being bored. My mother always said that I was a very *exigente* child, "demanding": *hablando mucho, preguntando de todo.* I was always talking a lot, questioning everything.

Typically, teachers would take a book and read from it in class, saying, "Today we're on page one to three, tomorrow we do four to seven." There was no planning, design, or agency of any kind. The Department of Education or the school had purchased this textbook, and so we had to see how many of these pages we could actually go through. And the history books in Puerto Rico were typically, "We are made of three races: Spaniards, Taínos, and Africans." But if you read the book chronologically, you never got to the African roots because that part was in the last pages of the book. We all knew about the Indigenous peoples and we all knew about the Spaniards who came, but God forbid we knew something about the Africans who came after. That's how that went every year.

But not for Mr. Ortiz. I ended up choosing to take my three years of English with "el Cuco." I remember that once I was really upset in his class, disappointed. And I don't like being disappoint-ed—by other people, but especially in myself. One day, when I had a quiz in Mr. Ortiz's class, I hadn't had a chance to study and I knew it. I remember going to the class and I was so disappointed in myself that I just sat there. I wrote my name on the test, flipped it over, and sat there with my arms crossed. He walked around the class and said, "Zaira, you done?" And I said, "Yeah, I'm done." So, he flips the quiz back over and said, "You didn't do anything. You didn't even try." And I said, "I didn't study, and I don't know what I'm supposed to do."

It was the first time in my life I saw a teacher pissed off. That made me feel the worst. He said, "Well, you're going to try. You're a smart student and the least you can do is try. You didn't study? Okay, that's what you learn for the next time. Not trying is never an option." That was one of those things that really got me thinking about who I wanted to be in life. I ended up deciding—thanks to Mr. Ortiz—that I wanted to be a teacher. So that stuck with me.

SAN JUAN WAS NOT AN OPTION

I didn't want to go to the University of Puerto Rico at Aguadilla, but I was forced to go there by my very Pentecostal mother.[8] When the time came to go to college, I requested my first choice, the ed-ucation program at the University of Puerto Rico at Río Piedras in San Juan, the capital city. But Lares is a town of families, it's a town of generations, and a town where no secrets hold. There's always someone watching you. So many people in the towns in the central region have misconceptions about what it means to venture out of the safety that you have in the interior of the island. They think of the metropolitan area as a place that's crowded, rowdy, noisy, with a lot of murders every day. According to them, someone's always

---

8. Aguadilla is on the west coast of Puerto Rico, approximately twenty-three miles from Lares by winding, mountainous roads.

getting drugged and raped on a corner. The two or three scary things that come out every other week in the news are typically what stick. And Río Piedras happens to be a campus that's nestled in that area.

So, she was in favor of Aguadilla because if I went there, I could commute every day. It was only a forty-minute drive north of Lares. Aguadilla had elementary and secondary education programs, but they had a focus on multimedia technology in education, which didn't interest me. I also hated the campus. It's ugly. Just poor, repurposed buildings that used to be military barracks for Ramey Air Force Base.[9] But, forced to choose between a school that didn't have the program I wanted in a location that I hated or nothing at all, I went to Aguadilla.

My mother was encouraging, she just wanted me to stay close. She was the first one in our family to go to college. And she did it because her mother made her go. Her first nursing book, which she still has today, was bought by her mother. That was the third kind of book we had in our house—nursing books. My grandmother was a single mom because the father of her children was an alcoholic. She made *almojábanas*—rice flour fritters—at a cafeteria, and people know her recipes to this day. She saved all her money from the sales, did everything she could so that my mother could go to school and become a nurse. My mom was her only daughter and she wanted her to do something more, and my mother wanted me to do the same thing.

I COULD BE MYSELF

College was my first time away from home where I could count on not having someone watching me. I was one of two people from

---

9. Ramey Air Force Base became operational in 1939 and played a significant role in the US Hemispheric Defense Strategy in World War II and the Cold War. In the early 1980s many of the former base's facilities were repurposed for public use. For more on the military in Puerto Rico, see "Military Bases" in the "Contexts" essay.

Lares in that program and I knew the other guy wouldn't say anything about me. So, for the first time in my life, I had a choice. I
could think about who I wanted to be and how I wanted to be per-
ceived. I didn't have to be Arvelo, not even Zaira, because you were
known by your family name, not your given name. So, if you said,
"I am Arvelo," the answer was, "From which family of Arvelo?" And
then people would ask who your parents and grandparents are, asking questions until they figured out who you belong to. People could
always trace where you were from. Always. So that was the first time
I could be myself, and I didn't know who I was. I didn't know who
I wanted to be because I was always told who I was supposed to be.
So, everything about it was exciting.

One day, right after I got to college, I walked down a hallway
in the English department and saw a box labeled "Free Books." Free
books! In Puerto Rico? I started looking through the books and
there were what seemed to be novels. But I didn't know, because I'd
only read one novel in Spanish in high school because you aren't
taught to read books for the pleasure of it. In that box, I found Kate
Chopin's *The Awakening*. To this day, that's my favorite book because it's the story of a person who had to choose between jumping
in the water while being scared or not jumping and always being
afraid. That's the moment I learned that knowing a second language
could change who I am. For the first time, I encountered this character that I would've probably never found in another type of literature from Puerto Rico. And for some time, Edna Pontellier, the
main character's name, was even the name I used online. So that was
the moment I knew I wanted to keep learning this language and be
a teacher, because then I could show other people that they can see
other worlds—*no otro trabajo, no más dinero, pero otra experiencia*.
Not that it got you other jobs or more money, but that there was
another experience through reading.

In college I ended up falling in love with Juan Carlos, who isn't
Christian, let alone Pentecostal. He was actually born and raised

in the States. For many people in Puerto Rico, that's a *gringo*, but if you ask him, he's Puerto Rican because his parents are Puerto Rican. But over there, where he's from in Connecticut, he would be called a spic. That was the guy I wanted to be with and, of course, my parents didn't like that. The first time my father saw Juan Carlos, he was wearing capri shorts and *chanclas*, or flip-flops, had a tongue piercing, no gel in his hair—unlike typical Puerto Rican men—a baggy top, and my dad was like, "Who is this guy?" Fifteen years later, we're still together.

WATER WAS EVERYWHERE

After Zaira finished her master's degree in English education, she and Juan Carlos moved to Indiana so that Zaira could continue studying. Once there, though, Juan Carlos often faced racist and prejudicial treatment, and was unable to find full-time work. It was only when they moved back to Puerto Rico that his career in electrical engineering took off. When they returned, Zaira began working as an adjunct faculty member at a local university, but she was quickly told that austerity measures affecting public education would prevent her from being hired in a secure teaching job. She left that position to begin an independent educational consulting company, specializing in business writing, translation services, and developing oral presentations. Her business opened in early September 2017, right before Hurricane Irma and then María made landfall in Puerto Rico.

Juan Carlos and I were living in a rented house in Aguadilla, behind the airport and Ramey Base. The night before the hurricane, I made rice and beans with pork chops, and I said, "We're gonna be fed." It made me feel good, like I was easing things.

Juan Carlos and I had done everything that we could on our property. I had prepared my emergency backpack: food, batteries, radios, medicine that we might need. I had granola bars. I had a forty-ounce canteen and gallons of water. We set everything up correctly. We even prepared two emergency rooms in the house. We put an air mattress in the room with the fewest windows. We figured that if the wind was a problem, we'd hunker down there. And if those windows gave in, we said, "We'll run to the bathroom where it'll be safe." Some of the cranks on the windows were broken, and we were afraid the windows would pop open during the hurricane, so we drilled screws in the corners of the frame so those wouldn't budge. We'd taken our cars to a nearby town, to a family member's house with a big garage, because we were afraid of projectiles and had no protected place to leave cars at our house.

We decided to stay in the house because it was our home together. My family has never gotten used to Juan Carlos, so this was our place as a couple. It's a cement house, the windows aren't glass—they're metal Miami windows with slats—and we locked them. There's no ocean nearby, no river, no lake, no apparent risk. We spent the whole day in that house just chilling. We were listening to the radio, but then every station started to die. FM died completely, then the only frequency we could get was AM and there was only one station we could get, Radio Una with Jensen Chaparro, who started saying that they had no information because nothing was coming their way, even with their huge antennae.

Around 3 p.m., I go into the bathroom and take a shower, not a problem, but then I flush the toilet, and notice that it's filling slowly, gurgling. I go to the bedroom and tell Juan Carlos, "Hey, *mi amor*, there's a problem with the water." And he says, "Don't touch that toilet again!" There was still running water, but he understood that the septic tank was flooded from the outside because it was in front of the house. And, outside, water was everywhere. Everywhere. We looked out the windows that led to our terrace, and there were rivers of water passing next to the house. We were thinking it was just runoff, water coming down from different places. But it was coming down with such strength that the tall grass—almost two feet high—was flattened by it. All you could see was water, but our house was high up. We have what would've been like a basement, but it was hollow. It had nothing underneath. Houses in Puerto Rico are often built on stilts, especially when they're on the side of hills.[10] So, the house was raised up, and it had nine steps to get to the front door. We're about ten feet off the ground, so we were never on ground level, ever. And the water was going toward the septic. That tank was already full, so I put a little stopper in the bathroom sink thinking that would keep the water there. You know, silly me.

The water started coming in under the front door around 5:30. It was September, so by that time it was almost pitch-black outside—the electricity had gone already—and the water started coming in. We were thinking, *It's the wind that's pushing some water in.* The hurricane was like a power washer gun pointed at every window, so we're thinking, *It's just a little bit of water*, and we went at it with a mop and towels, putting barriers against the doors, just like I assume the other three million Puerto Ricans were doing. And then we realize that what was coming under the door was a full flow of water. So, it hit us right then that there must have been twelve feet of water in front of our house. Because the water's coming in steady, not stopping. It's up over the stairs, across the porch, and at our front door.

When we got scared is when the back side of the house started getting water, too. Because our house is lowest in the front. So, for the water to reach through the back, it means that the water is higher than our house level. And we started getting water through both doors, the front and back. My husband decided to go to the bathroom for a moment to check on it, and I heard him cursing. He yelled, "Give me a shoe." And he told me there were cockroaches and critters just swimming in circles in our shower. The water was so high that the sewage from the septic tank was coming in through

---

10. Houses on stilts are common in Puerto Rico. This type of construction can be used in the mountains to facilitate building on a sloped site and can also protect against flooding.

the shower, the toilet, and sink. Juan Carlos said that he'd never seen the creatures that he saw in that shower, and I'm glad I didn't see them. We realized that they were starting to come into the house from there and I told him to just shut the bathroom door and forget it exists.

That helped with the critter situation, but then we had a larger problem: we weren't just seeing rainwater, we were seeing black water, sewage. At that point, the water was already at our ankles, and it stank. I was in my kitchen, standing next to my table, and I looked across my living room. And I could feel the water already coming. I had rainboots on, so I couldn't feel the water directly on my ankles, but my husband was cursing like there's no tomorrow. He's a germaphobe, and he was in chanclas. So, the black water is everywhere, around his toes, on his legs, and I just held onto the table. I spoke to myself in the third person, and I said, "Zaira, this is the moment where you need to remain calm and think logically, because you might have to make some very rough decisions tonight, and if you're not calm, you may do things that aren't responsible." So, I said, "Let me grab my emergency backpack, make sure it doesn't get wet."

By that time, the water was already coming inside my rainboots, almost at the top of my shins. While the water was low enough, I moved the air mattress from my office, our original safe room. The second safe room, the bathroom, was already locked and full of black water and critters. I moved the mattress by floating it on the water to the living room. It was a queen-sized air mattress, one of the really, really thick ones. Probably a foot and a half high. A family member gave it to us because it had a little hole and we'd taped it. So, it was a patched-up, hand-me-down air mattress that served as a raft for us.

At first, we were just riding out the storm. I had snacks, my husband brought towels and pillows. We were thinking, *There's so much land around us that the water will reach a level where it will flow elsewhere because there are acres of land in front of us and to our left.*

At that point, we didn't think we were in jeopardy. That didn't come until we realized that the mattress kept moving higher and higher in this stinking black water. I have a flashlight that does different intervals of light flashes and an emergency whistle that my husband's work gave him. So, I got off the mattress and walked through the stinking water up to my thighs and started doing signals to the house to my left because I'd seen my neighbors there during the eye of the hurricane. I'm thinking maybe they're still there. They have a second story that's higher than our house, so we thought maybe we could swim across to their house.

It was so dark inside our house; I had no idea what was around me. I think the scariest sensation was feeling the tiles lift. There was so much water, the tiles were coming loose and popping off the floor. So, as I'm stepping to the door to signal my neighbors, I fear that my foot is gonna go through a hole in the cement and I'm gonna get a cut with that black water all around. I lit my lantern, nothing. I blew the whistle, nothing. It was just my lungs against the hurricane. And it became clear right there that no one was going to hear us. That was the moment we realized we were completely alone. No one, anywhere, was going to hear us. And there was no cell phone reception. We'd turn our cell phones on every hour to see if we had a bar to send a message, to dial 911, anything. When I looked out that window with my flashlight for the last time, the only thing I could see was water on either side as far as the horizon.

At that point, we said, "No more drinking and no more eating," because we didn't want to have to go to the bathroom on our air mattress. And, of course, we still had to pee several times, because it was many hours. So, between the septic tank water, the water that came from outside, drowned animals that came in with the flooding, and our own piss in the water, there was barely any air in the house. And from then on, we just stayed there, not talking, not using the air. That was when we realized we could die.

I AM SO FREAKING EXHAUSTED

Every hour we'd look at the phone, check for a signal, turn it off. Wait one more hour, check, turn it off. I remember thinking, at like 11 p.m., as I was all the way up there on the water, seeing my house at this angle—from the top, the ceiling—*It's gonna be tomorrow soon. And everything's gonna be better.* Then midnight came, and I thought, *It's already tomorrow. It's gonna be over soon.* But all we could hear was the *blook, blook, blook* of the water. There was no air, there was nothing.

Finally, Juan Carlos says, "What's that? There's a light outside." We realized it wasn't a flashlight outside, it was the reflection of a flashlight from far away bounding across the water. And he had seen it catch the tinted glass of the tiny windows over the front door. I had my flashlight and got really close to the glass, flashing with the same intervals that the other person was flashing, so they could see it was a human being, not some weird flickering light. We realized, somewhere, there was someone else, but we couldn't see them.

We thought about trying to go through the front door, but outside there was between fourteen and sixteen feet of water and we were worried that we'd get tangled in fences or downed power lines or clotheslines. We were afraid we'd lose track of each other. We knew the lanterns would just turn off in the water, and we wouldn't be able to hear each other over the wind and rain. At that point, we were about fourteen inches from the ceiling—we couldn't sit up—and the water was so high that if we got off the mattress, there was no way to get back on. You couldn't. And hanging onto the mattress for hours was not an option. We would've drowned in black water as soon as our arms gave out. So, if we tried to leave the mattress and it didn't work, we were done.

We were so tired. We were on our backs for so long, twisting and turning, and everything hurt at that point. We tried not to move too much because we didn't want any sudden movements that might capsize us. We were worried about the risk of the mattress touching the metal curtain rings—was it going to pop? Or was one of the things that's floating around us going to puncture it? We stayed that way for almost six more hours. No one saw us. No one came.

When the sun came up and it was finally quiet—maybe 6 a.m.—I broke one of those tiny, tinted glass windows over the door and looked outside, and everything was water. That's it. It was water, and water, and water. To be able to look out the window, I had to press my head really hard against the mattress and deflate it a little bit so that I could look sideways. We were that close to the ceiling. And I'm holding on with my fingers to the curtain rod, so the mattress wouldn't keep moving back with the water. That's when I started blowing on the whistle again. I remember looking out at that strange angle and finally seeing tiny people all the way across that water and thinking, *They're gonna hear us.* And I whistle and whistle. I can even see two girls turn and point to where we are, but nothing happens. This goes on until 10 a.m. And I am so freaking exhausted by then, I doze off. I don't know how long until Juan Carlos wakes me and says, "I hear a noise." So, I pull the mattress again with my hand, and hold onto the curtain rod to look out that tiny window. Above me, I can see what looks like the bottom of a kayak, red and yellow plastic. And I hear a voice asking, "Are you okay?" There are two young men in the kayak, saving us.

Our front door is wooden, and it must have gotten swollen with the water. So, we decide that my husband will pull it while one of the men pushes. To do this, Juan Carlos has to slide from the mattress—so as to not tip it over or hit his head on the ceiling because we're impossibly close to it—into that super-cold shit water. But as soon as he's in the water, he starts shivering and hyperventilating to the point where the guy outside can hear him and thinks he's panicking. We have to yell through that little window to talk to each other, and I tell the guys that Juan Carlos knows how to swim, he's okay. It's just that the water is really cold and we're already cold because we were wet all night. It's so humid, and the air is so thick inside the house. There's something in the air. We were so tired of that smell. It's like it was inside us, like we wouldn't ever be able to clean that smell from our bodies. Juan Carlos lets go of the mattress, holds his breath, and dives into black water.

The guy from the kayak dives under that same water and starts kicking the door from the outside, but it barely moves. And he has to get air. Dive down and kick, come up for air again and again, till he's able to open it enough for Juan Carlos to pull with his hands. On both sides of the door, they kick and pull, come up for air, and dive again—all the while without opening their eyes underneath that dirty water.

When the door was finally open, I grabbed the backpack with all our important papers in it and passed it to the guy in the kayak. I slid off the mattress into the black water and pushed myself into the space where the door was. I put my hands on the top left and right of the door, and spread my legs the same way, holding them open so I wouldn't go underwater. Only two or three strokes swimming got me past our balcony to the plastic kayak. I held on to some wires at the back end of the kayak and was pulled along with my legs out behind me, careful not to let them hang down into the water. There were lots of things in that water. Whole uprooted trees—guava, lemon—barbed wire, electric pole wiring, fences. Lizards! I had lizards try to take a ride on me. I remember ducking so that I didn't hit the wires on a power line that was still standing. That's how high the water was. I was completely disoriented, had no idea where I was. The kayak just kept going over houses that were also underwater and I would look down at them.

THOSE GIRLS WERE SO BRAVE

Later, I learned that two twelve- or thirteen-year-old girls from a *caserío*, a subsidized public housing project, near where we lived kept insisting that there were people under the water. When we reached dry land, they were saying, *"Yo te lo dije que había alguien."* I told you there was someone there. They put their arms around us, and it started pouring again. Everyone else was running away from the rain, but I welcomed it because I was in dirty water for sixteen hours and knew I'd have no chance for a shower, no running water. And the girls, they just stayed there hugging us.

Those girls were so brave. Had they been some other girls, someone might have listened to them earlier. But they were young girls who lived in a caserío. They were wearing shorts that were "too short" and shirts that were "too tight" by some standards. They didn't have their hair perfectly done and they were just undereducated young girls who spoke in slang, unrefined Spanish. So, the police officers and firefighters ignored them. Everybody ignored them for hours until those two guys in the kayak—to this day, I don't know who they are—decided to go check it out. When it was finally safe to go outside, the girls were the only ones who heard us, and they kept on telling people until someone listened. Those girls saved our lives.

THOSE FIRST WEEKS

After the hurricane, I started filling out all the FEMA paperwork. I learned afterward from someone who has worked in disaster relief for many years that we filled them out wrong. Seeing the questions "Do you need clothes?" and "Do you need food?" I thought, *Well, I'm not hungry right now, and I'm clothed at the moment, although I lost everything.* So, I didn't put the checkmark that we needed things because we were unsure what the questions meant. And, of course, now we know that was the reason for us not getting the $500 emergency funds from FEMA. That was a big complaint we had about FEMA, that there wasn't a system put in place to determine people's needs. It was solely self-reported. I learned later that people who were actually in need could've gotten thousands of dollars, and that $500 could've actually helped us at that point.

Over a month later, we finally hear from FEMA that they're going to give us $700 so that we can find a place to stay, or we can stay
for free in an "approved" place. There was a phone number to call,
so I'd call it whenever I could get reception—after the hurricane,
reception was incredibly spotty, unreliable—and then you would be
placed on hold, and by the time a representative got to you, the call
would drop. They wouldn't call you back, and it was a whole mess.

When I finally got through, the lady who was helping me says,
"Well, I have one approved location here in V-I-E-Q-U-" and I just
say to her, "Let me stop you right there. Are you gonna send me to
Vieques?"[11] And she says, "Oh, is that how you pronounce it?" And
I'm like, "The point is not how it's pronounced, it's a different island. It's not the main island, it's a separate island. It's like me telling
someone in California to go to Hawai'i to find help." She's like, "Oh,
that's the only thing we have, except for some in the Virgin Islands."
I said, "How am I going to make it to the Virgin Islands?" So, we
took our own savings and have been living in an Airbnb. Paying for
it ourselves. The whole idea that FEMA provided for Puerto Rico is
a lie. It wasn't organized, and it wasn't covering the needs of people
who really needed it. Did some people benefit from it? I'm assuming
they did. I think that when you lose your property, to have a roof over
your head or have a bed to sleep in must've been nice for the people
who were able to get the help. So that was FEMA in those first weeks.

I WENT BACK

I went back to our old house for the first time in almost seven months.
One of my neighbors, two houses down—my Avon lady, Marí—started communicating with everyone else in the neighborhood who'd had

---

11. Vieques is an island municipality off the far eastern coast of Puerto Rico. It can
only be reached by ferry or plane, neither of which was working after the hurricane.
It is also an approximately three-hour drive from Aguadilla to the ferry launch if
the roads are open.

a loss due to Hurricane María. She found out that twenty-two families were affected by the flooding, including our own. So, she called
upon different agencies that are in some way related to funding that's
supposed to help people after a disaster and mitigate future disasters,
and asked them to come to a community meeting, to see what could
be done for the neighborhood. She called me and said, "Zaira, *tú sabes
tú no estás obligado.*" She told me that I wasn't obligated because I was
a renter, not a permanent part of the community. But I remembered
those girls who had saved us, and I said, "Yes, I'll come help."

In our case, there's evidence to suggest that some of the major
flooding in our community was related to activity that happened on
Ramey, the former military base. So, we needed to call upon agencies related to the federal government that communicate solely in
English. And I'm the one from that community who speaks English.
The communities that don't have an English speaker with a college
education: silence. Nothing happens for them.

I thought I was ready to go back. I thought I would feel absolutely nothing. But when I was driving down the road, I couldn't
avoid looking at our old house, even though I had planned to drive
right past. Three years of my life took place there. And I'm just looking at it, thinking, *That was my home. It used to be safe, welcoming.*
And it just hits me that even though I'm in my air-conditioned car
with the windows rolled up, I'm smelling what we smelled when we
were trapped in the flood. It was horrific! Like I'm never gonna be
clean. I don't know how to explain it, but there's this feeling in my
chest, like there's no air. And I have to just keep driving.

*In the years since we first met, we have kept in touch with Zaira, reach-
ing out on each anniversary of the hurricane, after some of the larger
earthquakes, and especially after the flash floods of Tropical Storm Isaías.
When each new disaster strikes, we check in to see how she and Juan
Carlos are doing. On the third anniversary of Hurricane María, we
messaged for quite some time, catching up and talking through some of*

*the ways her life has changed in the years since she survived the storm.
While her online business is still keeping her busy, Zaira and Juan Carlos
have moved to the mountains of Lares and live with her family to save
on rent. Juan Carlos is still working in Aguadilla, but they are both
worried about his job security. For now, though, they are enjoying free-
range eggs from all the chickens running around, picking endless* parchas
*from low-hanging tree branches, and taking long trips to the local lake.[12]
"Everyone is healthy," she tells us. "And, right now, that's the most important thing."*

I think that the body remembers. The third week of September will
just always be a lousy week for anyone who survived María. Our
human clock will feel it, always.

I've changed from that experience. When Isaías came to Mayagüez, all I could think about was what it's like to go back to a place
called home and not recognize it.[13] To have to tell yourself, "You can
do this." Square your shoulders and then walk back into what was
your house to see what you can salvage. All the while, your heart sees
what was your home superimposed over the mess.

That's what it's been like since María. When the earthquakes
started, I made beauty bags for the refugees.[14] I got a whole bunch of
old purses and filled them with anything that I remember not having after the hurricane: soap, deodorant, lotion, things to keep your
hair off your face, like a clip or a ponytail holder. And I got some
medicines, too, for colds, allergies, and headaches. I remember what
it was like not to have.

---

12. Parchas are passion fruits.

13. Tropical Storm Isaías made landfall in Puerto Rico on July 30, 2020, causing
widespread flash floods, mudslides, power outages, millions of dollars' worth of
damage, and at least five deaths.

14. An ongoing earthquake swarm in Puerto Rico began on December 28, 2019.
There have been thousands of earthquakes since then, the largest registering at 6.4.
For more on the earthquakes, see "Earthquake Swarm" in the "Contexts" essay.

EMMANUEL RODRÍGUEZ

BORN IN: 1991
LIVES IN: Mayagüez
Dental Technician

Emmanuel Rodríguez lives in Las Cuevas, one of many mountainous neighborhoods in the western municipality of Mayagüez.[1] People live in the mountains for many reasons, including cooler temperatures, natural beauty, and the wish to remain close to family and community. However, living in the mountains comes with some challenges, such as driving on narrow, winding roads that are prone to flash floods and mudslides. A network of these roads snakes through the mountain neighborhoods, leading to many places, including the center of Mayagüez where businesses and services are concentrated.

---

1. Mayagüez has a population of approximately 71,000.

Emmanuel is the primary provider for a family of six. He lives with his wife, father-in-law, nephew, and two sons. His younger son was born during Hurricane María. We meet with Emmanuel a few times in 2019, and he is almost always accompanied by his wife and other family members. He often has his baby, Ezequiel, cuddled in his lap as he tells his story.

I WAS MOSTLY AN INSIDE KIND OF PERSON

I'm the oldest of four. I was born in Mayagüez but raised in Passaic, New Jersey. I was around four months old when my mom, Sonia, and dad, Demetrio, moved to the States because my dad had a health problem and needed special care. I spent seven years in New Jersey. I was almost eight when my mom divorced my dad.

My dad used to abuse my mom. It wasn't just slapping; it'd be a punch or kicking. I'd try to protect her, but I couldn't do much. I was just a kid. If I tried to defend my mom, I'd also get hit. That really affected me. I had negative thoughts and I'd worry about my mom. Sometimes she'd have concussions or she'd faint or be swollen where he'd hit her. I'd also worry about protecting my sister and brothers, but he never did the same thing to them. Still, all of that really got to me.

After the divorce, my mom did stay in touch with my dad because, despite what had happened, she always wanted him to be part of the family. She wanted to help him keep his relationship with us kids. We never thought about hating him, none of us.

That same year after the divorce my mom remarried and we moved to my stepdad's house in Hialeah, Florida. My stepdad, Ramón, wasn't like my dad, at all. I never had a problem with him and we had a good relationship. He drove trucks for companies like UPS and FedEx. We moved a lot for his work: to Columbus, Ohio, where we spent three years; then Springfield, Massachusetts, for one year; then back to Hialeah for five years.

All those places! At first, I was scared, but I got used to moving around. As a kid, I didn't really head outside too much. I was mostly an inside kind of person. I liked reading, and still do, especially Stephen King and Edgar Allan Poe. Power Rangers and Legos were some of my favorite toys. I liked to construct things and loved puzzles. I also got along with my sister and brothers, but mostly I was the kind of person who just wanted to be in a quiet place.

I LIKE SO MANY THINGS ABOUT BEING A DAD

In 2010, when Emmanuel was seventeen, his mother and stepfather moved the family to Puerto Rico because they wanted to be closer to their relatives and his stepfather had a business opportunity with a member of his family. They settled in Mayagüez, and soon after the move, Emmanuel started dating his childhood friend, Darlyn.

Darlyn is a great person, really loyal and patient. When I was younger, I had problems controlling my anger. Growing up and seeing my dad's physical abuse of my mom affected me. Darlyn's not used to screaming or yelling. So, when she and I had a disagreement, I'd try to keep a distance from her. I'd get really mad and just leave. She would—no matter what—wait for me and say, "Just take it easy. I love you." She's always trying to find the positive in everything and she's always there for me. I eventually got treatment because of what I saw as a child and how it affected me. Now, Darlyn and I work together as a team.

Our first son, Yadiel Manuel, was born in 2011. At that time, I was studying to be a dental assistant. I was also doing odd jobs, working construction and cleaning—anything to support my family.

Darlyn and I weren't married yet and we were living with my mom and stepdad. Darlyn's sister was also living with us and was also pregnant. Her son, Andrew, was born only three months before Yadiel, so the boys are almost the same age. Darlyn's sister wasn't able to take care of Andrew and she left, so we've been raising him ever since.

Having my first son and taking care of two babies was a really big shock. At first I was afraid because I didn't know how much responsibility it would be. Some family members who knew my dad and how he'd treated my mom told me, "Hey, don't be like your dad." I was only eighteen when Darlyn got pregnant. I hadn't really thought about not being like my dad—or about being a father at all! But being with my boys and growing up with them has been very positive. We love watching movies together—especially *Minions*. But our favorite thing to do is play action figures together, or go outside and play ball. I like so many things about being a dad, especially watching my boys grow and seeing their joy.

SLAMMED AGAINST THE WALL

In 2012, Emmanuel and Darlyn moved into their current home in Las Cuevas, which belongs to Darlyn's father, Israel. In 2013, Emmanuel's mother and stepfather got a divorce and she moved back to the States with Emmanuel's siblings. That year, Emmanuel got a job as a dental assistant with Dr. Reinaldo Deliz, a dentist in Mayagüez. In 2014, Emmanuel and Darlyn got married. When the hurricane hit, in 2017, Emmanuel was still working for Dr. Deliz while Darlyn stayed home to care for the boys and her father, who is eighty-seven years old.

On September 19, the day before the hurricane, I took my wife to get her checkup. Darlyn was pregnant with our second son. The baby was due October 5. We had appointments regularly to get the sonograms done. We already knew the baby was a boy and we loved to see all his movements. The baby was healthy, so we left the doctor's and drove back to the house. That night, we started hearing strong winds, but we weren't too worried.

In the morning, we heard even stronger winds. The rain was intense and water started coming inside. The house is concrete and built into the side of the mountain on stilts.[2] It has one story with three bedrooms and a bathroom at the back. The front door opens to the kitchen and then the living room. There's also a second door to the outside off the living room. Water was flooding in under both doors.

I put two huge towels underneath the doors, but they quickly got soaked. I got more towels for mopping and a bucket to wring out the water in. I'd dump the water in the sink or bathtub and start mopping again. But the flooding got really intense. It started coming in the windows and under the doors even more. Around 11 a.m. I said, "That's it. I can't do it." By this time, I'd been mopping for over three hours and I was working by myself because I didn't want Darlyn or Israel to hurt themselves. I decided to stop because it was too much. I just let it go. Most of the house filled up with about five inches of water. Two of the bedrooms—mine and Darlyn's and my father-in-law's—were the only two rooms that were okay to be in.

Around 2 p.m., the winds were so strong that the front door started shaking. I told Darlyn, "The door's going to burst open." My father-in-law and I got the dining table and we held it against the door. I told my father-in-law to sit on the sofa. Because of his age, I worry about him a lot. So, Israel sat down and I held the door myself.

But then the door was shaking so violently that I couldn't hold it. It burst open and sent me flying. I was slammed against the wall in the hallway. The table was thrown up and hit the wall with a *boom*. Darlyn started screaming and crying. I shouted to her, "Go to our room! I'm okay." I took the kids to Darlyn and told them all, "Don't come out for any reason."

A lot of wind and rain was coming in. My father-in-law and I moved the table in front of the door again. Then, we dragged over

2. Houses on stilts are common in Puerto Rico. This type of construction can be used in the mountains to facilitate building on a sloped site and can also protect against flooding.

a freezer to put against the table. Once we got the door shut, we kept on hearing these noises. The winds sounded like voices—like screaming and growling. It was horrible, like something evil.

THE BABY WAS COMING

Israel started praying. I was also praying. It took me awhile to get everyone settled. I told Darlyn, "Just lay in bed, stay calm." The kids got some toys and went to my father-in-law's room. Israel and I stayed in the flooded living room to make sure the door held. Israel actually took a nap, which was kind of funny. I mean, how could he sleep during all that commotion? Despite the noise outside, things were calm inside until 4:30—that's when everything blew up.

I heard Darlyn screaming. I ran to our room. Darlyn was lying there holding her belly. She said, "Baby, I feel so much pain," and she started crying. I saw that her pants were wet, so I knew that her water had broken and I realized that the baby was coming. My anxiety went into overdrive. I didn't know what to do. I could hear the winds howling outside, but thought maybe we'd still be able to go to the hospital. I opened the door that wasn't blocked to see outside. I walked out a bit, but then the wind hit me so hard, I couldn't even see. Finally, there was a small break and I saw that a tangled power line and a huge branch had landed on the hood of my car. Massive trees had fallen and blocked both the roads from our house. I went back in to tell my family we were stuck.

Darlyn had calmed down a little bit. We waited and we prayed. The wind and rain continued. We were there like that, waiting, for almost three hours until around seven o'clock at night. Then Darlyn started feeling more pain. She was having contractions every ten minutes. She begged me, "Please, try to find a way out." So, I put on jeans, some old sneakers, a jacket, and a cap. And I went out.

I managed to move the branch and power cable off the car. Luckily the engine wasn't affected, so I started honking the horn and screaming for help. Neighbors heard and came over. I don't know how they got through all those branches in the dark. I told them, "Darlyn's about to give birth!" We checked for a way out of the neighborhood, but mudslides and fallen trees blocked all the roads.

My neighbors said they would keep trying to find an exit. Then they left and I was alone. I was terrified because there was no escape, no phone signal, no way to communicate for help, and even from outside, I could hear Darlyn screaming and crying. I had to do something. I went down some stairs that lead to the houses below us. When I got to the bottom, I started walking and screaming, "Hello! Is somebody there? Help me! Please! *Ayúdame!*" The neighbors didn't answer. So, I went on. Nothing. No one.

I kept walking until I met a guy in a pickup truck. His name was Joe and he was staying at his dad's house, just down the hill. It turned out he was a nurse. He hadn't brought medical supplies to his dad's, though, and he couldn't get through the road to our house, so all he could do was give me some instructions for what to do for Darlyn: "Don't let her sleep on her side. Keep her straight and put two cushions under her legs. Don't raise her head too much, but keep it centered. That way, her belly can stay in the same position."

With tears in my eyes, I went back to Darlyn. I told her I couldn't find help. It was almost nine o'clock. The whole time I was gone, she'd been screaming and crying. She wanted to go to the hospital. She started yelling, "Get me in the car! Try to do something!" But I couldn't do anything. I felt so helpless.

UP THE HILL BACKWARDS

Elevating Darlyn's legs helped a bit, and she was able to rest a little. I knew I had to get her out, so around ten o'clock I went out again. I met a neighbor who had an extra machete and we started cutting branches and clearing the tree that was blocking one of our roads. It was really dark and wet. I had to change my jacket a couple of times.

The funny thing was I had a raincoat in the car, but I didn't even think of it because I was so stressed!

Eventually we opened up that spot and I went inside to tell Darlyn. She cried, "Let's get out of here, now!" It was around 10:30 p.m. My father-in-law was watching over the kids, who were asleep, thankfully. The winds were really hitting us, but I got Darlyn into the car. I'd cleared a path close to our house, but the road was still a mess. Eventually we got down the hill, closer to the three roads we use to get to town. At the first road, there was this huge mess of bamboo stalks, so we went to the second road.

There, the road had collapsed on one side—just dropped off down the mountain—leaving only a small path for the car. I moved to the good side of the road and went a little further, but a massive tree had fallen. We couldn't pass and there was no way to turn around. So, even though it made me really anxious, I had to go in reverse. The path was so narrow, I was terrified we were going to go off the road and down the mountain. My wife panicked. "Watch out!" she yelled. I tried to comfort her, "Don't worry. Nothing's going to happen." I carefully reversed and made it up the hill backwards. Now, there was only one road left.

We tried getting out that way, but soon came to a big fallen mango tree. Darlyn was upset, crying. I was crying too. And praying. Throughout everything, my prayers never stopped. I was so afraid of what would happen to her and our baby.

I drove back to the house and got Darlyn settled in our room. It was around 1 a.m., and the contractions had lessened a bit, but around 4 a.m. she started feeling intense pain again. She was crying, "Help me! I can't take the pain!" She was lying on the bed and had pushed her pants down. I thought I might have to deliver the baby right there!

I placed a blanket on top of her and she closed her eyes for a little bit, but she was in pain and kept shifting around. I stayed by her side. The kids were still asleep, and my father-in-law kept checking on us. I told him, "There's nothing we can do. Let's hope for the best."

At seven o'clock we heard chainsaws. I went to look outside and saw some people were in front of my house, cutting the trees that were blocking one of our exits. I checked on Darlyn, and then I went and got Joe, the nurse. When he saw Darlyn, he put on some gloves, lifted up her blouse, examined her belly, and felt where the baby was. He said, "We've got to get you out of here because you're about to give birth and if that baby doesn't move into position, you might lose it." When he told us that the baby was in breech position, we burst out in tears.

Joe left to try to find some help. Around 9:30 a.m., two other nurses stopped at our house. They live on the next road over and had heard about our situation. They went in to check on Darlyn. One of them told me, "It's really bad. The baby's still not in the right position." They were saying that the baby might be dead. I was thinking, *This can't happen. We have to do something!*

I jumped in my car again. The strong winds had passed, but it was still raining. I drove in one direction and then another, trying roads that I hadn't checked before. It was slow going and I couldn't go far. I saw a lot of destruction everywhere. Just eight minutes from my house there was another landslide. This one was massive. The side of the mountain had fallen, and everything came down with it—dirt, trees, houses—all of that just vanished in the landslide.

I decided to go back. It was just too dangerous. But, when I was heading back, I saw a Mitsubishi Montero and the driver honked its horn at me. I saw Joe leaning out of the window screaming, "Your wife's here with me. Do a U-turn! Hurry! Follow me."

Inside the SUV were a paramedic and a doctor. I had no idea where Joe found either of them. The two nurses who'd been with Darlyn at our house were also in the car. Joe was driving really fast to get her to help as soon as possible. They had two groups of people on ATVs in front of the truck, screaming, "Move out of the way! We have a woman who's about to give birth!"

Darlyn thought that I was behind them in the car. But by the time I'd reversed and made the U-turn, I'd lost track of them. There was so much traffic now because, alongside all the cars, there were also bulldozers on the road. It was frustrating. But I knew they were heading to Perea Hospital because our doctor practiced there. I was honking the horn and yelling, "Please let me through!"

THREE DAYS BEFORE I COULD SEE THE BABY

When I finally got to the hospital around 2:30 p.m., they were only allowing limited numbers of people in. That day the generators were working properly and the whole hospital was lit. I made my way up to the maternity area and met with the doctor. He told me that Darlyn had given birth an hour ago, around 1:30 p.m., and that both she and the baby were fine. Once she'd arrived at the hospital, it'd been really quick. Thank God the doctor was there! Some doctors had just left the island when the hurricane was coming. Our doctor hadn't even gone to his house. Instead, he'd stayed at the hospital with his dogs throughout the hurricane.

After the doctor gave me the good news, he also asked, "Do you have the documents with you?" I was confused. "What documents?" He described what they looked like. It was the folder with the pregnancy records that the doctor gives you in case you have to give birth somewhere else. I said, "Oh, they're at the house." All I wanted was to see Darlyn and the baby, but the doctor insisted, "You've got to bring the documents to me. You can't see them until I have the papers." So, I had to go all the way back to the house without even seeing Darlyn and the baby. It was such a long drive. I had to go so slowly, watching out for traffic, trees, branches, and landslides.

I got back to the house around 4 p.m. I told everyone that Darlyn had given birth, quickly ate, put some blankets, clothes, and the documents in the car, and I drove back down. The traffic was really intense again, but once I got to the hospital and gave the documents to the doctor, they finally let me see Darlyn. She told me that the delivery had been really quick and the baby was fine.

He wasn't premature. He was almost eight pounds! She told me that he had brown skin and black hair. I thought, *Oh my God, a mini me!* I was so ready to see the baby, but I wasn't allowed in the newborn nursery.

The hospital suddenly closed. One security guard told me that there'd been an explosion nearby, and they didn't want to let visitors stay or enter, in case they'd been exposed to gases. They were worried about contamination or something. The explanation wasn't very clear, but I had to leave without seeing the baby. The next morning, I went to the hospital again, and I still wasn't allowed to see Darlyn or the baby. The maternity ward was open, but only women were allowed to go in. I don't know why. It was really strange. I told them, "I'm the father. I'm her husband." They said, "You're not allowed to go in." They didn't give me an explanation. I'm not a person to cause problems with anyone, so I just went back to the house. It was three days before I could see the baby.

On Saturday, I was finally allowed into Darlyn's room. When I saw Darlyn with the baby in the bed, I grabbed them, hugged them, and kissed them. We were finally together. Holding my son for the first time—oh, man, it felt so good. I had a blessing in my hands. It was beautiful. We named him Ezequiel Manuel.

WATER IS EVERYTHING FOR ME

That same day, we were able to leave the hospital. When we got back to the house, I got Darlyn and the baby set up in our room. But the chaos after the hurricane was challenging. We learned to eat the same things over and over: canned tuna, canned Carmela sausages, canned spaghetti, and canned ravioli. Also, getting gas for the car was an issue. I had help from neighbors; otherwise, there was no way I could get any.

There were also lines to get FEMA's help. They'd give us water and some treats—chips and sweets. They also helped out with stuff

for the baby. About three weeks after the hurricane, a government
truck came by the house with Pampers, formula, baby food, and
baby wipes because they knew that a baby was born in our area.
They'd come around, but you never knew when. Sometimes one
week, but then not the next. There wasn't a schedule that you could
rely on.

We still had no power or water, but our gas stove helped a lot.
For the baby, we'd heat up the water a little bit and we'd bathe him
in his bathtub. For the rest of us, we had a cooler that we used to
collect water from our neighbor's well and we used that to bathe.
I prefer living without electricity to living without water. Without
water I can't clean or mop as much as I usually do. I love mopping! If
everything's not clean and organized, I get really stressed out. Water
is everything for me. Picking up water every day took so much time.
Twice a day, I had to go down to the neighbor's house in the car to
get water. I hauled gallons and gallons.

The money thing was so stressful. Nobody expected the banks
to be closed. You couldn't use your cards in stores because there was
no signal.[3] I had some cash, but only because I'd gone to visit Dr.
Deliz at his home, and he and his wife kindly helped me out.

A WHOLE MESS OF PEOPLE

I don't get paid unless I'm working, and the office was closed because it'd been destroyed by the hurricane. The ceiling was gone
and the rooms were flooded. The water had been sitting there, so
it was dirty and smelly. There was mold climbing up the walls and

---

3. The point-of-sale systems that stores use to process payments require a cell phone
signal. After the hurricane, the majority of the archipelago's cell phone towers and
internet cables were destroyed, so stores couldn't process payments with credit or
ATM cards. For over a week (and in some places even longer), Puerto Rico's local
and transnational businesses operated on a cash-only basis. For more on the conditions after the hurricane, see "Aftermaths" in the "Contexts" essay.

spreading throughout the rooms. It looked like serpents crawling all over the office.

I'd go to the office and clean with the rest of the staff. I was really thankful Dr. Deliz let us work, but it was only part-time hours, so I was totally worried about money. I've heard that in San Juan a dental assistant might make $10 or $11 an hour, but that's the maximum. I started working at $7.25 an hour. Over the seven years I've worked for Dr. Deliz, that's been increased to $8 an hour.[4] My father-in-law, Israel, has a small pension, but other than that and my wages, we depend on food stamps.[5] Dr. Deliz told us to go to the Departamento del Trabajo y Recursos Humanos for help.[6] Going to the Departamento was really bad. All those lines!

The first time I went was October 18, 2017. I got there at 5 a.m. There were people who'd been waiting since three in the morning. The line snaked all the way around the huge parking lot. There were at least two hundred people. A whole mess of people, all waiting. When I saw that line, I was completely desperate. I just wanted to get into the office. But I had to wait two hours just to register, just to put my name on a piece of paper. When I finally got into the building, it was so hot. The rooms were completely sealed and there was no AC. There was still no power, and the generators weren't working. I was told to go away and come back another day.

---

4. According to the US Bureau of Labor Statistics, the national estimates for the median hourly wage for dental assistants in 2018 was $18.59.

5. The former US Food Stamp program is currently called Supplemental Nutrition Assistance Program (SNAP)—or Nutrition Assistance Program (NAP) in Puerto Rico—but people often still refer to the assistance as "food stamps" or "*los cupones*." Puerto Rico was part of the Food Stamp program until 1982 when it was reconfigured as a block grant. At that time, funding was substantially cut, and funding limits were imposed. For more on food assistance, see "Block Grants" and "Aftermaths" in the "Contexts" essay.

6. Departamento del Trabajo y Recursos Humanos is the Puerto Rico Department of Labor and Human Resources.

The second time I went back, I had an appointment. At that point, they were organizing people by social security number, so it was days before I could even continue the process. I got there at five in the morning again and had to wait three hours before I could give my documentation to someone. The office was overloaded and understaffed. There were packs of people making claims. And sometimes the computer system was down. Usually there are around twenty employees. In the weeks after the hurricane, only five to seven employees were working at the Departamento. I guess they had problems getting in to work too.[7] A lot of people were complaining, "Can't they do this faster? Why isn't the line moving?" Everybody was so agitated. It was really a bad situation. A lot of people had their kids with them. Some were older or maybe had a medical problem. But you couldn't cut the line. You just had to wait.

The third time, I had to wait a week before I could go back to finish filing my claim and get a card with information on it about when I would receive money. By this time they had power, but it wasn't reliable and they still had no working generator. I'd expect more from a government facility—they needed a generator that worked. If the power went out, they couldn't work. They'd cancel everything and send everyone away. That's what happened to me. I waited three and a half hours and the staff said, "The electricity isn't working, you have to go home. Come back tomorrow."

The fourth time, I had to wait in those long lines again, but I was able to finish the process. Once you got your papers filed, the government was supposed to deposit money in your checking account. But there were problems with the deposits. If you didn't get the money, you'd have to visit the Departamento again.

---

7. After the hurricane, the workforce was affected across the archipelago. Blocked roads and personal issues—loss of home, health issues, access to gas—impeded people from returning to work, and as a result offices and businesses were often understaffed.

I didn't get the money, so I had to go back a fifth time. The clerks said they couldn't find the document I'd filed. They thought that maybe it was stored somewhere else with other documents. Or maybe it was filed by last name or by social security number. It was all very disorganized. I wasn't the only one. A lot of people's paperwork got lost and they'd have to register all over again. And whenever you went back for help, no matter what—even if it was just to ask a question—you had to wait in that same long line.

THE BABY GOT SICK

On October 28, over a month after the hurricane, we finally got running water back in our home. Ezequiel was healthy and everything with him seemed good. But then around October 31, the baby got sick.

He was coughing and had a runny nose. His fever got very high, 103.6°F. The doctor said there was bacteria in his blood, and it was common to see that happen with babies, but other than that I never really got a lot of information. I didn't think about asking more questions; I was just trying to get through the days. Ezequiel was hospitalized for six days. He was taken to the pediatric ward, and we had to bring his bathtub, lotions, and clothes because the hospital doesn't supply that. Only one parent was allowed to stay with him. Since I was working at the office, Darlyn stayed with him. Sleeping alone and thinking about him and Darlyn in the hospital was hugely stressful.

My sadness during this whole time was mixed with frustration. The phones still didn't work well, so when Ezequiel was in the hospital, I'd have to go to the hospital just to know how he was doing. I also wanted to get things done, get things fixed around the house, but I just couldn't. I was driving all the time.

It was really bad having to get to work, the hospital, and the Departamento, and then having to make it back home. The traffic lights weren't working. To get to town I couldn't even use the usual road. It took two months for the government to fully clean up the area around my house.[8] They fixed one road, but it was still a very long route for me. I had to go all around a huge part of the mountain to get to town. Usually it takes fifteen minutes to get to work. After the hurricane, it took forty minutes. And to get to the hospital took an hour.

The city did its job as well as possible with what it had, but I think there would have been better services and the cleanup would have been faster if we were in the States. When I was younger and living in Florida with my mom and stepfather, Hurricane Katrina hit. It was almost a Category Four hurricane where we lived. The roads were all blocked and we lost electricity. But there, it only took a week to get everything cleared and the electricity stable. Plus we had trucks that would stop at our apartment and give us supplies. The aid was better organized and fast. But that's Florida, not here.

Living in Puerto Rico can be challenging sometimes. The economy is struggling, and there are problems in the health care system, especially with medical insurance and Medicaid.[9] As a dental assistant I see this from both sides—the doctors and the patients. I see what Dr. Deliz goes through just to get paid. And I also talk to the patients. For them, the insurance often doesn't cover the cost of the service, so they have to pay for the rest out of their own pockets. Personally, I don't find it that challenging living here because—even though there are problems—there is also always someone willing to help.

---

8. It took longer to clear roads in other areas. In November 2017, *Axios*, sharing FEMA's update on the status of Puerto Rico's roads, reported that of the island's 5,073 miles of roads, 2,932 miles were open, most of which were located in the outer ring of the island, not the mountainous interior. Six months after the hurricane, Oxfam reported that roads were cleared. With very limited public transportation, Puerto Rico is almost completely car-dependent.

9. Even before the hurricane, Puerto Rico's health care system had been struggling for a variety of reasons, including the economic instability of the archipelago, the migration of health care professionals, obstacles facing block grant–funded programs like Medicaid, and austerity measures. For more on the debt crisis, block grants, and austerity measures, see "Economic Contexts" in the "Contexts" essay.

Around the third week of November, five weeks after his first visit to the Departamento del Trabajo y Recursos Humanos, Emmanuel started receiving $150 every two weeks. On January 8, 2018, more than three months after the hurricane, he returned to full-time work at the dentist's office and stopped receiving unemployment benefits.

When we spoke to Emmanuel again in May 2020, he was still employed by Dr. Deliz, but no one at the dentist's office was able to work because Puerto Rico had been on lockdown due to COVID-19 since March 15.

Around March 10, we closed the dentist office, and I knew that I'd have to go back to the Departamento and go through the same long process again. On March 16, I filled out the forms online. I was really worried about what was going to happen. I had to pay bills and make car payments. At that time, no one was giving breaks for payments yet. Darlyn and I don't have medical insurance. I don't get coverage with my job. The government covers the kids, but my wife and I aren't eligible for Medicaid. We used to have it, but they took it away two months ago. If you exceed the limit for income, even by a dollar, they remove you. So now we have to pay for our own medications. And God help us if we have to be in the hospital because I'd have to pay for it in cash and we just don't have it.

Darlyn had a part-time job in a nursing home and she was still working a couple days a week, so that really helped. But around March 20 they let her go. She was disappointed because she couldn't help me. She said, "I don't want you to keep paying the bills by yourself." We always comfort each other, and we said, "We can get through this." But it'd been three or four weeks, and I was still waiting for money from the Departamento to come in. I was really desperate, especially having three kids at home.

This time around, we got our unemployment check six weeks after I applied for help. It was on April 27, and we get $198 every two weeks. We also got the federal money that everybody is getting around May 2, but there are still thousands who haven't received these benefits and are waiting for help.[10] Last week, I was that person. I didn't have anything at all.

Getting money was such a relief. But things are still difficult. I'm really afraid of another big earthquake.[11] It's also hard not being able to see family. But what I miss most is work. I like being active. And I love talking with patients. My biggest worry about this whole COVID shutdown was losing my job. But the whole time the office was closed Dr. Deliz said he would keep his staff intact and he did. On May 27, we started seeing patients again. I was so happy to go back to work, but with the pandemic and the earthquakes, everything is still very uncertain.

Almost five months after reopening, Dr. Deliz's office reduced its staff because of the impact of COVID-19 on business. Emmanuel was laid off on October 12, 2020. He sent out résumés that same week, and a week later he was hired full time by another dentist in Mayagüez.

---

10. In mid-May 2020, the US Treasury Department estimated that 87 percent of eligible Americans had received their Economic Impact Payment. The delay in payment to some residents of Puerto Rico was a result of "special rules" for people living in US territories.

11. An ongoing earthquake swarm in Puerto Rico began on December 28, 2019. There have been thousands of earthquakes since then, the largest registering at 6.4. For more on the earthquakes, see "Earthquake Swarm" in the "Contexts" essay.

RAMÓN LÓPEZ SOTO

BORN IN: 1942
LIVES IN: Aguadilla
Retired Builder

Ramón López Soto was born and raised in Aguadilla, a municipality in the northwest.[1] He lives in Edificio Víctor Hernández, a four-story concrete apartment building for seniors. In the hallway of the building, black and white photos of historical Aguadilla hang on the walls, showing workers in sugarcane fields and other industries. The cultivation of sugarcane has a long history in the archipelago, going back to the sixteenth century.[2] The sugar industry peaked in the first decades of the twentieth century, but by the 1960s it had begun to decline for a variety

---

1. Aguadilla has a population of approximately 50,000.

2. For more on sugar plantations in Puerto Rico, see "Transatlantic Slave Trade" and "The Spanish-American War" in the "Contexts" essay.

of reasons, including government policies. Ramón's first job was in the sugarcane fields.

Ramón spends much of his time in the building's garden, but if he is not there, he can often be found sitting at the entrance where he greets people. Because Ramón is mostly blind, he sometimes walks with a cane, but he does not always need it. He is very familiar with the building, its grounds, and his own apartment, which is on the fourth floor and has one room and a bathroom. His apartment is neat, his bed perfectly made. It is also uncluttered, but he does have pictures of his grandchildren, which he shows us with pride when we meet with him in the fall of 2018. Ramón has called the Víctor Hernández his home for over eight years, so it was especially difficult when he was forced to leave it and go to a shelter one day before Hurricane María.

I WASN'T SEEING AT ALL

I am blind. I can see a little from one eye, but mostly I can't see anything. I've been like this for more than ten years. I've had two surgeries, but the doctors say that if they keep trying, I risk losing the little sight I have left.

I got glaucoma from working outside so much. I've almost always worked outside, starting from when I was a kid, working in the sugarcane fields. Money was really tight in my family because there weren't enough jobs and the pay was poor. My father worked construction and earned really little back then—around seventy-seven cents an hour. Imagine that! There wasn't much to eat. One meal a day and some other little snacks, but at least we survived.

I attended school until seventh grade, and then I had to drop out so I could help support the family. I was so young that they wouldn't let me cut the sugarcane. Instead, I was sent into the fields to pick up the leftovers that the machine discharged, little jobs like that. This building where I now live was actually built on the land where I used to work. At that time, it was all sugarcane fields here.

By the time I was seventeen, I was working in construction like my father. Most of the time I had work, but sometimes I was unemployed for two, three months, until I could find something. Sometimes when there wasn't employment, I worked as a painter. I wanted a different job, but I didn't really have other opportunities.

I was a builder for almost forty years. The long hours I'd spent working outside and the brightness of the sun affected my sight. I lost my sight gradually. When I realized that I wasn't seeing at all, I was in the middle of building a house. I couldn't finish it. I stopped working construction in 2006. I requested social security, but they gave too little. I was able to work in a small store that sold drinks, beans, rice, motor oil—a little bit of everything. I stayed there seven years before retiring.

I DIDN'T WANT TO GO

I've lived in the Víctor Hernández building for over eight years. I live alone, but I have friends here and most of my family is in Aguadilla, so they're nearby. I have three children and seven grandchildren. My family visits me, but I have a helper. I spend a lot of my time working in the garden, planting beans, corn, cassava, and *gandules*, or pigeon peas.

When I received the news that a hurricane would strike the island, *válgame*, I felt bad, but I didn't feel scared.[3] My daughter came to see me before María hit. I didn't go with her or stay with family during the hurricane because I wanted to stay here. I like being independent. But then, one day before the hurricane, we were asked to evacuate the building. The building administrator informed everyone that we had to go to a shelter. I and four or five other people in the building didn't want to leave. I didn't want to go to a strange place I'd never been to before. I said that I couldn't go to a shelter because I'm blind. I can't

---

3. *Válgame* is an idiom commonly used in western Puerto Rico. The term is equivalent to "my goodness," "oh my God," or "geez."

even walk around if I don't know the place. I notified the shelter that I was blind, and the staff there said, "You shouldn't come here. It's not really set up to care for a person who is blind."

But the administrator said, "If you can't go to a shelter, you'll have to go to a hospital." I didn't want to go to a hospital either. When I refused to leave, she came here with two other employees and forced me out. She forced my friends out. She pressured us and said we had to leave and, if we didn't, she'd have the police kick us out.

We went to the shelter on September 19. There were a lot of us—twelve or fifteen—mostly people who had nowhere else to go. A school bus came and picked us up. Some people didn't have time to pack what they needed. When the bus arrived, one woman was still in her apartment. They were closing all the gates, and she was still in there, because they hadn't given her enough time to prepare. She had to leave without many of her things. The shelter was in the Escuela Superior Benito Cerezo Vázquez, a high school in the barrio Borinquen.[4]

The conditions were really terrible. I was in a classroom with about forty people. The room wasn't that big, about the size of two small apartments. There was no separate place for disabled people. Everyone was together, even the sick ones. There was no doctor. The windows had plastic on them, so there was no ventilation. There were no bathrooms close by. They were outside of the building!

SLEPT ON THE FLOOR

There were two women in charge of the shelter, a policeman, and two other women who helped. There were cooks who made us breakfast, lunch, and dinner, but they left at night.

---

4. The Superior Benito Cerezo Vázquez school is approximately one mile away from the Víctor Hernández building.

When the hurricane hit, the power went out. We didn't have a generator. We didn't even have a fan, nothing.[5] Because the windows were sealed with plastic, we had to leave the door open for ventilation. The classroom where we stayed was in the center of the building, so there wasn't much of a breeze, but because the door was open a lot of water came in. The place started flooding. The employees and some other people tried to keep the water out, but about a foot of water flooded the room in some places. My feet were all wet. People were screaming. I was scared. I thought, *What will happen to us?*

We passed hours without sleeping. Who could've slept? The shelter provided cots, but it was better if you just found a dry spot and slept on the floor. I never once used the cot and I was there for two days. It was really loud, and we could hear the wind outside. I felt it when things hit the windows. Everything was being blown by the wind—branches, metal, zinc roof panels. Many people were overwhelmed and screaming, sick people were screaming all night. An old man was sick, and since there was no doctor and no way to get him to the hospital, that man screamed and screamed, and didn't let us sleep the entire night.

Because the bathrooms were far and outside the building, we couldn't use them during the worst part of the hurricane. The women had to relieve themselves in pails inside the classroom, holding up cardboard to give each other privacy. If the wind calmed a bit, we'd use the bathrooms. We had to go outside often—in a hurricane—just to go to the bathroom! My clothes were all wet. At one point, I was on my way to the bathroom when a door blew open and hit me really hard. It threw me on the sidewalk. In the end, the bathrooms were flooded with so much dirty water that we couldn't go in there anyway.

---

5. The temperatures around the time of the hurricane ranged from a high of 82°F with 94 percent humidity to a high of 86°F with 84 percent humidity. By September 22, temperatures increased to a high of 90°F throughout much of the day.

This was my first time in a shelter. It was a surprise, and not a good one.

WE HAD TO BREAK THE LOCKS

Two days after Hurricane María, since the storm was over, we had to leave the shelter. I tried to communicate with my family, but the cell phones weren't working. There was no phone service or internet. Some of the people from my building were able to go with their families. But eight people were left, and a bus came to take us home. They dropped us off at the entrance of the Víctor Hernández building. They left us here. The building was completely sealed, boarded up with panels on the doors and everything. We had no way to get in and the administrator was nowhere to be found. There was no place to go. We had to stay outside.

Later that day, the police came and helped us take off the panels, but the doors couldn't be opened because they were locked from the inside. The administrator who was in charge of the building—and the only person who could open the doors—had disappeared. The police were looking for her because she'd abandoned the building and us.

We tried to open the locks. Someone forced the lock. He inserted a key and he kept trying to unlock it until he broke the lock. That opened the front door of the building. We were able to go into the hallway of the first floor but not anywhere else. The doors to the other floors were also locked. I live on the fourth floor, so there was no way I could go home. Even if we could get to our apartments, there wasn't a way to open the apartments because we didn't have the keys. It felt so bad being so close to my apartment but not being able to go in. We ended up waiting in the hallway for the administrator to appear.

The eight of us lived in that hallway for three days. It had been terrible at the shelter, but the worst part was those days in the hallway. Válgame, it was hot! There was no ventilation. And the floor was all wet. Water had come in on the ground floor, and it smelled because the water was dirty and also because of all the humidity. We had to mop the floor, just so we could stay there. We had no running water. We weren't able to bathe. Everybody was upset.

There was no refrigerator, no place for cooking. For a while, all we had was coffee that the neighbors brought us. Eventually, people from the shelter gave us food, since it still had a working kitchen. But we had no access to medication if we needed some. We were without electricity. The hallway was completely dark at night. The emergency lights that are supposed to turn on when there is a power outage were burned out. We were without beds and were sleeping on the floor. I already hadn't slept for two days in the shelter. And in the hallway we didn't sleep either. In total, it was five nights without any kind of good sleep. I was so tired.

The administrator finally arrived six days after the hurricane. It was day four of us being forced to stay in the hallway with nowhere else to go. But she came to take pictures of the damage to the building, not to look after us. She didn't want us to be in the building. She said we had to wait for the caretaker to come. But he didn't have the keys. She had the keys. I don't know why, but she just didn't want to open up the building. We couldn't convince her. Then she disappeared again. Eventually, we had to break the locks and enter our apartments by force.

WITHOUT WATER AND POWER

When I got into my apartment, it was such a joyful moment because I was finally home. As I went around checking on everything, I found that not even a drop of water had entered my apartment. It was the complete opposite of what had happened at the shelter! I was comfortable and it was so good to be in my own bed. I was finally able to sleep. But I was without water and power for the next thirty-seven days.

Do you know what it's like to be without running water for so much time? The building has a water tank, but the administrator—when she finally came back—refused to let us have water in our apartments. So we paid a man to bring us water, and neighbors also gave us water. Finally, the caretaker gave us access to the water reserve. Some men installed a hose, so we could get water on the ground floor and take it upstairs. But it was just good for washing, not for drinking. Since the elevator wasn't working, we needed to haul the buckets and trash cans of water up the stairs to our apartments. Because I can't see, I had to hold the handrails with one hand and carry the bucket with the other up four floors to my apartment. I helped other people carry their water up the stairs, too. We all helped each other out. Sometimes, I went up and down the stairs twenty times a day carrying water.

We had a generator, but the administrator only turned it on during the day. At night, she turned it off. It was completely dark, so we complained. Someone even came from San Juan and asked me, "When do you want to use the generator? Day or night?" and I said, "It has to be at night because we don't need it during the day. Why do we need a generator during the day?" He went to talk to the administrator in her office, and she said, "It has to be during the day," and nothing changed. The administrator was finally dismissed six months after the hurricane. She was fired for abandoning the building and us.[6]

For a long time after María, I couldn't communicate with my children by phone because there was no cell phone reception. When the roads were clear my family did come to see me. But even after all that had happened, I still didn't want to go with them and leave

6. A report by the Comisión de Asuntos del Consumidor y Servicios Públicos Esenciales (Committee on Consumer Affairs and Essential Public Services) confirmed that the elderly residents of the Víctor Hernández building were left without food, electricity, and running water. A criminal complaint has been made and the incident is being investigated.

my apartment here. I wanted to stay in my home. Everyone from the building helped each other. One neighbor was in charge of getting meals from the shelter for us, and we all helped with hauling water up the stairs. We supported each other. It was my friends from the building—David, Nereida, Milda, Lalo, Luisa, and others—who were key to my recuperation after the hurricane.

SHANIA TATYANNA
LIND GONZÁLEZ

BORN IN: 1999
LIVES IN: Mayagüez
Student

Shania Tatyanna Lind González spent the first twelve years of her life in Jersey City, New Jersey. Shania was adopted in 2011 and moved to Puerto Rico with her parents that year. While at first she struggled with the change, she now says, "My heart belongs to both places."

Shania is a chemical engineering student at the University of Puerto Rico in Mayagüez.[1] In the fall of 2018, we meet with her at a local park that is sandwiched between the university campus and downtown

---

1. Mayagüez is a western municipality with a population of approximately 71,000.

Mayagüez. The day is hot and humid, so we sit in the park's gazebo, enjoying the shade and a slight breeze.

Around the time of the hurricane Shania was producing vlogs about her life, which also included videos of her experience of the storm. In the videos and in person, her voice almost always remains calm as she recounts her struggles with foster care, family life, and her time during the hurricane. Before the hurricane Shania had been fighting with her parents. She spent the hurricane alone in a house in Mayagüez.

I WAS A PROJECT BABY

Before the hurricane, Mamá and I were fighting a lot, so instead of going to stay with my family in Arroyo, I stayed in Mayagüez.[2] When I'm not in Mayagüez, I feel like an alien. Like there's something seriously wrong with me. It's definitely easier living here. It's a university town with a lot of young people and, in general, we're much more accepting. Plus, the people I surround myself with here are also queer, so I don't feel discriminated against. But when I leave Mayagüez and go to smaller, rural towns, it's very noticeable how different I am. Like I don't belong.

I was a project baby. My birth mom, Joyce, is Puerto Rican, but she's from New Jersey. I was born in Jersey City. When I was born, my birth dad was like, "No, that's not my kid." So, for the first five years of my life, it was just my mom and me. We had an apartment in Jersey City with Section 8.[3] We lived in the Curries Woods housing project on the fifteenth floor in one small-assed apartment.[4]

---

2. Arroyo is a southeastern coastal municipality with a population of approximately 17,000. It is approximately ninety miles away from Mayagüez.

3. Section 8 is a federally funded program that provides low-income households with rental assistance.

4. Built in 1959, the Curries Woods towers were Jersey City's largest subsidized housing project at that time.

My mom was neglectful. I can't remember eating real food. She'd get me chips or Twizzlers and stuff like that from the corner store. I never used to shower. I didn't know how to brush my teeth. My hair was a mess. My mom would never do my hair. I saw pictures of me when I was with my mom, and my hair was really sad then. My mom was abusive. She'd hit me and kick me. She was crazy. She'd do stuff like wake me up at midnight to go for long walks. Cops were always coming and going in and out of our apartment. I never really understood why; I was so young that my memory of this time is blurry.

My sister, Janessa, was born when I was five. Her father was my stepdad. But then my mom cheated on him, and we moved in with my mom's parents. My grandma was a drunk. I don't have memories of her being sober, just of her forcing me to dance salsa with her in the living room.

Not too long after us moving in with them, my mom stole money from my grandma. My grandma caught her and was mad. A couple nights later, my mom woke me up in the middle of the night and said, "We're going to leave." She took me and my sister, who was in her stroller, and we were leaving the building when Grandma came out behind us. She was screaming and beating up my mom in the street. She was pulling stuff out of my mom's pocket. I was too young to even understand what was going on, but that night my grandma called the cops on my mom. When the police came, they took us away to foster care.

A SHIT-TON OF FOSTER KIDS

In foster care, my sister and I were moved around a lot. A Dominican lady taught me how to shower. She said, "You need a shower every day. This is how you shower." She taught me how to brush my teeth and how to braid my hair. Eventually we ended up with my foster parents María and Anastasio. But we weren't with them the whole time. We'd go to other homes and then come back to María. We were even with my birth mom for a year. I was around seven. My mom was in this rehab center for women who are recovering from drug abuse that allows you to raise your kids. They provided us with breakfast, lunch, and dinner. They had a school. It was a nice place. But supposedly they caught my mom on camera kicking me in the stomach and hitting my sister. So, we came back to María's.

María never told me why she was a foster mom, but she always had a shit-ton of foster kids coming and going. A lot of different kids and babies would come, and then get adopted. Or they would throw a fit and María would get mad and have DYFS come and pick them up.[5]

María and Anastasio also had daughters of their own, but they were older. One of their daughters lived on the bottom floor with her sons, who were around my age. I could see the bond between María and her daughters and grandsons. But I didn't feel like she bonded with me. I always wanted to play Monopoly or read books together—normal mother-daughter stuff—but that just didn't happen. She worked in a legal office in New York City and was always busy. We never did anything together. I didn't feel like I could trust her, to tell her about my day or things like that. I remember one time I had a nightmare, so I went to her room and I told her, "I can't sleep. I'm scared." And she said, "That's stupid. Go to your room." And she shut the door in my face. I just wanted a hug or a kiss or something, but she never gave me one. I never really felt motherly love from her. And I never really interacted with Anastasio, either. He'd just wake up, go to work, and that's it. When you're a foster kid or adopted, the difference can be very marked. Sometimes, no matter how much you want the love to be equal, it doesn't feel that way.

My sister and I would visit with our mom every second Thursday at the DYFS center. By law, the birth mother is allowed to visit with her children under supervision. Sometimes she wouldn't come

---

5. DYFS stands for Division of Youth and Family Services, New Jersey's child protection agency. In 2012, it was renamed Division of Child Protection and Permanency.

to the visits, but when she came, we'd have fun playing board games. I'd tell her about school and my problems. I liked going to see her. She'd hug me and tell me, "I love you. I'm going to do better. I'm going to get you back." So, I really thought she was going to do that. I kept a journal where I'd write about how much I missed her, how I wanted to go back to her, and how I didn't like anyone else. I'd write about how these foster parents weren't my real parents and stuff like that.

One by one, I saw other foster kids go back to their parents or get adopted by other people. We didn't. In the end, we spent so much time with María that I got accustomed to her. She and Anastasio were parental figures because they gave me a home and they fed me. I call María *Mamá*, but I didn't have an emotional bond with her.

THINGS THAT DIVIDE US SHOULD BURN

María and Anastasio adopted my sister and me in 2011. Around that time, we stopped communicating with our biological mom because Mamá just didn't let us. I think it caused her insecurity as a mom. We weren't allowed to have contact with any of our birth family.

That same year, Mamá was retiring and wanted to move back to Puerto Rico because she was born here. We settled in Arroyo. It was so different here. I didn't feel like school was challenging. I'd tell Mamá, "School's too easy. It bores me." The material they were giving me in class, I'd already studied three years before in the States. There were kids in the sixth grade who didn't know how to multiply and divide. That shocked me. But it's not their fault. It's the system. I didn't feel like I was learning anything new, but I easily got good grades.

In high school, though, I had the best time of my life. I even had a boyfriend. It was my first relationship and it was beautiful. I fell in love with him. Mamá didn't suspect I was gay because I had a boyfriend. She's Pentecostal and would always talk about gay people in a bad way. She'd say things like, "All those homosexuals are going to go to Hell. It's in the Bible. It's wrong. It's not natural."

That relationship lasted until college and then my boyfriend and I went our separate ways. I think I've been *gay* gay since college. By then, I could never watch straight porn, and sex with men was never pleasurable. But when I'd look at girls or watch lesbian porn, I'd feel mad guilty about it. Like, *That's wrong! That's the Devil!* At first, I thought, *Oh, damn, I can't be gay. I don't want to go to Hell.* But I don't like men, and I can't force myself to like something I don't.

It was weird telling Mamá I'm a lesbian because, at that moment, I didn't care what she thought. It was only a few weeks before the hurricane. I just said, "Listen, I'm gay." But she made a big deal out of it. She said, "Why is God punishing me? You went to church. You read the Bible. You know what's going to happen to you. You're going to go to Hell." She was mad extra.[6] I really didn't fight back or anything. I was like, *Whatever, you're just going to have to deal with it.* I told her my sexuality is my sexuality. No one has to give me their opinions on that. My parents should care about my well-being, not my sexuality.

But my family criticizes me for things like using men's cologne and wearing men's shoes—or what's considered to be men's shoes—because who puts gender on clothing, *cabrón*?[7] It's just clothing; it doesn't have a gender. Why the division? I don't feel we should be divided. All things that divide us should burn.

So, yeah, before the hurricane, Mamá and I were fighting about a lot of things—me being gay and smoking weed and being rebellious—but it was also because I was talking to my biological mom. I hadn't had contact with her for years because Mamá wouldn't let me. But after I moved out of Mamá's house, I was on Instagram

---

6. "Mad extra" is slang for being overly dramatic or excessive. When used by youth to refer to adults, it can also mean judgmental or close-minded.

7. The literal translation of *cabrón* is "male goat." In Puerto Rican Spanish slang, depending on the context, it can be understood as "dude." For more, see the glossary.

and one of my cousins found me and put me in contact with my mother. Mamá accused me of going behind her back. It was just a miscommunication, but we fought over it. I've always been very independent, always taken care of myself, so I told her, "I'm an adult and I can make my own decisions. I don't need you!" So I wasn't even on speaking terms with my family when the hurricane came.

ONE PACK OF RITZ CRACKERS

All the people I knew from university had left to be with their families. I didn't have a girlfriend at that time. I was living in a rented room in a one-story, three-bedroom house by the campus. One room was always locked and the other was my housemate's, but she was an exchange student from Spain and was gone for months at a time. She wasn't there before the hurricane, so I was alone. I was aware that there was a hurricane on the way, but I thought it would just rain for a few days. I didn't know that there'd be no electricity and so much destruction. I didn't know I had to be prepared or anything like that. I didn't have food or water. When the hurricane came, I had one pack of Ritz crackers, a candle, and not much else.

From inside my house, the hurricane just felt like a lot of rain. I mostly just stayed in my room. A little water came in, but the house wasn't flooded, just a bit wet. The worst part was not having running water or electricity. It was dark with all the windows closed. Sometimes I'd open the window to look out, and I could see my neighbor's house getting all messed up. Her *techo*, her roof, was made of zinc, and it was peeling off with the wind. I was surprised at how powerful the storm was. I'd never seen something like that.

In my room, I'd eat one cracker at a time, so they could last me longer. If I was really hungry, I'd just sleep. There was nothing to do in my house except read. I was reading *The Hundred-Year-Old Man Who Climbed Out the Window and Disappeared.* All I wanted to do was read in peace, but my one candle burned out. So I went out into the hurricane to look for light. I walked a little and found a building that had a red emergency light. I sat on the curb under that light and read. I was getting rained on, and it was crazy. So I went back to my house.

When the storm quieted down a bit, I put on some flip-flops and walked to the plaza to see if there was damage. It was still night. It was all dark and a mess. Trees were fallen on the ground everywhere, stop signs were knocked over, and traffic lights were dangling at face level. I'm like, *Oh my God, look at this!*

I spotted a light at the sports arena, the Palacio.[8] I wanted to read my book, so I walked over. The Palacio was being used as a shelter. I went in and later the guards wouldn't let me leave because of the storm. My house is close by. I could've just gone home, but they wouldn't let me. I had to stay there all night. I hated it. It was so loud and disorganized. There was a pile of cots—you'd pick one and put it wherever you wanted. If there was space, put a cot there and sleep. Imagine a circular arena full of a bunch of beds and people lying on them.

There were so many people in the Palacio. It was very crowded. Oh, my Lord, I saw everything there. There was a shit-ton of people and no privacy. I saw families with babies and kids. The babies were crying. It was really sad. There were also crackheads and addicts who'd go to the bathroom to do drugs. I was so scared that I slept right next to the guards, but that was the worst because during the night, everyone would go up to the guards to complain about some-body else. There was a lady who was yelling at a guy because the guy kept wanting to have sex with her. She was saying, "He's sick *de la cabeza*, in the head. I'm telling him *no*, but he keeps *molestándome*, bothering me." The security guards started taking the guy out. Then they all started fighting. The lack of order led to the craziest things. I only stayed there that one night.

---

8. "Palacio" is short for the Palacio de Recreación y Deportes Germán Wilkins Vélez Ramírez, which is a Mayagüez stadium with a capacity of 5,500 people.

I EMPTIED OUT MY PIGGY BANK

Shania recorded videos of the first few nights and days of the storm. She shared a few with us. One video shows Shania the next morning walking away from the Palacio. The predawn sky is cloudy and gray. Shania steps around broken trees. She is crying when she says, "It's a little scary. This hurricane has left Puerto Rico so messed up."

The morning after the hurricane I went to the bank to take out some money, but it was closed and none of the ATMs were working. I was starving, so I emptied out my piggy bank and managed to get three dollars.

Because I couldn't get money from the bank, I went back to the Palacio. During the day, you could come and go freely. You had to leave by night, or you'd get locked in. I showered there a few times and there was always food—cafeteria food like rice and beans. I went there every day for a few weeks, until we got electricity and power back in Mayagüez.

I also went scavenging for food from supermarkets like Mr. Special and Pueblo. Those stores were powered with generators, so they were open. They were only accepting cash, though, which I didn't have access to because the banks were still closed. So, I just stole. I mostly had a vegan diet, so I took healthy foods that I couldn't get at the Palacio.

Sometimes, I'd go to the Palacio just to be with people. When I went there, though, everyone was just sitting around moping, doing nothing. There was electricity in the arena, but no signal for phones. We were all bored. There were some thirteen-year-olds there who I interacted with a lot. They were funny. I'd bring books from my place and we'd talk about books and college. They especially liked *The Hundred-Year-Old Man.*

Mamá was the first person I talked to on the phone after I got a signal. It was almost a month before we were able to get in touch. She was really worried because she hadn't heard from me in such a long time and just wanted to know if I was okay. Just hearing from me made her super happy. She told me that she and the rest of my family had actually tried to come and get me but couldn't because of the blocked roads. It felt good to hear from them.

A BIG NO-NO

Mamá actually came to see me around the end of October, before classes started again, and we talked it out. She was like, "I'm here to take you back with me. You're not going to stay in Mayagüez." And I'm like, "No, I'm not going with you." But I talked and cried with her.

We talked about a lot of things that I was going through and her issues as well. One of her issues was about videos I'd made and posted online. I had a bunch of them, showing my day-to-day experiences. Before the hurricane, the videos were just of me going out and doing stuff. Some of them had my girlfriend at the time in them. The videos during and after the hurricane pretty much centered on the destruction and my reaction.

The last video I posted was actually of me crying over something about Mamá. In the videos, things weren't always pretty. I wasn't like, "I'm 100 percent okay. And my parents love me, and everything is great!"—because I'm a normal person who has problems. It was just my life, but Mamá didn't like it. Also, my family's very traditional, so those videos of me with my girlfriend—that's a big no-no.

Some of Mamá's friends had seen my videos and were criticizing her. She wasn't happy at all. She felt like I'd embarrassed her by "exploiting" myself online. She thinks that if I share my problems publicly, they're going to reflect badly on her—it'll look like she didn't raise me right or take care of me. If I say, "I was starving. I only had three Ritz crackers," my mom says, "What will my friends think of me? They're going to think I don't care about you, that I left you with no food and no money, that I abandoned you!"

In the end, Mamá told me to take down the videos and I did. I mean, who's going to fight after we just got destroyed by a hurricane?

It was just like, "I'm so happy to hear from you. I don't care about the fight we had—at least you're alive! You're not dead!"

We talked with Shania via Zoom at the end of May 2020. She spoke to us from her new apartment where she lives alone. Puerto Rico had been on lockdown due to COVID-19 since March 15, so Shania had been sheltering in place by herself for two and a half months.

I've been doing good actually. I'm alone, but I'm not necessarily sad about that. I enjoy my own company. I'm much more at peace when I'm away from Mamá. My relationship with my adoptive family is what it is. I understand that they're old school. The way that they did stuff back then is not necessarily how people do things now. So there's still friction. Mamá's always mad at something. If she can't find anything to be upset about, she'll make something up. Nothing positive comes out of her mouth. No compliments. No "you did a great job." It's always, "you're stupid" or "you're dirty," stuff like that. So I just keep my distance. My adoptive dad can't stand being at home because Mamá's always on him for some shit. He's like, "Why are you always screaming?" He's very peaceful actually. He likes to be on his *finca*, his farm, and that's what we bond over—plants and animals, but it's not like we're very affectionate or close.

   I've actually seen my birth mom since the hurricane. She came to visit me last summer. She's been supportive and loving, and she's asked for forgiveness. She's very antiviolence now. She told me that she'd finished rehab. She doesn't do street drugs anymore, but she still does drugs. When she came here, she couldn't go a day without something. She feels like she's grown so much because she doesn't do crack or heroin. She's changed to oxys and palis.[9] To me, it's the same ballgame. She has crazy addictions. She's addicted to gambling. She's

---

9. "Oxy" is short for oxycodone, which is a prescription pain medication. "Pali" is short for the generic drug paliperidone, which is prescription-only and commonly used to treat symptoms of schizophrenia.

addicted to a bunch of shit. Every time we talk on the phone, she's looking for advice. She has a lot of problems. I'm not one to entertain problems. I'm one to focus on the solutions. Last time we were on the phone she said that talking to me was like talking to a psychologist. She's kind of like a teenager, like she never really grew up.

Right now, I would say that instead of concentrating on where I am or my family, I'm more focused on where I'm going and the general direction I want to take my life. I'm working on myself. I'm content and peaceful. I feel grateful.

WINDY DÍAZ DÍAZ[1]

INTERVIEWED IN: San Lorenzo
Retired Health Professional

*Windy's full name is Fredeswinda. "It means storm," she explains, when
we first meet in her home in San Lorenzo, which is located in a mountainous region in the southeast.[2] Windy's home is a modest one-story
white cement house of about 700 square feet. She bought the house new,
almost thirty years ago. A covered carport shelters the entrance to the
house, and Windy has created a little garden in this outdoor space. She*

---

1. To protect Windy's privacy, some personal information has been omitted at her
request, including place of birth, birth year, and other identifying details such as
locations and family members' names. Windy also chose to illustrate her story with
a portrait of her dog, Chispy, by her side.

2. San Lorenzo has a population of approximately 36,000.

has flowers, plants, and herbs growing in containers on wheels so she can easily move them herself from her wheelchair.

Windy is in her fifties. In 1986, she had an accident at work, but that was only the beginning of her multiple health problems. Her health continued to deteriorate, and when we meet with her in November 2019, she had been in a wheelchair for almost ten years. She lives alone, but a neighbor comes to check on her daily and clean once a week. Windy's dog, Chispy, a ten-year-old, fifty-pound white bull terrier, keeps her company and follows her everywhere. For most of our conversation, Chispy lies at Windy's feet. But whenever Windy becomes emotional—as she talks about her frustration over the lack of care and planning for people in wheelchairs or her sorrow about how worried her son was when he couldn't communicate with her for weeks after the hurricane—Chispy sits up and gives Windy her full attention, watching her closely, nudging Windy's hand with her nose or resting her head on her owner's lap.

WE DON'T HAVE TIME FOR SADNESS

When I was young, my mom and dad were both working. When my mom would come home from work, she also had all the housework to do. She'd say to me, "Okay, you have to deal with this." I was only around seven or eight years old, but I was the oldest child, so I helped my mom. I'd come back from school and take care of my brother and sister. There was a lady, a neighbor, who would check on us, but mostly I was alone with my siblings. I'd cook, take care of the house, do everything. I was a Girl Scout and went to meetings on Saturdays, but that's it. I didn't have time to do other things.

It was my great-grandma who taught me how to cook. And her daughter, my grandma, used to cook a lot, but nobody in my house baked. I learned how to bake by myself. I loved to cook and bake. My toys when I was growing up were little stoves, little kitchens. I had an Easy-Bake Oven! Cooking and baking and cleaning—those were the things I knew. I wasn't a kid; I was a little mom.

Taking on responsibilities so early makes you strong. We're strong women in my family. We work hard. My mom is a strong lady. My grandma was also a strong, strong lady. She had a big family to care for and she showed us how to deal with things just by what she did, how she lived. She showed us how to care for and raise a family. It was all about helping the kids grow up into good people. She showed us our strength. That we have to think, work hard, and deal with whatever is happening at the moment. We don't have time for sadness. We're strong women.

I DON'T FEEL MY ARMS

Windy has been widowed twice and raised her son on her own. Her son was four years old when she had the accident that led to the discovery of the multiple health problems she would face.

The accident happened in 1986. I was at work. I was a veterinary technician. It was lunchtime, but I needed to find a file for a doggy who was having surgery, so I went to the room where we kept the files in a large cabinet. To open the drawers, you had to pull them from the top. I pulled a drawer open, but it was so full the whole filing cabinet tipped over. I put my hands out to stop the cabinet, but it kept falling, broke my wrists, and landed on my chest.

I was pinned under the weight of all those files. At that time, I weighed about three hundred pounds. Now, I'm 110, but back then I was a full-figured lady. I kept trying to push the cabinet up with my hands. I said, "I can't, I can't." My wrists were so big and swollen. I tried to push with my legs, but I had all this pain in my back. My adrenaline was so high. I was so pissed off. You know what I was thinking? *I have to move, to get free, because tomorrow is Father's Day, and I still have to go buy a present for Dad!*

People in the office tried to help get the cabinet off me, but it was too heavy. I was pinned under the cabinet for around an hour before another client came into the office and was able to push the filing cabinet back and pull me out. I said to my boss, "I have to leave. Look at my arms!" My right arm was red and my left one was blue. Both wrists were badly bent forward in a horrible position.

I called my mom. She said, "What's happening?" I told her, and she and my dad took me to get checked. By this time, I wasn't in pain. I actually couldn't feel my hands and arms. But I didn't have time to be scared; I had to figure out how to deal with the situation. First, we went to El Hospital Industrial, but they sent us to the emergency room.[3] There, they took X-rays, and a radiologist said, "You have multiple fractures. We have to put casts on both your hands." I had four fractures in my left wrist and six fractures in my right.

After about three months, the doctors took off my casts. I said, "Listen, I've got a problem. Check my hands. I don't feel my arms. Something's wrong with me." I was so worried.

I HAD TO FIGHT

Over the next months, Windy had more problems with her hands and arms, and also her legs, which continued for a year. She experienced pain and numbness, and her fingers started to curve inward. Doctors put plastic splints on her hands to try to open the fingers. She was admitted to the hospital several times. She had physical therapy, two surgeries, and was given nerve blocks to manage pain.[4]

In one month, they gave me nineteen shots to block the pain. With the nineteenth needle, I went into shock for seventy-eight hours.

---

3. El Hospital Industrial, known as Industrial Hospital Services in English, offers medical services to workers who have suffered accidents at work or have occupational-related injuries. It is in San Juan, approximately twenty miles away from San Lorenzo.

4. Nerve blocks are injections of medication on or near nerves. They are used to control or prevent pain.

After I recovered, I talked to the doctors. I said, "It's been a year. You do surgery on me, you give me nineteen blocks, why don't you bring a neurologist or a neurosurgeon to talk to me? Maybe they'll know why I don't feel my legs, my arms. I'm not crazy." What do they do? They send me to a psychiatrist.

I actually said, "Oh, thank God! Now, someone is going to hear me!" When I saw the psychiatrist, I said, "Look, I'm not crazy. Touch this hand and touch the other one. One is hot and one is cold." He touched my hands and said, "You're not crazy. Something's wrong with you." I said, "Finally! Thank you."[5]

After that, two neurosurgeons were brought in to see me. They sent me for a test. When they got the results, they sat down to talk with me. I said, "I want you to tell me the truth. What's going to happen to me in the short term, medium term, and long term? I need to know because I have a young son at home and I have to prepare him." One neurosurgeon said, "Honey, you have to lose a lot of weight because you're going to be in a wheelchair." I asked, "When?" He said, "We don't know. Right now you don't feel your arms. Later you're not going to feel your legs. You're going to be in your bed one day and try to get up, and you're going to fall down, and you'll never feel anything again."

The neurosurgeons told me that I was born with nerve dystrophy and that it just keeps degenerating. It's in my blood and in my spinal cord. The condition was there when I was born, but was dormant until my accident woke it up. They told me, "It's not a mess now, but it's going to be."

---

5. Windy is referring here to how the proper diagnosis was mismanaged and delayed. Even before the hurricane, Puerto Rico's health care system had been struggling for a variety of reasons, including the economic instability of the archipelago, the migration of health care professionals, obstacles facing block grant–funded programs like Medicaid, and austerity measures. For more on the debt crisis, block grants, and austerity measures, see "Economic Contexts" in the "Contexts" essay.

When the doctors talked to me—told me the truth—I just looked at them. They were afraid of my reaction. They told me they were waiting for me to start screaming and crying. But I didn't have time to cry. I had to fight. I had to prepare my young son for life. I had to show him how to clean, how to fight and be strong, how to be a good husband and a good daddy. I had to prepare him for challenges like María and all the things that can happen in life. My health was so bad, all I was thinking was, *If I die, my son will be alone.* My family helped me take care of him while I was in the hospital and of course they would take care of him if something happened to me, but I wanted him to be as strong as possible, as quickly as possible. I had to train him.

I showed him how to cook and clean. He said, "Mom, this work is for girls." I said, "Listen, the chores and jobs, they don't have a sex. If you have money, you can pay for cleaning. But if you don't have money, you have to clean, mop, feed yourself, do the laundry. If you have a wife and she's sick or you have a baby, you have to do all that."

When he was little, my son could play. But I showed him how to play so it would help him when he grew up. Through play, I taught him how to cook and clean. I did give him hugs. There was love in the house, but I still had so much to show him. I was trying to make him strong. I felt like I didn't have time.

PLANS A, B, C, AND D

Over the years, Windy's health deteriorated. By the time she had to use a wheelchair in 2009, her son was grown and already living in the States, where he had moved to in 2005.

Windy has quadriparesis, which is a weakness in all four limbs. Unlike quadriplegia, people with quadriparesis may have some mobility or feeling in their limbs. Windy has no feeling in her arms and legs, but she is still able to move her arms. In addition, her right lung is sometimes partially collapsed. "Honey, it's a long story," she says, as she tells us that at the hospital, they have three binders full of her medical records.[6] In her bedroom, she has an oxygen tank and other equipment set up around her bed. "That's my little hospital," she says. Despite these challenges Windy lives independently. She spent the hurricane at home alone except for the company of her dog, Chispy.

The doctors had told me that it was going to get harder and harder. I have a lot of conditions. I've been in a wheelchair a long time, almost ten years. In 2011, I had a stroke on the left side. That was bad. Now, I have a problem with my lungs and because of that my situation is going to get even worse. The doctors said that by now I'd be bedridden. But I'm a fighter, I don't have time to be worse. The best thing in my life is that I'm positive.

When María was coming, I wasn't too worried. We're on an island; I'd lived through hurricanes before, so I knew what to expect. When Hurricane Hugo came in 1989 and Hurricane Georges came in 1998, I showed my son how to deal with any hurricane or severe tropical weather. This time with María, I didn't tell my son until the last moment because I didn't want him to worry. Finally, I called him, and I said, "Honey, this is coming." He was upset. He said, "Mom, I can come to Puerto Rico. I can help you." I told him, "Remember, I'm always prepared. I have my plans A, B, C, and D." I have to be prepared because I don't have a generator or anything, so I always have a system.

My neighbors helped me put up the aluminum shutters to protect the windows. I prepared my desk. The radio was there and a whole bunch of batteries. I had little battery-operated lights in the corners of all the rooms. I have two electric wheelchairs. The one

---

6. Only some of Windy's many other medical conditions include thoracic outlet syndrome, chronic obstructive pulmonary disease, Tietze Syndrome, multiple sclerosis, severe polyneuropathy, chronic coagulation problems, peripheral vascular problems, osteoporosis, cerebral thrombosis, reflex sympathetic dystrophy, and costochondritis.

I usually use has lights for nighttime, which also helps when the power is out. I pulled out my extra wheelchair and put it in a corner of the kitchen in case I needed it. I made sure both were charged.

I was stocked up with food and water. I prepared an area with food and water for my baby, Chispy. She's my helper. I have a small gas stove, so I prepared an area by the table for cooking. By the sink, in the kitchen, it was all set up with water. I had two water containers with taps set on the side of the sink and smaller plastic containers that I could use to fill them. I had more water in the sheltered area outside, in two of those big plastic storage containers. One had bleach in it for cleaning. In the bathroom, under the sink, I had a little container of water for washing. I had two buckets for washing and one smaller pail for flushing the toilet. It was all set up so it would be easy for me to take care of myself in the bathroom.

In the corner of the living room, I set down a little foam cooler, and inside that I put a plastic cooler. Why? Because I like my coffee and I need milk. In the country, when our grandparents didn't have electricity and they'd need to keep their milk and food fresh, where did they put it? In the water. Because water will keep things cool. So I didn't have ice for my coolers, but I put water in them and then I poured the milk in an empty water bottle and put it inside the coolers, and it stayed fresh for days. You can also reuse the water from the coolers to flush the toilet or clean.

A few days before the storm, I was all set up and then I was waiting. But the problem was I didn't know exactly what time the hurricane was coming. That day, I didn't have power, like much of Puerto Rico. I did have a little radio, but the information wasn't good. At no moment did they say when the winds would start, so I was sitting here with the door open!

At almost eight o'clock, it was dark. I heard some winds. Chispy was trying to get my attention, barking. Then, all of a sudden, water started coming from the tap in the sink. I have a pipe on the roof that connects from the bathroom to the kitchen. The hurricane took

out part of that pipe and water started coming in through the kitch-
en tap. Then, I was hearing winds—big, big winds. I said to myself,
What's going on? It was María.

MY WHEELCHAIR TIPPED OVER

I was dealing with the water coming in, trying to stop it and clean
it up. I managed to plug up the tap, but then I fell down. My wheelchair tipped over. It went *bang* against my leg. I didn't notice I was
hurt because I can't feel anything in my legs and there was no blood
or cut. My wheelchair was broken, so I started to crawl across the
floor. I was trying to pull myself to my other wheelchair, which was
just across the room, maybe about ten feet away. It was so hard because I can't feel my legs and my arms. I can move them a little, but
I don't have much strength. I was trying to move sort of like a snake.
Chispy was trying to help, pushing and pulling me. I was crying.
I couldn't breathe because of my collapsed right lung. It took me
almost two hours to get to my other chair. When I got to the chair,
I used Chispy's body to pull myself up to sit in it.

It was almost 10 p.m. I could hear the winds. The sound was
like howling, like a ghost in the middle of the night. I could hear
all the trees breaking and falling outside. My dog could sense that
the storm was bad. She wanted my attention. I said to her, "This is
María. This is the storm."

The door was still open. I hadn't had a chance to shut it. It was
hard to try to close the door. Every time I tried to close it, the wind
stopped me. You have to control yourself. You can't cry. You can't
panic. Finally, the wind shifted direction and it actually helped me
pull the door closed.

The winds got bigger, stronger, so I went to the middle of the
hallway, which is in the middle of the house so it's the most protected. I wanted to get down lower, but if I get on the floor, I can't get
up easily. My dog was trying to protect me. She stood up, putting

her front paws on my knees, but she's so heavy that I couldn't let her stay there.

I couldn't sleep. Nobody could sleep. María lasted too long.[7] The storm was screaming. The winds were hitting the windows. The aluminum shutters were shaking, but I felt secure because I'd opened my windows a bit. People say, "Close your windows!" But I don't do that. My grandfather used to say that when you're in a strong hurricane, you have to leave two windows open—one for the winds to come in and the other for the winds to go out. If you don't open the windows, the pressure will build and the windows will be sucked out. I had a window cracked open in the back and a window open in the front, in the protected area. I got a little water coming in, but not much, because you know what I had done? I put plastic shower curtains over the windows, tucking them in between the screen and the window frame. I'd done that in my apartment during Hurricane Georges. It worked then and it worked now, too. The water didn't come all the way in; it just stayed in one corner of the living room.

At about two in the morning the storm started changing. It was so silent. We say in Puerto Rico that when the hurricane comes, you hear big, big sounds. When you don't hear anything, the eye of the hurricane is here. Some people think that because the sound is gone, the storm is over. They open their doors. But it's not safe. I say, "People, don't go out! Close your doors because you don't know what's going to happen." There was the calm, the eye of the hurricane, and then all of a sudden the winds came back. They came from the other direction and it was worse.

I looked outside. There were branches flying. I could see the palm tree across the street just bending to the ground and bending back the other way. I could hear other trees breaking. I have two tall pines beside the house. I planted them not long after I bought the house, so they're about twenty-five years old and over two stories

---

7. The winds and rain caused by Hurricane María lasted for longer than thirty hours in Puerto Rico.

high. Before the storm, I had called someone to trim them, but they were going to charge me $600. It was too expensive. So María cut them down and blew them around.

In the morning around six or seven o'clock, I looked outside again. You know where my pine tree was now? In the front of my house! The tree was blocking the handicap ramp! I couldn't leave my home. I was trapped.

The winds were a little quieter, but it was still raining a lot. Fallen electric cables were on the ground everywhere and the street was flooded. There was about two and a half feet of water in the front of the house. In the back, all the fallen trees had broken my fence. When I saw all the damage outside, I thought, *Thank God.* Because I was safe inside my house.

"TEACH ME MORE OF DOMINOES"

Two days after the hurricane, my dog was licking my leg, almost as if to say, "What's going on with you here?" I looked down to check and saw that I had a bruise from when I'd fallen. But there was nothing I could do at the time. The ramp from my house was blocked, and because there was no phone signal, there was no way to call a doctor. In general, I was feeling bad. I couldn't breathe well. I had equipment for oxygen at night, but you need power to run it. I also had an asthma treatment, but you need power for that too. Luckily, that could run off a car battery and one of my neighbors brought me to his car to give me a therapy.

My other neighbors who had a generator also helped charge my wheelchair. It takes at least five or six hours to charge. My neighbors would come at ten at night to take it and bring it back around six in the morning. Once it's charged it will last for about four days. I only had a little cash, but I still gave them five dollars. They didn't want to take the money. I said, "I know you need it for gas for the generator and you're helping me. Please, take it."

Most people tried to help each other. One of the most important things I always say to God is "I need to help others." I'm in a wheelchair, but I'm still here. I thought, *I'm going to help the mamás.* It was the same week of the hurricane and the kids in the neighborhood had no school and nothing to do. I thought I could help keep the kids busy and it would help the mamás to know that their kids were here and having fun. I used to be a teacher, so I asked all the kids in the neighborhood, "Who wants to take classes? I'll teach you—English, mathematics, whatever." The kids talked to their moms and it was all arranged. They would come three times a week, stay from nine in the morning to one in the afternoon, and bring their lunches and water with them. In the end, there were about ten kids who came—boys and girls, ages five to ten.

I taught them reading, writing, and math. We played dominoes to learn mathematics, strategy, and logic. One of my favorite moments was when this little six-year-old girl said, "Teach me more of dominoes." She is the sister of one of the older boys. I asked, "Why?" and she said, "Because the boys say they are smarter than girls. Learning more will make me the smartest." I told her, "It doesn't matter whether you're a boy or a girl. It's how smart you want to be."

One time when I was teaching logic, the kids were curious about how I was managing with no running water or power. They asked me, "How do you do things? You're in a wheelchair, how do you wash your clothes?" I said, "How does the washing machine work? It washes by moving the clothes. *Wishy-washy, wishy-washy.* I do the same thing with my clothes in the buckets in my bathroom."

Then they asked, "Okay, how do you dry your clothes?" I can't wring them out because my hands and arms are weak. So I go outside to the water tap and I twist the wet clothes around the tap and the water comes out. I worked with the kids for a couple weeks after the hurricane. The parents were happy.

I FELT INVISIBLE

Nobody from the government checked on me. No one came, no one helped, no one. In San Lorenzo, there are hardly any wheelchair-accessible areas or ramps, and the officials don't have a list of people who have disabilities. There are a few of us, but they don't know who is disabled and where we live. They can't get to us if there is an emergency. I didn't know if they had shelters we could've gone to because they didn't contact me. I felt invisible. I felt vulnerable. I felt angry.

It was bad for me. I was without running water for a month. Electricity was a problem. I couldn't use my computer. I couldn't call anyone. I didn't have contact with my family, with my son. I couldn't go out. I was trapped. People were trying to clear the streets, so branches and debris had been piled up in front of my house. Nobody came to clear the tree blocking the ramp.

About four weeks after the hurricane, the Red Cross came. I heard people speaking in English so I went outside. There were two ladies and two gentlemen. I thought they might need help, so I asked them if they needed something. They were looking at a paper and then at me. They said, "We're looking for you." "For me?" I asked. They had my picture, my address, all the details to come here to my home. They asked, "When was the last time you spoke with your son?" And I said, "The morning of the day that María came." Then they said, "Your son sent us." I always say God is my hero, but I have another hero too—my son.

The people from the Red Cross had a satellite phone. They gave it to me and said, "Your son needs to hear you say something." I knew what he wanted to hear. I called him and said these four words: "Baby, I love you." My son said, "God bless you. Mum, you're okay!" It was such happiness. He was so excited. Then he asked, "Are you really okay?" I said, "Honey, I'm okay because I'm speaking with you." He said, "Let them check you and then we'll speak again."

I told the people from the Red Cross, "Come inside!" It turned out one of the ladies was from Philadelphia. The other lady was born in Puerto Rico but living in New York. And the two guys were Norwegian. They spoke Spanish. I was fascinated because their Spanish was so good. They checked Chispy. And they asked me if I was eating, if I was feeling well, if I needed something. One of the ladies was a nurse, so she could see I was dehydrated and that I needed electrolytes. I have a condition that eliminates electrolytes from my body. She also checked my leg that had been hurt when I fell. It wasn't cut, but there was a dark bruise and a rash. I showed them that I was cleaning it and putting antibiotic cream on it. They called my doctor on the satellite phone and I explained everything. The doctor told them what I needed. So they went to the drugstore and brought back Powerade and personal hygiene products.

Then they called my son back and said, "We checked your mom and the dog. The dog is doing better than your mom, but she's okay. She's a little dehydrated. But she has water and milk and we brought her all the stuff she needs." The people from Red Cross also went to the mayor's office to try to get help for me. It was only then, a few days later, that the town came to clear the tree and debris that were blocking my handicap ramp.

After that Red Cross visit, around five weeks after the hurricane, people from the church nearby started to bring me water and food. But during María, so much of the food that was being handed out was bad for me. I can't eat rice or beans. It bothers my stomach. And what are the first things that they bring to you? Rice and beans. I lived on mashed potatoes and little cans of chicken and vegetables. The only thing that I took for myself from the food people brought was cornflakes and sausages. I could eat that. Sausage is nice, but the rest I couldn't eat, so I said, "God, how do I help others? I need to do something." So, with all the food that was given to me that I couldn't eat, I prepared little bags for the neighbors.

Also, about five weeks after the hurricane, a woman from the city offices came to see if I needed a generator. She said, "We have a generator. Do you need it? We could give it to you, it's available."

It would have been good to have power for the oxygen treatment at night because of my right lung, but I said, "Honey, I need it, but maybe a sick child or a person who is bedridden needs it more. Give it to them." This woman didn't come in an official capacity. She only came because she knew me.

The lack of government response was devastating. Days, even weeks after the hurricane, the government did not help. I have a deep instinct inside me that tells me this is wrong. People with medical conditions, with handicaps, in wheelchairs, the elderly—the government didn't help. How many people died?[8] How much of the money that came to Puerto Rico was given to help people with handicaps? The army was over at the mall to give out food. Tell me, how—in the wheelchair—can I go to pick up food? The mayor's office didn't come around here to see if I needed help. That was the root of my anger. The mayors have money. Why don't they use it to help people in wheelchairs? People with problems? They help the "important" people, but the people in need—they kick our butts. I felt forgotten. I *was* forgotten. Not by my family or neighbors, no. But by the people who are supposed to take care of the community—the mayor and the government.

People like me have to help others. Because no one shows us how to help ourselves. For example, in an earthquake, what's the first thing you're supposed to do? People say, "Move, drop to the ground, take cover under your desk. How are people in a wheelchair supposed to do that?" So, I'm writing a little book called "The Vision of the Hurricane from Wheels." It's to show others in wheelchairs or with medical conditions how to prepare for an emergency. I actually gave a workshop in San Juan about that and about how emergency workers

---

8. For months after the hurricane the government's official count of deaths caused by María was sixty-four. In August 2018, the official death toll was revised to 2,975 people, making María among the deadliest hurricanes in US history. Research shows even this revised number may be greatly underestimated. For more on the death toll, see "Aftermaths" in the "Contexts" essay.

can better support people with disabilities like me. Emergency people from San Juan were there and so were people from San Lorenzo's City Hall. The mayor and the civic workers of San Lorenzo all know me because I taught them how to deal with wheelchairs and the special transportation vehicles that they have for people with disabilities— how to load and unload the wheelchairs, so they aren't damaged. I'm educating them on the challenges people with disabilities face and on how to treat us properly. That's the teacher in me. I love to teach.

I'm happy that God gave me the courage to be the way I am, that God gave me the family that I have. I'm proud of my son. I'm proud of who I am and for trying to help others. It's like the strong women in my family—my mother and my grandmother—showed me strength because they were doing the things they needed to do for their family.

I want to help others see that María was a big, big deal. When María came, Puerto Rico was devastated, but the island still stands up and helps others. Right now Puerto Rico is helping the Bahamas.[9] A person can stand up, but an island can also stand up with heart and courage.

We checked in with Windy by phone in June 2020. She had been sheltering in place due to COVID-19 since March. Windy's health conditions make her especially vulnerable to viruses.

My health is not okay. Three weeks ago I had a lot of pain and headaches. I called the doctor and they gave me some medications, but that didn't help. So last week, a nurse came to the house and gave me three injections—to manage my condition and for my pain—and that helped. They gave me a prescription and my neighbor took to

---

9. Category 5 Hurricane Dorian hit the Bahamas on September 1, 2019. It is the most powerful storm on record in the Bahamas and left widespread destruction. By September 4, Puerto Rican organizations were already sending aid to the Bahamas, citing the need for an early response to natural disasters.

me to the pharmacy at Walmart. When we arrived, there was a whole bunch of people there. I was afraid. When I got home, I washed my hair, my clothes, everything! I don't want to get sick. When my neighbor does my grocery shopping, I put newspapers on the floor in the garage, and she leaves everything she buys there, and then it takes me three hours to disinfect everything. It's exhausting. People may think I'm just sitting here doing nothing, but I'm always busy.

My neighbor comes every day to check on me. I don't have other visitors, but my son calls me. Last week, he sent me the most beautiful photo of my granddaughter taken for her high school graduation. I also talk to Mom a lot—she's seventy-nine now. She lives in a different town, but before COVID we still tried to see each other every month. But now, she can't go out and she doesn't have anyone to visit her. So, twice a week we have dinner together over the phone. The last time we did this, she used her good crystal glasses, and I wore special clothes and put on my jewelry. I made salmon and mashed potatoes, and she made fish, a salad, and a potato. She said, "We didn't even know what the other was going to make for dinner and we made the same thing!" I said, "Mom, we can pretend we are in the same restaurant together and we ordered the same thing." It was a funny moment. I have to laugh.

NILDA RODRÍGUEZ COLLAZO

BORN IN: 1942
LIVES IN: Toa Baja
Retired Factory Worker

Nilda Rodríguez Collazo lives in one of the most densely populated com-munities in Puerto Rico, Levittown, which is in the municipality of Toa Baja on the western side of San Juan.[1] Her two-story home is framed by a manicured hedge that is low enough for neighbors to see easily into her small yard and ask her, "¿todo bien? Is everything okay?" We enter her house under the three archways that frame her front door. Inside, there is not a lot of furniture, but there are family photos everywhere. Pictures of her brothers and sisters, their parents, and her beloved niece, Nereida, cover every available surface.

---

1. Toa Baja has a population of over 74,000. San Juan is the capital of Puerto Rico and the largest city in the archipelago. The population is approximately 318,000.

After working in factories for years, Nilda has worked hard to make
her house a comfortable home for her and Nereida, who has Down
syndrome and is now bedridden. Nilda has dedicated her life to caring
for her niece despite having only nominal financial support and limited
social services to help her.

A CAMPESINA

I was born in Aguas Buenas, in a community called Monte Llano.[2] I
come from a big family, with a lot of siblings. There are nine of us—
seven from my mother and father, and two more on my dad's side from
a previous relationship. In birth order my siblings are Federico, Ana,
Genara, María Luisa, Audria, María Antonia, Ángel Luis, José Antonio, and me, Nilda. My mother's name was Purificación, and her
nickname was Pura. My father's name was Pantaleón. My parents come
from Cayey.[3] When my father came to Aguas Buenas in the 1900s, he
moved to a cattle ranch owned by Spaniards who lived in Bayamón, in
the La Morenita neighborhood.[4] They had recruited him in the mountains and hired him to oversee their estate. There weren't many Spaniards with the kind of lands we had when I was growing up. It was a
big farm, three hundred or four hundred *cuerdas* (three or four hundred
acres). My father kept his own cattle, too, and planted whatever he
wanted there.

Because of his skill, he made enough money to return that property to the Spaniards and bought his own farm, La Finca El Don

2. Aguas Buenas, the town of the "clear waters," is a municipality in the eastern-
central side of the Cordillera Central, the mountain range that bisects Puerto
Rico. It has a population of almost 25,000 and is approximately twenty-five miles
south of San Juan.

3. Also in the Cordillera Central, Cayey is approximately twenty miles south of Aguas
Buenas. Cayey marks the start of la Ruta Panorámica, a 165-mile-long scenic highway.

4. Bayamón was founded by the Spanish in 1772. It is the second largest municipality in Puerto Rico.

Pantaleón, where he grew tobacco and other crops and kept live-stock. He built us a house up on a hill overlooking the crops and animals, and we moved from the Spaniards' estate to our own land, where I developed into the human being I am today. I always say that I am a campesina, or country girl, because I love everything that comes from nature.

A COW INSIDE MY PLAYHOUSE

My childhood in nature was just perfect until Hurricane Santa Clara came to visit in 1956.[5] It came in the middle of the night and everyone in my house was sleeping when the gusts of wind started. Dad had closed every door and window and locked them before we went to bed. He told us, "Don't open any doors. Let the hurricane take whatever it wants." Our house had four rooms and I slept on the windy side of the house, nearest to the kitchen. There was a strange sound coming from the kitchen, like *trah-trah-trah!* It woke me up, but nobody else noticed and they stayed sleeping. It sounded like the rain was pounding directly on the kitchen door. How could that be? I called out for my mother and father, but they were still sleeping. I banged on their door, crying, "Listen! Listen to the rain! The kitchen is gone!"

That woke them quickly. My mother realized what was wrong and shouted to my father, "*Viejo*, the storm is already tearing off ev-erything.[6] Listen!" Then my brother José Antonio woke up, then my brother Ángel Luis, then everyone else. "If the kitchen is gone, it's gone," my father said. "The door to the kitchen stays locked."

When the strong gusts of winds passed, my father said to us, "You're not going outside because in a hurricane there's a *bonanza*, the calm when the eye passes, and then the storm starts again. A zinc

---

5. Hurricane Betsy, known as Hurricane Santa Clara in Puerto Rico, made landfall on August 12, 1956.

6. *Viejo* is a term of endearment that means "the old man."

panel could blow off a roof and hit one of you. Stay inside the house. I'm going to go out and check the damage."

But Mom opened up a window to see what happened, and, when we looked outside, we saw a cow inside my playhouse. The cow had almost its entire body inside the little house. The house was six feet tall, gabled with a pitched roof, all made out of wood that was left over from other projects. It had one little window and the door in the middle. I designed it, and my brother, José Antonio—we called him Billy—built it for me. I didn't have any paint, so I decorated it with leaves and flowers. They'd eventually blow away, but I kept replacing them. It was very pretty! But we'd never shut its door, so it remained open throughout the hurricane. The little playhouse didn't fall apart, but the kitchen did!

"EVERYTHING WAS LOST"

When it was all over and he decided it was safe, my father gave us permission to *novelerear*, or look around, so that we could see how the farm survived. But we could only go out to the balcony because there was a lot of broken windows, glass, and debris all around. We looked up at the mountain in front of us, and all of those houses on the mountain had fallen down. The people in them were our neighbors and they worked with us on the farm. We looked down at the fields and all our crops had been flattened. Our plantain trees were ruined. A grapefruit tree, which was leaning over the playhouse, had all its branches broken off, but the trunk stayed strong.

Except for the kitchen, our house was fine. The walls were made of cement, but the roof was made of zinc. The zinc roof didn't get torn off because when my father built it, he used a technique where he pounded in thick nails through the zinc and boards, and then he bent the nail tip back against the wood for extra support. But outside was different. My father looked around and told my mother, "*Vieja*, everything was lost. Let's see if we can find any chickens still alive. We can make a little coop. We can even cook *asopao* now. And we can start to rebuild the kitchen tomorrow." Not many people know how to call chickens. It sounds like "*pi-pi-pi-pi-pi-pi*." My dad called the chickens and some came. Not all of them, though. A lot had died. He grabbed one and killed it, and we made asopao.

Then he went to see our neighbors and said, "Let's build a little kitchen out of zinc panels where all of us can fit. Go to the fields, and pick up bananas, plantains, *yautía*, anything you can find on the ground, and let's make a good lunch."[7]

After the new makeshift kitchen was finished, Dad went down to la finca where he grew the tobacco. He came back and said to my mother, "Vieja, we lost a lot." Everything we built to harvest and dry the tobacco at the finca was gone. The walls of the drying house were made from *pencas* of palm trees, and a lot of these leaves were destroyed.[8] The main structure was okay, but everything else was gone. So, Dad told the people who had lost their houses that while they started to rebuild them, they could sleep at la finca. "Go hang your hammocks," he said. "Sleep there."

WORKING, WORKING, WORKING

Almost a year after that hurricane, in 1957, my sister Audria—we all called her Lula—asked my father for permission to take me to Chicago where she'd been living for a long time. She and her husband worked long hours and had two little girls, Migdalia and Lorena Espada, and needed help to take care of them. My father rarely let me go anywhere so it took a lot of begging. But he could see that things were difficult after the hurricane. So, I left school and went to Chicago with my brother Billy to help out Lula. She worked in a factory that made electronic

---

7. *Yautía* is a root vegetable also known as taro.

8. While palm leaves—*pencas* or fronds—vary in size, many are six feet long and are traditionally used as building materials throughout the Caribbean, although they are infrequently used in contemporary Puerto Rican structures.

devices, and her husband was the head of a company that made frames for paintings and photos. After a year, Billy couldn't stand the cold and went back to Puerto Rico. My sister and I made a deal that I'd work during the day and she'd work during the night, so that we could both have jobs and care for the children. I was fifteen years old.

A friend of my sister got me a job at Western Electric. Back then, saying you work at Western Electric was something special. They made cables, telephones, everything that had to do with communication and electronics. They made pieces for NASA! I worked there for two years, and at that time, my motto was, "If you do something, do it right!" I started to identify with that work. It became a part of me.

During that period, I had to ask three times for time off. One time my sister María Antonia was in an accident on a public bus in Puerto Rico. The second time was when I needed a foot operation. The third time was when my father died in 1966. They gave me a week of leave. When I returned, I continued working, working, and working. I'd come in at 7 a.m. for overtime on Saturdays and stay until five or six in the afternoon.

SHE NEEDED MY HELP

My mother kept sending me sad letters, though, saying how much she missed me, how lonely she was, and how she needed my help with Nereida, my sister María Luisa's daughter.

Nereida was born with severe Down syndrome. I was seven years old when Nereida was born, and I remember everything. I carry the memory of her as a baby lying weakly in her crib. She couldn't move. The family would take her to a doctor in Caguas who gave her medications and told us to move her legs and arms often so that they would grow stronger.[9] My sister had to leave Nereida with us, and went with her older daughter, Lourdes, to Cayey. María Luisa

---

9. Caguas is approximately five miles from Aguas Buenas and fifteen miles from Cayey.

wanted to start over and we had relatives there that she could stay with. After a time, Lourdes also came to live with us, and both girls were raised by my parents.

My parents grew very fond of Nereida, but when María Luisa finally divorced the girls' father, Miguel, she decided that she wanted to take her two daughters with her. My father told my sister that she could take Lourdes, but not Nereida. He said, "She will be raised by me and your mother." My sister said that Nereida was her daughter and it was her right to take her. My father agreed but said that he knew that María Luisa would leave, look for a job, and not take care of her daughter. "This child needs care twenty-four hours a day. And we will do it! Not you." So, my sister left, and Nereida stayed.

When Nereida was young, she always carried a purse and wore sunglasses. Near my parents' house there was a store where my mom would buy some small stuff. For groceries, she'd go into town, but if something was missing, she'd make a note and give it to Nereida, who would go to the store and give it to Don Félix, the store owner. He would give Nereida whatever my mom put on the note, and she'd return home with the little package in her arms. She was very active when she was young.

When Lourdes was grown, she didn't care for Nereida the way my parents did. She got married, made her own family, and moved to Ohio where she lives currently. Lourdes doesn't help her sister at all. Then my father died. He was in poor health, but really died from old age. My mom was alone with Nereida for three years, but when her health declined in 1969, she wrote to me in Chicago that she wanted me to come and help take care of Nereida.

I LOVE BOLEROS AND RANCHERAS!

At first, I lived in a house in Caguas owned by Billy, who was living in San Juan. My mother continued to get older and sicker, so we had to bring her and Nereida to the house, too. One of my cousins was the head of the International Telephone and Telegraph, Inc. (ITT) branch in Puerto Rico, where they made phones. Since I had experience in Chicago with cable systems, he was able to get me a job there. It was on the road from Caguas to Río Piedras.[10]

I was glad to be so close to San Juan because Billy, Lula, and I liked to go out to nightclubs here in Puerto Rico to dance and listen to music. I would work hard all week and take care of my mom and Nereida at home, then go out with my sister and brother on the weekends to have a good time. Ocho Puertas in Viejo San Juan on Calle Fortaleza was my favorite nightclub. It was where the best artists would go and where I could dance and sing all night. I love boleros and rancheras![11] I had a very social life and we'd meet a lot of artists. I met Demetrio González—I have a photo with him on my wall. I also met Javier Solís, who is my favorite; Gloria Mirabal—I have a photo with her, too; and Carmen Delia Dipiní, who lived here.[12] Billy worked in the Sheraton Hotel and when famous artists like Tom Jones would come to perform, he'd get me front-row seats.[13] Tom Jones would dance and drop to the floor, and he'd grab my hands!

---

10. The Río Piedras neighborhood of San Juan is home to the flagship campus of the University of Puerto Rico system.

11. The music and dance style referred to as bolero has its origins in eighteenth-century Spain but has become a Latin American and Caribbean phenomenon. Ranchera is a traditional type of Mexican music that is heavily influenced by folk music and predates the Mexican Revolution.

12. Demetrio González (1927–2015) was a Spanish-born actor and singer who starred in Mexican ranchera films. Javier Solís (1931–1966) was a Mexican singer and actor who was part of the group of singers who developed the bolero-ranchera. Puerto Rican singer Gloria Mirabal (1918–2000) was known for her wide vocal range. Carmen Delia Dipiní (1927–1998) was a famous bolero singer from Naguabo, a town in the southeast of Puerto Rico. She was inducted into the International Latin Music Hall of Fame in 2002.

13. Tom Jones is an award-winning Welsh singer and actor.

THE HOUSE WAS SO UGLY

I worked at ITT until 1971. I left after I suffered a workplace accident when heavy equipment and computers fell on me. I had to endure a long recovery for my back, but I also received compensation. I decided to buy a house.

At first, I wanted to live near Lula in the city of Carolina, but that wasn't God's will.[14] I walked with my sister almost every day through the neighborhood of Villa Carolina, but I didn't find anything that I felt was home. The houses were all fine physically, but it was more of a spiritual feeling that I couldn't find.

One day my friend, Adelina del Valle, who lived in Levittown, Toa Baja, told me that I should start looking for houses in other areas.[15] "Maybe in Levittown?" she asked. But I told her that if God wanted me in Levittown, it would have to be in Cuarta Sección, the fourth section, because it was the only part of Levittown I liked. Adelina responded that it was going to be difficult because the people who have property there don't usually sell, as it's such a quiet place. I had faith, though, that I would find a house.

I went every day to Cuarta Sección to see if there were For Sale signs, but there wasn't a single one. One day when I had slept over at Adelina's house, I got up early in the morning and told her, "I'm going out for a little while." I drove around a section called La Brisa Oeste, "the West Breeze." There was a two-story house, with a light pole out in front that had a small For Sale sign on it. I leapt out of the car and knocked on the door, but there was no one home.

Luckily, there was a neighbor who had the key to the house. The neighbor told me that the owner of the house had bought it with his fiancée, but she'd dumped him. "He was so depressed that he just

---

14. The city of Carolina is just east of San Juan and is the home of the Luis Muñoz Marín International Airport.

15. Levittown is a planned community in Toa Baja and is considered part of the San Juan metro area.

walked away, but he gave me the key just in case someone drove by who was interested." He was also very honest in telling me that I'd have to invest a lot of money in repairs for the house. It looked abandoned. All the paint was peeling off. Nonetheless, I quickly called Adelina, who dropped everything to come look at the house. She asked me, "Have you done the impossible?"

When we arrived at the house, she entered first with the neighbor, and I stayed in the car. When she came out, she shook her head and told me that the inside was covered in mold and dirt. But when I stepped out of the car, walked over, and put my hands on the frame of the front door, I felt the confirmation of my celestial Father that this is where he wanted me. I started crying. I told my friend, "This is the house I want." She looked at me as if I were crazy and said, "You haven't even gone into the house, or seen its condition. All the wood inside is rotted. You can't buy this house!" But I just told her, "This house is the one."

We asked for the owner's phone number and I called him. He said, "The house is priced at $16,500." I had to respond, "God has spoken to me, and told me that the house was meant for me, but I only have $15,500. I am $1,000 short." He confided that he only wanted that money to go on a trip to Mexico with his mother to heal his broken heart, so he'd talk to his mother and get back to me.

Later that same day, I got a call from him accepting my offer. Very quickly I went to my lawyer and arranged for an inspection of the house. Everything was approved so fast and I signed the papers. But because the house was so ugly and in bad condition, I didn't tell anyone about it at first. When it was pretty and clean, I told everyone that I bought a house and they could visit anytime.

SHE BECAME INCAPACITATED

After I moved to Levittown, I'd go back to my brother's house in Caguas three times a week to clean and help my mother out around the house. One day she asked me, "Promise me that when I die, you'll take care of Nereida." I told her, "Of course, Mamá. I'll take care of you both."

I brought my mother into my home and cared for her for the ten years that she was bedridden. Over time, Nereida's condition got worse until she became incapacitated, too, and she has been bedridden for twelve years. She became blind in 2000 and cannot speak. Her doctor, who's now like family, comes to the house. Nereida needs oxygen, respiration therapy, and a suction machine for phlegm, and there are lots of medications I need to give her. She is beginning to suffer from renal failure.

It's expensive taking care of Nereida, because Social Security only gives her approximately $500 a month for her care. Before that, when her father was alive, they would only give her $178. After he died, they increased the sum. Almost every medication she takes has a large deductible, and the power bill is very high because of all the equipment she needs. I took out a medical insurance plan for her from Triple-S Salud that I pay for with whatever money comes to me, but nowadays medication is so expensive.

Nereida's father, Miguel, never had much contact with her when she was a child. When he got older, he felt that he should meet his daughter properly, but he lived in New York. When he retired in 2010, Miguel came to Puerto Rico to be with Nereida. He showed up at my house in Levittown.

He was already living in Cayey, and after that visit, he began to come every Saturday. When Miguel came, he would sit down next to Nereida and sing to her. Then they would play dolls together. Miguel would say, "Nereida looks so happy here and she does well in this house. There's no other place for her." He came to visit her every weekend until he died in 2012.

Caring for Nereida takes up most of my time now. She lives on the first floor and we keep all her medical equipment and supplies there, too. She has the biggest room in the house because I wanted to put a small bed in there so that I can sleep next to her. I give her the medications and therapies there. Even though it's the biggest room, it can't hold everything, and I have to keep some supplies upstairs. When I finish giving her breakfast, I start to think what to give her for lunch. When I finish her lunch, I start to think about dinner. I live in her room and in the kitchen. At night in bed I'm very tired. I have my own room downstairs, but usually sleep in the bed next to *la nena*, my girl. I don't lie down until I finish every task for Nereida.

I WAS FLOATING

On the night of Hurricane María, a friend of mine, Aida, stayed with me because she lives alone and was afraid. That night she was sleeping while I was seated in a chair. I didn't sleep, because one of us had to stay vigilant. I kept awake guarding the house, so I heard everything. The winds were so strong that I thought the cement blocks were going to detach from the walls.

The winds would go *crak-crak-crak-crak*, sounding louder and louder like a subway until Aida woke up and started praying on her knees. She thought I was sleeping, but I was just sitting, listening. I told her, "Calm yourself, nothing is going to happen. God is going to take care of us." When dawn came, we gave thanks to God for surviving and had breakfast. We had no damage, my house survived fine, and we had electricity because my neighbors on both sides had generators and they threw me cords that allowed me to plug in. Aida went to check on her own house.

The day after the hurricane, September 21, around 6:30 or 7:00 at night, I was giving Nereida her routine medications and applying her breathing therapy. Everything was calm. But then, I heard my neighbor, Tito, yelling, "Nilda! Nilda!" I stopped the therapy machine and moved to the window. "What is it? What's wrong?" I called. He cried, "Open the door. The water is at my back. I've come to save the girl!" I just stood there for a moment, wondering what was happening.

I couldn't move. I was frozen in the doorframe. He hurriedly explained to me that he was driving around looking at the aftermath when he noticed that the streets were filling up with water. At first, he thought that the sewers were overflowing, but as he looked on, he started to see that the roads were flooding, and the water was running down here to the houses. He shouted at me, again, "Nilda! Come on! Look at the water. It's already over my ankles! I'm here to save *la nena*, Nereida. Come on!"

He rushed past me into the house with his stepdaughter, Amaría, behind him and they picked up Nereida. They grabbed my girl and put her on Tito's shoulders, and he carried her up the stairs that way, placing her on a bed that I have up there. Water was entering the house through the windows and the doors, and through the kitchen door that has a window. The water pouring in through my lower windows looked like a waterfall.

He ran back down the stairs, and both of them kept helping me. He brought up an oxygen tank with the little oxygen machine attached to it. I managed to bring up the phlegm suction machine and some diapers. Thank God some medications were already safe upstairs along with bottled water and some other supplies. We grabbed more of Nereida's boxes and quickly took them upstairs before the water rose too much.

I continued to take the small machines upstairs, but many of the things were already underwater. After Tito helped me carry the heaviest things, he said, "I have to go home to see what I can save over there." I continued trying to save things. I started to throw framed portraits upstairs, but a lot of them were lost. I had all the tables filled with them, because I'm a fan of photography. I started throwing them on top of a cupboard, to at least get them high up, but a lot that were in my room were already ruined. *Mi adrenalina estaba a millón!* My adrenaline shot up to a million! In about half an hour the first floor of the house was flooded. When the water reached my waist, there was a moment when my feet could barely touch the floor and then I was floating. I said to myself, "Let everything go. It's not worth it. Get upstairs." When I climbed to the top, I sat down and watched the sofa floating around the house.

The room upstairs that Tito carried Nereida to has an interior set of stairs, which is unusual in Puerto Rico. I had converted that room into a living space with a kitchen area, a bathroom, and a kind of bedroom. It could be an apartment since it has a set of exterior stairs to enter the room from outside. Tito came back to check on us and told me that many houses were flooded. Almost every other house in Brisa Oeste has only one floor, so most of them were underwater from the flooding. He said that the families were in the street with nowhere to go. "Tito," I said. "Round them up and get them here. Look, I have room."

They sat for hours, two women crying throughout the night and others praying. But the water stopped at the top of the stairs and never came in. We stayed safe and when the waters went down the next morning, the refugees went to their homes to throw out everything. Nereida and I stayed in that upstairs apartment for four months, while I slowly cleaned the rest of the house.

When my house flooded, the water also brought with it insects, seashells, sand, and dead fish. I found one in the shower, and my neighbor found two big, dead fish. They stank! The neighborhood of Levittown has been in existence for more than fifty years and it has never flooded. We learned later that when the river flooded and hit the ocean, the storm surge pushed it back on us. It was a mixture of the two waters, the river and the ocean, that flooded us. The surge was so big that the river didn't stand a chance.

I lost the furniture, the cabinets, the exterior doors, and the bedroom doors. My niece, Mildred, Billy's daughter, bought me new window screens. She bought me the chairs we're sitting on right now because I had to throw out the other dining chairs. All the beds downstairs were lost, the cupboards, everything—sentimental objects, photos, and important documents. The doctor had been to see Nereida right before the hurricane and left the prescriptions. I had filled them that morning, and they were gone. The food from the fridge and every food item that was stored at a low height was lost. I threw out everything.

FEMA sent a representative here approximately three or four weeks after the hurricane, and I filled out all the papers with Mildred, who lives nearby. A lady who was assigned to my case measured everything with a tape measure to see where the water reached. She took photos of everything that was ruined—the cupboards, the cabinets.

The amount that FEMA approved after that visit was very little. Every neighbor lost everything, it wasn't just me, and they gave all of us very little. Some received $500, others $800, and I received $1,800. My reimbursement was higher because of the medical equipment. I estimate that I lost a lot more than that, though. I lost two blood pressure monitors, two respiratory therapy machines, and the machine to extract the phlegm stopped working. I lost the five hundred dollars' worth of medication that I'd bought the morning of the hurricane. FEMA was just not with me. They weren't here for the people. The lady that came to measure things said to me, "They're going to give you a big amount, because you lost everything, especially medicine." She said that they were going to consider everything, and they did not.

The government sent me a letter telling me that I was denied further aid but that I was eligible for a loan. So, I called Mildred to tell her and she said, "Tití, let's appeal again." But I asked her, "Why should I appeal? They only want to shove a loan at me." My neighbor warned me, "*Mira*, they just want to tangle you up." What they want to do is indebt people. So, I felt in my heart that I shouldn't appeal anything. They're going to deny my request again so that I'll take out a loan.

I DIDN'T LET THE TERROR CORNER ME

A day passed, and I couldn't give Nereida her breathing therapy because there was no regular electricity. The mayor of Toa Baja, Betito, helped my community in particular.[16] His cousin works for the city and she is a close friend of my neighbor. Because of that connection, the paramedics arrived quickly. They went up the stairs and taught me how to give Nereida therapy with an oxygen tank, without the machine we lost. It was hard at first, because I was alone, and I had to go up and down a lot. The stairs aren't easy. I had the little kitchen upstairs, but the sink was downstairs. I never once thought of taking her to the hospital and leaving her there, though. The paramedic said, "You're taking good care of her. She's well hydrated, looking very healthy and can continue as she is."

The experience and all the damage marked me, but I didn't let the terror corner me. My trust was in God. Mildred and I cleaned the walls of Nereida's bedroom and disinfected the whole room. Tito repainted it for us. The insurance company sent me another hospital bed and I prepared the room. By the time the room was ready, though, my car had stopped working because the ignition was broken from the flooding, so my friend came and took me to a private ambulance company.[17] A young lady came out to meet me and asked, "What can I do for you?"

I told her, "I'm one of the people from the Cuarta who lost everything after María, and I have my girl, Nereida, who is immobile, in a room upstairs. I repainted the bedroom and I want to bring her downstairs today so that she can sleep in her own room. But I can't do it by myself. I need help." The lady hugged me and said, "Well, I'm going to help you. All the ambulances are in the streets, but

---

16. Toa Baja's mayor's full name is Bernardo Márquez García.

17. Prior to Hurricane María, public services were unreliable due to austerity measures imposed by the Financial Oversight and Management Board. After the hurricane, they were often unavailable. For more on austerity measures, see "Economic Contexts" in the "Contexts" essay.

there is one that we are cleaning. Soon the men who are out on calls will be coming back. When we're finished cleaning and the men arrive, you give me the directions because we are going to help you!"

I asked how much the service was going to cost me, because I was very short of money at that time and insurance wouldn't cover the private ambulance. But she said to forget it. They weren't going to charge anything to bring my girl downstairs to her own room. The paramedics came to the house that day. They used Nereida's bedsheets to make a hammock—one grabbed the sheet at her head, the other at her feet, and they brought her downstairs. I already had her bed made up and everything. My friends were here, and it was a celebration. Nereida was happy, more comfortable, when she was laid down on the bed. She snuggled into the new pillow and started giggling softly. When I saw that she was happy, I was really happy, too. I cried tears of joy. I was so grateful that Nereida's condition remained stable throughout the ordeal, because God gave me the blessings of my neighbors, friends, family, and these complete strangers.

Because of the COVID-19 pandemic, Nilda and Nereida stopped receiving guests in March 2020. We talked to Nilda by telephone in June 2020 to find out how they were doing.

Nereida's condition has gotten worse. The doctors and I take care of her excellently, but it gets harder for her to breathe and swallow. I'm still taking caring of her day and night. I never stop, and I never will.

Nilda confided that this year of the pandemic has been the hardest of their story together. In April 2021, Nereida passed away.

RAFAEL RAMOS DÍAZ

BORN IN: 1966
LIVES IN: Camuy
Police Captain

Rafael Ramos Díaz is the chief of police in the town of Arecibo.[1] He joined the police force in 1996 to take care of his growing family. When the hurricane struck, the city was flooded by both ocean waters and the Río Tanamá, which crested its banks and sent three to four feet of debris-filled water running through the city.[2] The Puerto Rico Civil Defense Unit, US Army, Puerto Rico National Guard, and the people in

---

1. The city of Arecibo is approximately nine miles from Rafael's home in Camuy. It is located on the northern-central coast on the Atlantic Ocean. According to US Census data, almost half of Arecibo residents currently live in poverty.

2. The source of the Tanamá River is high in the mountains in the town of Adjuntas. It flows through Utuado and down into Arecibo where it meets the ocean.

charge of the waterworks at the Autoridad de Acueductos y Alcantarillados worked, together with the police, to pump out the floodwaters. In the days after the hurricane, Rafael divided his time between evacuating people from their homes, providing first aid, distributing food and water, and watching over the supply of fuel at the gas stations.

WE WORKED NONSTOP FOR SEVEN DAYS

Our biggest problem was the gas. All the gas in the stations was gone by the third day after the hurricane. Many of the trucks that were supposed to refuel the stations had been stored away in preparation for the hurricane, and when the drivers did go out to deliver gas, they were robbed everywhere they went. It didn't matter if they were on highways or rural routes. Eventually, the oil companies made a deal with the police that every tanker would need to be escorted by a police cruiser from their town, or else the trucks would only go to the San Juan metro area.

Gas station owners had to go to their local police station to request an escort for the truck, and then the owner had to go with those officers to the Bayamón depot outside of San Juan.[3] It didn't matter where you were located, you had to get over there. It cost about $10,000 for five thousand gallons of gas. Since everything was handled by cash, when the day was over an officer had to also escort station owners to the bank so that they could make the deposit without being robbed. We worked nonstop for seven days. We were supposed to have twelve-hour shifts throughout that first week, but sometimes we would work almost twenty hours in one shift.

While we Puerto Ricans are used to the heat, it's different to stand outside in the sun all day. We couldn't sit in our cruisers, we had to be out in the streets helping people. We used sunscreen and had the benefit of the uniform hat as a sunshade, but sweat kept

---

3. Bayamón is forty-six miles from Arecibo in the eastern region of the island, just south of San Juan.

running down my forehead into my eyes, stinging them. It poured down my neck and back and drenched my shirt. We'd been given permission to work in Class B uniforms—our everyday clothes with our hats on and badges displayed, carrying our weapons. Most of us wore jeans, though, because there was no water or electricity to wash our clothes, and jeans still looked okay after a few days without washing. No one dared put on a bulletproof vest. Wearing that would've felt like having a fur coat on.

Any gas station that was open had a few cops guarding it. Every store and many houses around the gas station that I was assigned to guard had generators running. They were growling all around me: *grrrrrr, rrrrrr.* It was like they were each competing to be the loudest. The air was thick with diesel and the stench was just suffocating. The smell was almost as bad as the heat itself. The number of cars surrounding us made the heat and smell even worse. The noise and stench of all that gas made me want to run inside for some cool air, anything to refresh myself. I stayed, though. I had a job to do.

We were lucky that a lot of people brought us water. It was easy to get dehydrated quickly in those days. My biggest problem wasn't being hot, though. It was that my feet swelled up from standing in the heat so much. When you're under the sun for that long, you begin to feel the sweat running down your body, all the way down your legs. Your socks soak up all that sweat, which basically keeps your feet soaked all the time you're out there. My feet felt as if they were on fire, and my synthetic leather boots sure didn't help. I tried to find someone to relieve me every once in a while, so that I could go out back and take my boots off for just a few minutes. When I finally had the chance to take them off, my feet were pale and swollen due to my diabetes. It felt so good to let them free, even for a little while. But then I needed to put on that used, sweaty pair of socks again and stick my feet back into my boots and get to work.

AN EMPTY GAS CANNISTER IN EACH HAND

At that time, FEMA was *secuestrando* the gasoline.[4] They'd go to the owners and buy their entire supply of gasoline, sometimes taking control of the whole station. At first, the owners were reluctant to sell their gas to FEMA, but after the governor officially declared a state of emergency, FEMA could more easily obtain the gas. Then the station owners had no choice. Some of them didn't mind because FEMA was paying for the fuel, but others were upset because all the gas was given to first responders and there was none left for the people.

Thankfully, when people could get gas, the prices stayed the same as before the hurricane because the Departamento de Asuntos del Consumidor froze them.[5] Still, sometimes a day or two passed without any gas arriving at the stations. One time, about three days after the hurricane, a truck with twenty thousand gallons arrived at a Total station in the town of Florida, but five or six hundred people were waiting in line for that fuel.[6] We told station owners to warn customers that there wasn't going to be enough for everyone. Many times, the owners rationed the gasoline at twenty dollars per person so that everyone could get something, but that gas was for generators as well as cars and there just wasn't enough. It led to fights everywhere.

Another time, around one o'clock in the afternoon, a gas truck arrived at the station I was guarding. As it pulled inside the station, I watched the peoples' eyes lock onto it, their gaze following the truck to the tanks. It had been raining lightly, but the rain stopped, and within minutes we were drenched in sweat again. Some people

---

4. *Secuestrar* means "to hijack."

5. Departamento de Asuntos del Consumidor (DACA) is the consumer protection agency of Puerto Rico.

6. Florida is one of the smallest and least populated towns in Puerto Rico. It is in the northern-central region. It does not have its own police force and is therefore covered by the officers from Arecibo.

had brought umbrellas to shade themselves from the sun and many were sharing with their family members or strangers standing next to them in line. I liked seeing that. But most people wore shirts with no sleeves, their skin slowly getting redder while they waited.

It takes a long time to measure how much gas is already in the tank and how much is needed. The driver has to use a wooden stick to measure—like those metal ones that people use to check motor oil—and verify how much gas was left in the station's tanks. New tanks have buoys for those purposes, but most older gas stations use that stick.

As the gas delivery was getting set up, I saw a car enter through the exit of the station and drive past the whole long line. A woman who looked to be in her late sixties got out and walked slowly toward me with an empty gas cannister in each hand. She walked past everyone who had been waiting hours for their turn and came right up to me. She looked so exhausted, her shoulders slumping and her face sad. "Officer, I have an emergency," she told me. "My husband has lung cancer and I need gas for the generator so that I can turn on his oxygen machine and heart monitor."

I looked over to her car. Her husband was in the front seat. He had oxygen tubes up his nose and his mouth was hanging open. "Is he okay?" I asked, but I wasn't looking at just her and her husband. I was also looking into the crowd behind her and seeing that people were all staring at us. "He is," she replied, "but he can't breathe without his machine. Help us. Please!"

I could see that some of the people around us were frowning and looked upset. Somebody touched my shoulder and I turned to face a man who seemed to be in his forties. His hair was all greased up with sweat, and his cheeks and nose were deep red from the sun. He was holding an empty canister in one hand, gesturing with it while he spoke loudly, "Hey! She has to wait like everybody else, no matter what. I have my own conditions and I'm waiting in line. She has to wait, too!"

"Sir, her husband has lung cancer and can't breathe without his oxygen machine. Without the gas for their generator, he will die," I explained as I motioned another officer to escort the lady to the pumps so she could get her gasoline. The man was very angry and kept getting angrier. He didn't want to calm down and stop yelling. At that moment, the lady's troubles didn't matter to him. I had to walk him back to the line explaining, "That man could be your family. You could be the one driving around asking for gas. And if you were in her situation, believe me, we would help you the same way."

Fights like this happened often. Too many people had to wait in the heat for too long. And sometimes there was nothing to give them. I kept thinking: *How do I get a person to come to their senses? How can I calm them down? What words can I use?* But I can't judge them. I don't know them. I do know that everyone has their own story, their own trouble. I just had to keep my eyes on the whole situation and try to keep everyone as calm as I could.

VIVIENNE MIRANDA RODRÍGUEZ

BORN IN: 1980
LIVES IN: Rincón
Wellness Center Owner, Farmer, and Doula

Vivienne Miranda Rodríguez lives in Rincón with her husband, Ricardo, and their sons—Inti, who is ten, and Anuk, who is eight. Before the hurricane, the boys attended a local public school, which had been fighting against closure for the past few years. Like so many other schools on the island, it was eventually shut down due to ongoing cuts to public education.

Vivienne is a licensed massage therapist, yoga teacher, and birth doula. Ricardo is an agronomist, working for Envirosurvey, a group that has been replanting deforested areas on the island. Vivienne and Ricardo also co-own and operate several small businesses, including two

119

guesthouses; Centro La Paz, a yoga studio and wellness center in Rincón; and Finca Hekiti, an agroforestry cacao farm in Las Marías.[1]

Vivienne's yoga studio served as a base for her relief efforts, and it is where we first meet with her in April 2018. The studio has white walls and open spaces, and is filled with light. Outside, wind chimes stir in a gentle breeze, but in the distance the sound of power tools and hammering can be heard, a reminder of the rebuilding that still continues seven months after Hurricane María.

BE PART OF THE CHANGE

I was born in Quito, the capital of Ecuador. My father's from a large port city in Ecuador called Guayaquil, and my mother was born in New York to Puerto Ricans from Sabana Grande, a small town in southwest Puerto Rico. When I was less than a year old, we moved back to the States.

I grew up in San Jose, California. As a little girl I was a big dreamer. A bit of a tomboy. Always rebellious, kind of a loner. I loved to go out and play in the rain or ride my bike. There were big mustard fields, vineyards, and orchards by my house. I used to walk around the orchards and pick apricots off the trees and get honey sticks from the beekeeper. I have a younger sister, Danielle, who was born in California. She was more of a homebody. I was always very protective of her. I still am.

My favorite memories as a child are the trips my family took to Ecuador. We'd get off the plane and hear the vegetable vendors calling, *"Tomate, tomate!"* They announce all the fruits and vegetables that they have for the day from a bullhorn. And the smells—it smells like the Andes—like clouds, like eucalyptus. Like lemon oil for the wood polish—so many things that remind me of childhood. In Ecuador, it was all love. Lots of hugs and kisses. There, it

---

1. Rincón is a western coastal municipality with a population of approximately 15,000. Las Marías is located at the west end of the Cordillera Central mountain range.

was instilled in me that family comes first, and charity begins in the home. So, everything for me goes back to family and interconnectedness with people.

I have a very good relationship with my parents, Vivian and Carlos. My mother and I are very similar, so when I was young, we were always butting heads, which is a big reason why I went off so early. I was seventeen when I moved back to Ecuador by myself. I stayed there six months and then I moved to New York because I was starting university there. Then I went to Spain, then back to California. I was so independent largely because of my father's influence. He promoted exploration and self-sufficiency.

Both my parents are big on the whole idea that if you don't like something, be part of the change. The minute I'd start complaining, they'd say, "What're you going to do to change it?" That would either shut me up or I would say, "Okay, I'm going to do this."

A TROPICS GIRL

I was nineteen when I first came to Puerto Rico to visit my mother's family. I loved it. I'm very much a tropics girl. I like the laid-back feeling and the sense of family.

I was twenty-six when I met my husband, Ricardo, in 2006. I was on vacation and had come to Mayagüez to visit some friends. Ricky was their housemate. He grew up in the southeast between Maunabo and Caguas, but he'd come to Mayagüez for university and then stayed on the west coast.[2] We had an immediate connection. Ricky's very calm and sincere. I think that was a big attraction. We were inseparable while I was here. At the time, I was studying at De Anza College in California, so we maintained a long-distance relationship for a year. And then he asked me to marry him, and I moved here.

2. The municipalities of Maunabo and Caguas are approximately a hundred miles away from Mayagüez.

Ricky was always very clear. He said, "If you're going to be with me, it needs to be in Puerto Rico." And me? I kind of float. I've lived in a lot of different places. So, I said, "Okay, sure. Why not?"

When I was pregnant with our first son, Inti, we were living in a little shanty in downtown Mayagüez. It was one of those houses where you sneeze, and your next-door neighbor says, "*Salud.*"[3] Then, when Inti was about a year old, we moved to Rincón. We found this house up in the hills, in Barrio Río Grande. It's a typical Puerto Rican house—square and cement. Kind of like a bunker.

Inti is a mini-Ricky, an old soul. He feels everything and is very emotional. He loves to read a lot of books at the same time. Now, he's reading *Harry Potter, Indiana Jones,* and *Rosie Revere, Engineer.* He's very inquisitive. He observes everything. Anuk is a mini-me, a fireball. He's super cuddly and loving but very defiant and rebellious, very smart. It's kind of hard because he learns things so quickly, his school doesn't challenge him. He's a big class clown. He loves skateboarding and any physical activity. He loves animals. He'll lie with our dogs and just look at them.

In 2015, I bought the yoga studio, Centro La Paz, where I'd been working. In 2016, my sister, Danielle, moved here from Mexico and joined the business. She was going to run a small café from the studio and provide food. Danielle's an amazing cook. She loves sweets. She makes chocolate avocado pudding and mint chocolate chip cookies. Chocolate, chocolate, all the way.

September 2017 was the first time Danielle's side of the business was going to have a full season with all the tourists. And September is her birth month, too. So, Hurricane Irma was her birthday present and then María happened.[4]

---

3. A courtesy that could be translated as "bless you" but literally means "good health to you."

4. Hurricane Irma made landfall in Puerto Rico two weeks before Hurricane María. It killed three people, caused substantial damage, and left a million residents without power.

"YOU HAVE NO IDEA"

I'm from California. I know about earthquakes. With earthquakes, you don't know when they're coming. So, before Hurricane María I thought, *This is nothing. At least we know it's coming.* But my husband kept saying, "You have no idea." Because he's been through several hurricanes. Ricky said, "We're going to be without water and electricity for months." With Hurricane Georges his family was without electricity for six months and without water for a year.[5] He remembers that really clearly. So, he started preparing everything—stocking up on water and on gas for the car and generator, and getting candles and food, putting up storm shutters, and strapping things down. There was a sense of urgency. Some people already had their electricity and water out from Irma. So, people were already a little desperate.

Then María happened—and it was long. It was over thirty hours. Constant strong, strong wind and rain. It felt like it would never end. The safe room was our sons' room, which is the most protected. The windows had metal storm shutters, which we'd closed, so it was dark, but we had candles. We were all together—Ricky, Inti, Anuk, and Danielle—taking naps, playing games, drawing, and eating snacks.

My boys are constantly eating. The little one, Anuk, kept saying, "I want a snacky." And we were thinking, *Oh my gosh, maybe we should save these snacks.* Because of the level of destruction going on outside—we knew that there wouldn't be access to much food after the storm.

The biggest thing I remember is the howling. It was like someone was screaming the whole time. It was nerve-racking hearing those intense sounds. We have solar panels and I could hear them going *dat dat dat dat dat* nonstop. Everything was being torn apart

---

5. On September 21, 1998, Hurricane Georges made landfall in Puerto Rico as a Category 3 hurricane, leaving approximately 80 percent of the archipelago's population without water and electricity.

outside, slamming against the house or falling on the roof. I kept saying, "Wow, this is intense. Wow, it's really loud. Oh man, the wind's really strong!" And Ricky kept saying, "I told you so."

It was very humid. It smelled like leaves and wood and moisture. One small window in the bathroom didn't have metal shutters, so we'd look out there to see what was going on. There were these gusts of wind, and all of a sudden everything would either bend or break. We saw trees being ripped out of the ground. I'll never forget seeing the first tree that went. It was Inti's bay rum tree. He'd planted it with me when we first moved to the house when he was only a year old. Ricky said, "It's gonna break. It's gonna crack." And you could hear it going *kk-kk-kk-kk*. And it just snapped in half.

As soon as that tree fell down, Inti broke into a panic and was crying and screaming, "That's my tree! I hate this hurricane!" I had to calm him down. I said, "You're safe. We're going to be okay. We can plant more trees. It's okay, it's okay." I was trying to calm him down, like any mom in a moment of crisis. You try to make your kids feel safe, even if you're scared or nervous. But you're dealing with your own internal struggle: *What's going to happen? What's going to come after this?*

NO GREEN ANYWHERE

When the hurricane passed, all of a sudden it got really quiet. You didn't hear anything—no birds, no animals. Just a constant light rain. It felt really humid, like a sauna. The rain clouds were different shades of gray and white. And it was so strange; we could see what looked like the border of the hurricane—all the clouds—moving away in one direction, in a spiral.

The first thing Ricky said when he got outside was, "This is so much worse than Georges." Electrical posts had been knocked down. Our trees—banana, plantain, avocado, *achiote, guanábana*—were broken or ripped out of the ground. One of our solar panels was smashed. On the ground there was glass, plastic, branches, and leaves. It was just a mess. We started taking inventory of all the things we needed to do. Then we saw our neighbor's house at the top of the hill behind us. Their windows had imploded, the doors and roof had been ripped off, and the cement had been smashed. When we saw that, we felt an urgency to help. We thought, *Who needs help and what do they need?*

People started coming out of houses and they were all doing the same thing—clearing trees. We got our machetes and the chainsaws and focused on the road that goes from our house to the plaza. About three or four of our neighbors also came to help. It's usually a five-minute drive in a car. It took five to six hours to clear the road.

When we got back to the house after clearing the road to the plaza, we thought, *Now what?* We didn't know how long we're going to be without food. It was avocado season, so we gathered up hundreds of avocados. We were eating avocados like they were nuts.

In the days after the hurricane the view from our place changed. There was no green anywhere. It was just dirt with sticks, which were all the trees that had been snapped. It looked like porcupine hills.

We weren't able to find out any news of what was happening around the island. There was no phone, no radio, no TV, no internet. We have one of those emergency radios—nothing. I kept thinking, *I hope everybody's okay.* The minute we got in our truck and started driving, I realized everybody was not okay.

TWO HUNDRED SANDWICHES

About two weeks after the hurricane, Vivienne and Ricky were able to visit their cacao farm in Las Marías, which is in a mountainous region approximately twenty-six miles from where they live in Rincón. Landslides blocked access to their farm, so they had to hike in. Over 90 percent of their cacao trees were destroyed. They'd lost their harvest, but because cacao is a noninsurable crop, they received no compensation from the US

*Department of Agriculture's Puerto Rico Farm Service Agency, which
provides various programs and services to farmers, including insurance
and disaster assistance. The agency does have a Noninsured Crop Disaster
Assistance Program, which Vivienne and Ricky are enrolled in, but they
have not received compensation from that either, despite having submitted all required documentation.*

We couldn't call anybody for about two weeks. One day, all of a
sudden, my phone started beeping. It was one of the first phones to
get a signal. Anybody in Rincón who found out we had service was
coming over to call their loved ones.

The first person I talked to was my mother. She was freaking
out. She said, "What are you doing there? You need to come back
to California! At least be responsible and send your sons." This was
something we really battled with. Ricky grew up here. He didn't
have family off island, so he didn't have the opportunity to go to the
States after a hurricane. We decided to keep the boys with us and
wait to see what would happen.

But things were difficult. I couldn't work. No one was going to
come do yoga or get a massage. All my doula clients left the island
because there wasn't—and still isn't—good access to medical services. We didn't have anything to sell from the farm because everything was torn apart. I can't stand being indoors, so I thought, *How
can I be of help?*

Because my phone worked, I was able to ask for donations from
family and friends in the States. Around the end of the first week of
October, I started receiving supplies, which included baby formula,
first aid kits, batteries, solar lamps, flashlights, clothing, diapers. The
post office wasn't open, so I'd meet private jets in Aguadilla.[6] I used
my yoga studio as a center for people to pick up goods. The majority

---

6. Rafael Hernández Airport is located in Aguadilla and is both a civil and military airport.

of the people I spoke with hadn't seen any official help—not FEMA, not the municipality, not the military.[7]

In the beginning of October, one of my clients who is part of the Mesón family of El Mesón Sandwiches, a local restaurant chain, reached out to me and told me that they had shut down the Mayagüez restaurant specifically to make a thousand sandwiches a day to distribute to communities in need. The people at El Mesón were very insistent about making sure that the food was getting to the people who needed it and that it was getting to them while it was still fresh.

A lot of people were eating beans, Chef Boyardee—anything canned. With no power, most people didn't have another way to heat food. Even if you have a generator, what good is it if you don't have gas or the money to buy gas?[8]

On October 9, I started delivering sandwiches. Ricky was doing other relief work, helping people clear fallen trees with chainsaws, or he needed to work on our land or home, so I was alone with my boys. We'd pick up two hundred sandwiches, and we'd drive through Añasco and Mayagüez, which were majorly flooded by the Río Grande and the ocean, and we'd distribute those sandwiches to people.[9]

Sometimes El Mesón would give me cold juice to go with the sandwiches—which was amazing! Most people had no ice, no refrigeration, so getting a cold drink was something special. When

---

7. The US military was deployed to Puerto Rico on September 27, about a week after the hurricane. In general, aid arrived first in parts of San Juan and was slower to reach other places on the island, like the mountainous interior.

8. Gas stations, banks, and ATMs remained closed or provided limited services, making it sometimes impossible to purchase gas or get money. For more on the conditions after the hurricane, see "Aftermaths" in the "Contexts" essay.

9. Añasco and Mayagüez are municipalities south of Rincón. Añasco has a population of approximately 26,000, and Mayagüez has a population of approximately 71,000.

people saw what we were offering, their faces would just transform. My boys kept talking about that—how people's faces changed when we gave them a sandwich or a cold drink.

I'll never forget one woman who was home with her two children. Inti won't forget either—he always talks about it. The neighborhood where this woman lived was between two bodies of water, the bay of Mayagüez and the mouth of the Río Grande. Everybody was flooded there. And it still was full of water. We were outside of the house at the front gate. Both my boys were standing beside me. The woman was about my height. She had dark-brown hair, almond eyes, light-almond skin. She looked a lot like me. Her kids—a girl and a boy about the same age as my boys—were beside her. I asked, "Have you had lunch?" The woman said, "No, but we were about to eat some *pegao*." Pegao is the crispy, almost burnt rice at the bottom of the pot.

We gave her sandwiches and she started crying. She couldn't stop hugging me. And my boys started crying too, because it was a human moment, mother to mother. And her kids were just so happy because they were going to eat. It left a big impression on Inti. We left them, thinking, *Is she going to be okay? Are those kids going to have food tomorrow? Who's helping?*

MUD AND DEBRIS AND SEWAGE

The supplies that I was getting from family and friends overlapped with my work with El Mesón. It was perfect because while I was distributing sandwiches, I could ask, "What do you need?" And then— say I had a bunch of formula or first aid or women's supplies or clothing—I could distribute those supplies.[10] I'd start around seven or eight in the morning and finish my day around five or six in the evening. It depended on how deep in the mountains I'd get.

---

10. Vivienne was also active with Levantando el Valle Relief in Añasco, a nonprofit organization formed by locals who wanted to help their community.

A big part of the relief work was people just wanting human contact. They wanted someone to hear them. Puerto Ricans would rather suck it up and take care of themselves before asking for help, which is the opposite of what's been in the press, unfortunately. People are very proud here. So, it could be difficult coming up and asking, "Are you hungry?" Instead, I'd ask, "Have you eaten?" Or, "Do you have water?" And a lot of them would say, "No." So then I could give them food and water and any supplies I had. If they had medical needs, I'd tell the medical teams we were working with, and they'd go back and attend to the people. It was nonstop.

I tried to focus on the elderly, and there were a lot of them in need. I'll never forget this older woman who was easily in her seventies. Lines were engraved in her face. She was really beautiful and distinguished looking. She lived in Añasco and her house was completely flooded. It was surrounded by three feet of what we call *babosa*. It's not even mud. It's mud and debris and sewage, and it's really heavy and thick and hard to clean up. It went in her living room, bedroom, everywhere. She was living there alone. She couldn't clean it. She was waiting. A lot of people were just waiting. Because they kept thinking, *The municipality will come or the government or the sanitation department*. But they just kept waiting. The only people that were doing things were locals.

So, I asked this woman, "Have you eaten?" And she said, "I'll take what you have, but here, have some bananas." She had these little *guineos*—tiny, sweet bananas. I said, "No, you keep that." And she was really upset because she just couldn't understand why I wouldn't take the bananas. She's like, "Don't give to me without taking something." That whole experience was very humbling.

SICK FROM THE WATER

We had wanted to keep Inti and Anuk here in Puerto Rico with us, but then the boys, my sister, and I got sick from the water. We had abdominal pain, fever, diarrhea, and headaches. With no running water at our house, we were going to natural springs and filtering the water. But just because it's a natural spring doesn't mean it's crystal-clear clean. Everybody was going to the springs, but a lot of people were getting really sick.

Finally, we decided the boys and Danielle should go to the States. For myself, leaving was never an option as our properties and businesses are here. Ricky and I needed to make things work again here while ensuring the boys had access to school, food, and health care. On October 15, we ended up going to San Juan to fly the boys and my sister out.[11] I have never seen that airport so packed. It was chaotic. Wall-to-wall people with baggage, like they were not coming back. This was a mass exodus.[12]

When the boys arrived in San Jose, my mom did everything. She got them Medicaid because they had to go to the doctor. So did my sister. The doctor told them they were all sick because there'd been fecal matter in the water they were drinking.

My mom also got the boys into a public school right by her house. It was an amazing school. The boys were playing sports. They were healthy again. They were with my family. So that was a relief.

My conversations with my sons were very short because the phone service here was so bad. Anuk, he's very independent, so he was like, "I'm great. I love it here. I'm staying." But Inti was having a really hard time in the beginning. He said, "I'm Puerto Rican. I want to be in Puerto Rico. I want to be with you. I don't care if there's no water or no electricity." He's older, and it was really hard for him to be away from us because he was worried about us.

---

11. The Rafael Hernández Airport in Aguadilla is the closest large airport to Rincón, but flights off the island were reduced and demand was high, so often the only option for people on the west coast was to fly out of San Juan, which is approximately ninety-six miles away from Rincón.

12. The Center for Puerto Rican Studies estimates that almost 160,000 people left in 2018 as a result of the hurricane. For more on depopulation, see "Migration" in the "Contexts" essay.

It was hard for us too, but we sent our boys to the States for many reasons. They were sick. There was no school, food, gas, water, electricity, and no reliable way to communicate. Even when I started getting a cell signal, it was very inconsistent and the lines would get crossed. So, there was no way of knowing what was happening or how to plan for anything. All the banks were closed. There was no access to money. There was a constant sense of urgency and uncertainty.

On one hand, having the boys off the island was a good thing because it allowed Ricky and me to refocus our energies and figure out how to make a living. But on the other hand, there was such an emptiness. I'm a mother of two young boys. They encompass so much of my time and energy. To not have them all of a sudden, it was like, *What is this reality? It's not mine.* So, I shifted that energy into other things. I completely dived into relief work.

A LITTLE CONTAINER OF PRINGLES

The mail service started working here about a month and a half after the hurricane. As soon as I could get mail and I could get on Facebook, I started posting about the situation here and asking for what was needed.

We never got enough. You know, those two hundred sandwiches I'd get per day would be gone in an hour and a half. Gone because you'd get to what looked like a small house, and you'd ask, "How many people are living here right now?" And they'd have eleven people. Someone would say, "My aunt and uncle's house was totally destroyed. Everyone had to come and live here."

I went back to Barrio Playa in Añasco a lot of times. It's a small community. The families have been there for generations. People were so angry. They were exhausted. They were weak because they weren't getting the nutrition they needed. They weren't bathing like they used to because there was no running water. It was very hot, very humid. It was dirty because the river and ocean surge had caused flooding up to twenty feet in some areas.

The week of the hurricane, before the storm, emergency service people went into these neighborhoods that were going to flood. I'm not sure exactly who they were, but they were from the government, either the feds or the local emergency services. They said, "We need you to evacuate." And people said, "We don't have anywhere to go." The evacuation people said, "Then write your social security number on your arm with permanent marker so we can identify you after the storm." That's what they were telling people.

After the hurricane, that entire valley of Añasco and Mayagüez looked like a lake. And it stayed like that for weeks. When you went into these people's houses and saw the line of mud where the water had gone up to—it was six to eight feet high! Everything was destroyed. Nothing could be salvaged.

People were desperate. They kept asking me, "What organization are you with?" or "Are you with FEMA?" They were so surprised when I'd say, "I'm just a person doing this." FEMA eventually started setting up in this area. But it was weeks after the hurricane. I ran into the military a few times. They had water tanks where people could bring their containers to fill. They'd give out little boxes of what were supposed to be rations. We'd go get a box to see what people were getting, and it would be a little container of Pringles, a Chef Boyardee can. It was all junk food.[13] And it was literally a little box that could last one person maybe a day.

The military was not going into the interior roads of the island. They, like FEMA and the emergency centers, were mostly set up in the centers of town, which could be very hard for people from

---

13. Nutritionists noted the amount of candy and chips being distributed, and also that fruit and vegetable items exceeded recommended limits for sugar and sodium, respectively. Military MREs (Meal, Ready-to-Eat), while useful in emergencies, are highly processed, have a high content of preservatives, fat, and carbohydrates, and are low in fiber. For more on food aid, see "Aftermaths" in the "Contexts" essay.

the interior to reach. Some people, especially the elderly, don't have access to cars and there's no public transportation. Also, people had no idea where the help was because there was no communication. People were not being reached.

NOT THE TRUTH

Inti and Anuk were in California for two and a half months, which felt like forever. We still didn't have electricity or water, but for us that had been enough time being separated as a family. On December 20, we went to California for Christmas and to bring back the boys. Danielle decided not to return to Puerto Rico.

My parents picked us up in San Francisco. We drove back to San Jose, and then it was time to pick up Inti and Anuk from school. It was really emotional. The boys were happy and so proud to introduce their parents to their friends and their teachers.

But being in San Francisco was just nuts. We were coming from no stimulus, no news, limited communication, a shortage of food and supplies, and then all of a sudden, we were confronted with the wealth of Silicon Valley and the Bay Area. It was strange just going to the grocery store and seeing such abundance. After having nothing in Puerto Rico, it made me angry, but you can't get angry at what people don't know.

When people heard that we were from Puerto Rico, they thought that they knew the reality of what was happening on the island because of what they'd seen in the news, which was not the truth. The media presented the situation as if the government were taking care of things and doing all this outreach. But most of those pictures in the news were from San Juan. In the first few weeks after the hurricane, we hadn't seen any of that help on the west coast. And the death count that was announced by the president was so off.[14] Hundreds of people disappeared. All you needed to do was go to any of the neighborhoods that bordered the Río Grande or the coast and talk to the people there. Locals know each other, so they knew people were missing. They didn't find bodies. People just disappeared.[15]

Being in the States was very, very overwhelming. In Puerto Rico, I hadn't stopped. I was physically strong from all the lifting and walking, but I'd lost weight and was mentally exhausted. All I wanted to do was lie in the sun in the park and watch my kids play and read. All I wanted to do was be with my family.

We were in California for three weeks. We brought our sons back to Puerto Rico in January. Before we left, we had a talk with the boys. We said, "We want you to know that the island is better than when you left, but it's still struggling." Inti was so ready to come back. He said, "I'm Puerto Rican. I love my island. I want to go home." But the thought of coming back was hard for Anuk. He said, "I really like California. I like my school. I love you, but I don't necessarily want to go back." We could understand that. The public schools in Silicon Valley are definitely a whole level up from the schools here. They've got learning programs that kids don't and won't get here. It's a big conflict. As parents, we wanted our sons back on the island, but we also wanted them to have those kinds of opportunities in school here. Why is it that Puerto Rican kids can't have educational opportunities?

---

14. For months after the hurricane the government's official count of deaths caused by María was sixty-four. In August 2018, the official death toll was revised to 2,975 people, making María among the deadliest hurricanes in US history. Research shows even this revised number may be greatly underestimated. For more on the death toll, see "Aftermaths" in the "Contexts" essay.

15. On October 16, 2017, three weeks after the hurricane, 109 people were still listed as missing. "People Listed Missing in Puerto Rico since Hurricane Maria Hit Island," Missing Persons Center, https://missingpersonscenter.org/index.php /component/k2/item/4-117-people-listed-missing-in-puerto-rico-since-hurricane-maria-hit-island.

FIGHTING TO KEEP THE SCHOOL OPEN

Schools remained closed for weeks and sometimes months after the hurricane for a variety of reasons, including damage to infrastructure or lack of running water or power. Hurricane María also exacerbated the problem of ongoing school closures in Puerto Rico. Puerto Rico's Departamento de Educación (DE), the Department of Education, had been closing schools even before the hurricane, often citing low enrollment as the primary reason, but austerity measures have also played a large part in recent closures.[16] In April 2018, the DE announced the closure of 283 public schools, approximately one-quarter of the public schools in Puerto Rico.

When we got back, Inti and Anuk's school still didn't have water and electricity. From the middle of September until the middle of January it was closed. Then the director said, "We can't keep waiting." So, they brought in cisterns of water. None of the schools got generators. But as long as the kids could go to the bathroom, then school was open.

The boys love their school. It's called Escuela Genoveva and it's been around for generations. It's a small-town school. Everybody knows each other. It feels like a family. But we have to leave it because the DE has decided to close almost three hundred schools. And our boys' school is one of them.

I can tell you why they want to close our school. It's prime real estate. The school is in a neighborhood called Puntas.[17] It has a massive amount of land surrounding the building and there's an ocean view. Puntas is being bought up. We have two guesthouses, and as soon as we had water and electricity, we opened them up again. Every single guest who came to stay after the hurricane was here to buy

---

16. For more on austerity measures, see "Economic Contexts" in the "Contexts" essay.

17. The Puntas neighborhood has many of Rincón's most popular beaches, and while it has long-time local residents, it also has a substantial expatriate population.

property.[18] It's scary because Puerto Ricans can't afford to pay rent or buy a house here anymore.

We've been fighting to keep the school open for three years now. The first time, in 2016, the parents and staff had to camp out at the school because—even before the DE made the official announcement that the school was to be closed—they were coming at night and taking away gas tanks and equipment. If we didn't stop them, they'd be able to say, "Oh, your school's not up to par because you don't have this equipment." Equipment that they took in the middle of the night!

We went to town meetings to fight for our school, but the mayor only lamented the closure of the school. So, we joined with the Teachers' Association and other public schools that were also being threatened with closure.[19] Together, we sued the DE. Not all of the schools won. We did.

But in the summer of 2017, once again, we were notified our school was closing. They said to keep a school open, the facilities and programs needed to be up to date. We complied with all DE criteria for non-closure.

They sent investigators to each school to see if the criteria were being met. They showed up at six in the morning. The director of the school wasn't there, the secretary of the director wasn't there, none of the students were there, the teachers weren't there. The janitor was there. They talked to the janitor.

We were notified our school would be closed, so we fought again. This time with calls, emails, and by going to the office of the

---

18. According to the real estate website Point2Homes, online searches for real estate in Puerto Rico increased after the hurricane. Point2Homes surveyed the visitors to the Puerto Rico section of the site and found that 97 percent of the respondents were US mainland residents. For more on Puerto Rico's post-María housing market, see "Disaster Capitalism" in the "Contexts" essay.

19. The Teachers' Association, also known as Asociación de Maestros in Spanish, is one of the unions in Puerto Rico that represents teachers.

secretary of education. And it worked. We got to keep the school open for the second time. But just this week we were notified again that the school would be closing.[20]

We've managed to protect the school from closure for three years, and of course I am fighting for it again, but now there's no way. The decision has been made and fighting the system takes a lot of time. You have to take off from work. You have to pay for gas to go wherever a meeting's going to be held, which a lot of times is in the metro area. You need to be able to make calls and write informed documents. A lot of people still don't have internet. And a lot of the schools that are being closed are in areas where people don't have cars to get around. People are fighting to get their homes rebuilt, to pay the bills, to get jobs. We are all so exhausted. We're fighting to keep our kids strong. We don't have the fight in us for this anymore. And that is why they're closing schools now. Because there's not going to be a fight.

If you ask the DE why they are closing schools, they say it's because of the mass exodus, that the schools are under-enrolled. And then it's all about money. There's this "debt"—in quotes—that Puerto Rico needs to pay back. The first thing to be cut is public services, education being one of them.[21] I think it's really sad because what type of future generation are we going to have when they're constantly getting this sense of *I'm not important enough to matter*?

THE FEELING OF HOME

Six months after the hurricane, most of the people I've done relief work with have continued working. They're still providing food,

---

20. They were notified of this final school closure in April 2018.

21. Puerto Rico has been experiencing an economic decline since 2006, which culminated in the Puerto Rican government-debt crisis of 2014 and the archipelago filing for bankruptcy in 2017, just months before the hurricane. Since then austerity measures have been imposed, affecting public education. For more on the debt crisis and austerity measures, see "Economic Contexts" in the "Contexts" essay.

water, and medical aid. They're building people's roofs and houses. They're clearing roads. Sometimes we have to be really creative.
Like, *Oh, we don't have water. What do we have to do? Well, let me
take out the center of a satellite dish, turn it upside down, connect it to
a pipe, and run it to this basin. And there, I can collect rainwater.* Junk
turns into treasure when you need it.

I definitely get frustrated with the inefficiency and bureaucracy
here, but everywhere's like that—nowhere's perfect. I think that if
you don't like what you see, make it better where you are. I say this
because I am second-generation Puerto Rican, and I see the heart-
ache in my grandmother's eyes when I talk to her about Puerto Rico.

My grandmother moved to the States when she was in her twen-
ties—she's in her eighties now. She came back only once to visit the
island several years ago. I took her to the beach, and she was like a
little kid. There were almonds on the ground, and she said, "What
is wrong with people? This is food." She took a rock, broke open
the almonds, and ate them while lying in a hammock. She grew up
sleeping in a hammock.

The song "En Mi Viejo San Juan" talks about the person who
leaves the island but whose heart remains in Puerto Rico.[22] This is
the migrant story, right? They go to find a better life, but the heart
never leaves home. I always remember the chorus: *Adiós, adiós, adiós,
Borinquén querida.* My grandma cries every time she sings it because
it's saying, "Goodbye, goodbye, goodbye, my beloved Borinquén."[23]
It's a ballad about the mountains and the rivers and the people and
the flowers and the scents and the sounds and the flag, and it's a
sense of *patria*.

Patria is a word in Spanish that you cannot directly translate
into English. You can't say, it's my homeland—that's so cut-and-dry.

22. "En Mi Viejo San Juan" was composed by Puerto Rican singer and songwriter
Noel Estrada.

23. Puerto Ricans often call the island "Borinquén," which is derived from
"Borikén," the Indigenous Taíno name for the island.

Patria is so much more romantic than that. Patria is the feeling of home, of homeland. It's the feeling of walking into your grandma's kitchen to the smell of *sancocho*. Of grating *plátanos* to make *pasteles* for Christmas.[24] Of sleeping in a hammock during a summer night.

One of my favorite traditions here is Three Kings Day on January 6. The evening before, some people do *promesas*, making promises for the new year. We dedicate them to the Three Kings, and do a sort of pilgrimage, staying up, playing music, and singing. It's a celebration of hope, and I think it shows what being Puerto Rican is all about. There's still uncertainty in the air, but that spirit is slowly returning to the island.

---

24. *Sancocho* is a Puerto Rican stew or hearty soup made of root vegetables, beef, and pork. *Plátanos* are plantains. *Pasteles* are a dish often eaten during the Christmas holiday season consisting of a green banana and root vegetable dough stuffed with meat, olives, eggs, raisins, and other ingredients (depending on local preferences), wrapped in banana leaves and boiled.

JOSÉ GARCÍA SEPÚLVEDA

BORN IN: 1965
LIVES IN: Aguada
Pastor

José García Sepúlveda is the pastor of the Iglesia la Familia (Family Church) in Rincón, where he has been ministering for more than twenty years. He lives in Aguada, a town just north of Rincón, with his wife and their four children.[1]

When we meet with José in December 2018, the crisis center that he established after the hurricane is still operating. We talk with José in his office, a small room at the back of the church's modest white building that is reached by passing through a dim hall containing shelves filled

---

1. Aguada and Rincón are municipalities on the west coast. Rincón has a population of 15,000 and a significant expat community. Aguada has a population of approximately 36,000.

141

*with clothes, diapers, and many small cans of Beanie Weenies—just
some of the donations that the church continues to distribute among
families in need more than a year after María.*

A SEVERE FINANCIAL RECESSION

God put it in my heart that we needed to open a crisis center. This
was in 2014, before Hurricane María, when we were seeing a severe
financial recession on the island and there was no light at the end of
the tunnel.[2] So many people were struggling. I knew of elderly people who only got $100 or $200 in pension or social security benefits a
month. No one can live off that. They were having to sacrifice things
like food or personal hygiene items in order to cover doctor's visits
and much-needed medicines. Families also weren't earning enough.[3]
Many were leaving because there was no other choice. There was a
great exodus in the two to three years before Hurricane María. I
think close to a hundred thousand people abandoned the island.[4]

When I saw so many families struggling, I could relate. My wife,
Damaris, and I have four children—two boys and two girls, ranging
in age from ten to twenty-one years old. We've got a full house, and
pastoral ministry is not a well-paying job. If you're looking to come
into the ministry to get rich, you're in the wrong line of work!

---

2. Puerto Rico has been experiencing an economic decline since 2006, which culminated in the Puerto Rican government-debt crisis of 2014 and the archipelago
filing for bankruptcy in 2017, just months before the hurricane. For more on the
debt crisis and austerity measures, see "Economic Contexts" in the "Contexts" essay.

3. According to US Census Bureau statistics for 2014–18, the median annual
household income in Puerto Rico (in 2018 dollars) was $20,166, compared with
$60,293 on the mainland United States. The percentage of persons living in pover-
ty in Puerto Rico was 43.5 percent, compared with 10.5 percent on the mainland
United States.

4. According to the US Census Bureau, from 2015 to 2017 the Puerto Rico population decreased by 147,946 people. For more on depopulation, see "Migration" in
the "Contexts" essay.

I've actually known this kind of struggle since my childhood. My parents were born on the island, but when they married, they moved to the States seeking a better life. So, I was born and raised in Brooklyn, New York. Bushwick, the community we were living in, was going through its worst moment. Our home was in a three-story apartment building and our landlord wasn't paying the heating bills. In dead-cold winters, I remember cuddling up with my brother and sister—sometimes the entire family—in one bed, fully dressed, with socks on our feet and on our hands, under five blankets just to stay warm. We'd wake up early in the morning to warm our hands over the burners of our gas stove.

Bushwick was also very dangerous. This was during the 1970s and the crime rate in New York was high. Drugs and gangs were everywhere. Apartment buildings very close to us were being destroyed by arson.[5] We were living in fear. Every time we heard a siren, we'd wake up frantic and ask ourselves if it was our building that was on fire. Families were moving out as fast as they could. My parents knew that we couldn't continue to live that way. They decided to move back to the island. They wanted a better life for us.

WE HAD TO OPEN A CRISIS CENTER

José was thirteen when his family returned to Puerto Rico and settled in Añasco.[6] He struggled with the move from a big city in the States to a small island town and turned to the church for comfort. Because he knew how to play a little guitar, he became the local church's musician.

---

5. In the early 1970s, fires burned nightly in Bushwick, primarily due to acts of arson committed by apartment building owners who were setting fires to their own property to collect insurance money. The fires continued for years, escalating during the blackout of July 13, 1977. For more on the history of this neighborhood, see "The Death and Life of Bushwick" by Steven Malanga, *City Journal* (Spring 2008), www.city-journal.org/html/death-and-life-bushwick-13083.html.

6. Añasco is a western municipality south of Rincón with a population of approximately 26,000.

José met Damaris at church. Eventually he studied theology and became the pastor of the Family Church, located in a small neighborhood of Rincón called Stella, which is composed of a mix of older, modest homes belonging to longtime residents, and more recently built condos and vacation houses.

With so many people struggling because of the recession, I knew we had to open a crisis center. About a year before the hurricane, I put that in prayer to God and—without anyone else knowing what I'd asked for—Richard McDonald, a man from our community, came up to me and said, "Pastor, I feel in my heart that the keys to my property should be handed over to you, so that you can use it as you feel in your heart." I told him, "You've got to be kidding me!" But he wasn't. He gave us permission to use the property, and God reminded me, *Didn't you want a crisis center? This is where you're going to set it up.* The property had a small wooden house, a trailer, and more than an acre of land in the neighborhood of Calvache, which is only about a mile from Stella, the neighborhood where our church is. I registered the crisis center as the Casa de Misericordia, the House of Mercy, and we were just about to open the doors when the hurricane hit.

OUR DREAMS WERE BLOWN AWAY

After the hurricane, I had to wait four days before I could go to the church in Stella because the roads were blocked. My home is concrete and thankfully had been spared, and when I got to the church I saw that it, too, was undamaged—even though the winds had blown off the entire roof of the house next door. It could have fallen and crushed our church, but instead it fell in our parking lot without damaging anything other than the fence. It was a miracle that we still had our church.

But later that same week, people who live in Calvache, where the House of Mercy crisis center was going to open, told me that one of the old gigantic trees on the property was blown off its roots and had crushed the little wooden house. It was completely destroyed. I questioned God, *Didn't you ask us to build a crisis center? Didn't you want us to help these families in need?* I didn't know what was going on. María really shook us all. It seemed as if our dreams were blown away with María.

Things were chaotic. There was a lack of water, electricity, phone service, food, and medical services. There was no refrigeration, so food poisoning was a risk. There was no trash pickup. Garbage was piling up, so there were more rodents around where people live.[7] The lack of running water created serious sanitary issues. Dirty water was making people sick. The risk of leptospirosis was high due to rat feces and urine.[8] Life on the island during those days was very dangerous. And there was desperation everywhere.

I knew that the church in Stella had been spared so we could focus on the people in need. The hurricane was on a Wednesday, and that Sunday I told my wife and kids, "We're going to reopen the church." There was no power or water. All I had was my acoustic guitar. When I arrived, twenty or thirty people were already waiting. I played guitar and everyone was singing and we were so joyful that we were still alive.

After the service, I told people, "We have to do something." We didn't have a generator. We didn't have a backup water system, like a cistern. We simply had the desire to work. So that Monday, a small group of six people showed up—they were exactly the people we needed. I asked the volunteers two questions: "What do we have?" and "What can we do?" The answer to the first question was that we

7. The Puerto Rico Solid Waste Authority estimated that Hurricane María "created 6.2 million cubic yards of waste and debris." For more on the conditions after the hurricane, see "Aftermaths" in the "Contexts" essay.

8. Leptospirosis is caused by *Leptospira*, which are bacteria in the urine of rodents and other animals. Outbreaks occur after surface waters become contaminated following heavy rainfalls and floods due to storms and hurricanes. For more, see the glossary.

had a kitchen with gas stoves, a couple of grocery items on the shelf, and about $3,000 in the bank account. "Let's open a soup kitchen," I said. "Let's start serving hot meals to people who don't have food."

Most ATMs weren't working and the banks were only authorizing $100 per person. But I know a couple bank employees, so I was able to request a withdrawal of $400, and with that we were able to make our first purchase of groceries. A lot of the stores were closed, but Sam's Club still had some canned items on their shelves. It was enough to get started. We weren't looking to offer elaborate menus. People just wanted food! On September 25, five days after María, our soup kitchen opened.

NOTHING BUT THE CLOTHES THEY WERE WEARING

People came to the church for food, but our volunteers also delivered around seventy-five meals a day to local neighborhoods. Many said that we were the first to arrive with help. In some cases, this was two weeks after the hurricane. That surprised us even more. And this wasn't the remote communities up in the mountains. We went to the housing projects in town, which are walking distance from the plaza. But the fact that they're closer to town didn't make them less vulnerable. Everyone had needs. It didn't matter where you lived, who you were, or what your social class was. Even those who had money needed help—what good is money if you can't get it from the bank and there's no food or gas to buy?[9]

We thought that the first responders would be the Red Cross or FEMA or some other much larger organization, but help from FEMA didn't come here until more than a month after the hurricane. In the first few weeks of the emergency, the Red Cross

---

9. For weeks after the hurricane, banks, stores, and gas stations remained closed or offered limited services. ATMs and point-of-sale systems that stores use to process payments also did not work. For more on the conditions after the hurricane, see "Aftermaths" in the "Contexts" essay.

and other humanitarian organizations were helping, but it wasn't enough. You'd wait no less than thirty to sixty minutes to get rations of food like MREs, dried pasta, trail mix, crackers, cookies, and canned items like tuna, sardines, and spaghetti and meatballs.[10] And sometimes what you got wasn't enough to get you through the week or even the day, especially if you had a family.

Around two weeks after the hurricane, we got notice that the coastal community of Tres Hermanos in Añasco needed help. Members of our church live there, so we visited them and we simply couldn't bear what we saw. It was complete desolation. It seemed as if a bomb had exploded. The flooding had been so intense, the first floors of these homes had been completely underwater. There was still a foot of mud and debris in the homes that had to be cleared out with shovels. Everything in their homes was destroyed. They had nothing but the clothes they were wearing.

That was when we understood that we had to go beyond simply providing hot meals. We were going to use every single item on our shelves and every single dollar in the bank to help as many people as we could. We made cards with information about our location to hand out to people, so they could come to the church and be served on a daily basis.

Word spread about what we were doing and help started to arrive at our doorstep. The Red Cross provided fresh fruit, groceries, and some other items. From La Cooperativa, a bank in Rincón, we received a truckload of baby formula, which was very much needed. We received donations from churches, and from friends and church members who were living in the States. They sent money and packages with clothing, solar-powered lamps, batteries, and personal hygiene items.

---

10. An MRE (Meal, Ready-to-Eat) is a shelf-stable, individually portioned meal. Originally designed for the US military, MREs are now also sold as an emergency preparedness item or as survival food.

We didn't really have any space to put the supplies. Since María had destroyed our planned crisis center in Calvache, all we had was two rooms at the back of the church in Stella. The rooms were around twenty feet by twenty feet each, and this small space is what we ended up using as our crisis center. Sometimes the supplies came in faster than we could distribute them. We piled box over box. We needed to organize. We began by purchasing one shelf, but that wasn't enough, so we purchased another and another. Eventually the two rooms were completely full. We had grocery items and baby supplies. We had diapers of all sizes from infants all the way to adults. There was also over-the-counter medicine, bedding, housewares, and clothing.

Our volunteers were always looking for ways to fit everything. We'd have close to eight volunteers a day, but it really wasn't enough. My wife and the kids were at the church just about every day, either helping in the kitchen or in the crisis center. I often went on the deliveries. I'll never forget how everything was so silent when we'd go into these communities. If you didn't hear a power generator, it was complete scary, eerie silence. You didn't hear the noise of a TV or a radio. You didn't hear the cry of an infant. Many families with babies had fled or sought safer places to live until the emergency had passed.

GHOST TOWN

That Christmas was one of the saddest I've ever seen because there were no decorations, no music, and no celebrating. Typically at Christmas here, you'll see lights on every porch and hear music everywhere, especially with the *parrandas*.[11] We'd walk into communities like Tres Hermanos and it was like walking into a ghost town.

---

11. *Parrandas* are a Puerto Rican holiday tradition in which a group of friends and family gather late at night to surprise others in their homes with music and song. Food and drinks are shared, and often several homes are visited in one night, the group growing as the night progresses. For more, see the glossary.

You'd ask yourself, *Do people live here?* If you did see people, no one was talking. Everyone was speechless because of the devastation.

So, I told my team, "I want to do a Christmas banquet." I wanted to bring people together, serve them a Christmas dinner, and also offer them a financial contribution. When monetary donations came in, we'd been setting aside the majority of the funds to help people who needed it. This was our chance.

We searched for a venue and knocked on the door of this little hotel in Tres Hermanos. The owner had seen us working in the community every day, so he was happy to let us use his place free of charge. We contacted a person to make food for the event and asked them to cook for around three hundred people. We invited those who'd been hardest hit, and that evening we had people come from all the communities we'd been helping.

We served everyone a Christmas meal of *arroz con gandules, ensalada de coditos,* and roasted chicken.[12] We had live gospel music. People were dancing, singing, and laughing. They were happy. We did this early in December, around the seventh. For most people, this was their only Christmas celebration because they didn't have the money to do anything themselves. We also gave every family that attended $100. The families came in all sizes; most had around four or five people. We gave out around $6,000. People were overwhelmed with joy and tears. But you knew in your heart that it wasn't enough.

One of the things that this hurricane brought to light is how serious the social crisis on our island is—how many people are living in poverty. After the hurricane we walked down every road we could because we wanted everyone to get a plate of food or a bag of groceries. And by doing that, we discovered that there were so many people living in such poverty. We visited one house that was very dilapidated. It had hardly any paint on it and was slightly off its

---

12. *Arroz con gandules* is a Puerto Rican dish made with rice and pigeon peas. *Ensalada de coditos* is a Puerto Rican macaroni salad.

cement foundation. You could see through holes in the wooden pan-el walls. Inside, the floors seemed too weak to step on. The kitchen had a small metal sink and a few pots and dishes. They had a very old portable stove hooked up to a cylinder gas tank, and the walls were black, entirely covered in grease. The bathroom wasn't func-tional; the faucets were broken. The bedroom consisted of a very old mattress on the floor. Rodents, roaches, and insects roamed freely in and out of the house. In spite of all their poverty and need, the people who lived there offered us coffee!

People were living in such inhumane conditions—conditions that simply are not acceptable. And they were living like this before the hurricane. After the hurricane, the situation was even worse be-cause they didn't have water or power.

It's been a year since the hurricane and we know of people who are still hurting. They're often the people who—even before María—simply couldn't get through the month because of their financial situation. This time it was María. Next time, maybe it's another hurricane or maybe an earthquake.[13] I don't know. But we want to be prepared; we want to be there for our community. There's still much to be done.

---

13. An ongoing earthquake swarm in Puerto Rico began on December 28, 2019. There have been thousands of earthquakes since then, the largest registering at 6.4. For more on the earthquakes, see "Earthquake Swarm" in the "Contexts" essay.

LOREL CUBANO SANTIAGO

BORN IN: 1980
LIVES IN: San Juan
Community Organizer

Lorel Cubano Santiago is just finishing up with a customer when we walk into Colectivo PerlArte in the spring of 2020. PerlArte is a community-owned gallery that Lorel runs and helped to found after Hurricane María. The gallery is located in La Perla, a small, economically impoverished but culturally and historically significant neighborhood adjacent to the much more well-known Old San Juan.[1] PerlArte is easy to spot because of the brightly colored mural that covers the front of the gallery. The mural depicts a woman lying in a wooden boat, which floats in the air over blue water. The community of La Perla is nestled

---

1. Old San Juan is a historic district of Puerto Rico's capital city, San Juan, which has a population of approximately 318,000.

in her lap. One pink house falls from the boat, but the woman's hand is cupped, ready to catch it.

The gallery is one long, narrow room with no windows. Sunlight streams in through the open front doors, but most of the interior is dim. The walls and shelves are full of paintings, mosaics, sketches, jewelry, and vejigante masks.[2] Printed T-shirts hang from a rack in one corner and two wall-sized, communally created paintings are on display at the back of the room.

We sit on the back balcony among stacks of rum barrels that will be transformed into bomba drums for one of PerlArte's community programs. Lorel's story is about herself, but it is also about the neighborhood of La Perla in which she has lived and worked for over six years. Although La Perla is located minutes away from the port of San Juan, where the majority of aid was being delivered to the island after the hurricane, Lorel and her neighbors received little help from federal or local governmental humanitarian relief operations.

A MIX OF BOTH CITY AND DIRT

I come from humble beginnings. I grew up in Manatí.[3] We lived in a small house in an *urbanización*.[4] While I was growing up, both my parents were in college, so I saw them study and work and struggle.

I'm a mix of both my parents. My father, José, eventually ended up working in the pharmaceutical industry, but he's a lawyer and a psychologist. He's into reading books and he's always studying.

---

2. The vejigante is a demon from medieval Spanish folklore who has become intertwined with Taíno and West African mythologies in Puerto Rico. During the Carnival festivities in Ponce and Loíza leading up to Ash Wednesday, revelers often wear vejigante masks made of papier-mâché, coconut husks, or gourds.

3. Manatí is a northern coastal municipality with a population of approximately 37,000.

4. An *urbanización* is a planned community. For more, see the glossary.

That's what I got from him. My mom, Carmen, is a registered nurse, and she did a lot of work with hospice patients. Watching her as a little girl, I saw her passion and love for the elderly. That's where I get my love of community.

We traveled all the time between my dad's family and my mom's family. My father came from San Juan, and my mom came from the mountains, from around Utuado.[5] So I know the city and I know the land and the mountains. I'm a mix of both city and dirt.

I had very urban experiences as a child because we'd visit my father's family in San Juan. My father comes from Puerta de Tierra, a neighborhood just outside of Old San Juan. This community has been left in poverty and the people there are disenfranchised. But I have good memories there. My big sister Tania, my big brother José, and I would spend time with our grandfather. His name was also José—I have a lot of Josés and Carmens in my life!

Grandfather used to walk a lot and he'd take us to get ice cream at a local place, Colombo's Frozen Yogurt. It was far away, like three miles to get there. And then three miles back! I was only four to six years old, but he'd keep us going, talking as we walked. Oh, we burned energy on those walks. The ice cream tasted pretty good after a hot walk under the sun. My favorite flavor was chocolate. It's always chocolate for me. I'll eat chocolate anything!

My grandfather died when I was young, but I still have these memories of Puerta de Tierra. My father grew up there and studied in San Juan. His whole life was here. That's why I have a sense of belonging to San Juan.

Some of my favorite childhood memories are of going to visit my mom's family in the country in Utuado. Her family is large, with nine brothers and sisters. Aunt Josephina—we call her Tití

---

5. San Juan and Utuado are both approximately thirty miles away from Manatí. San Juan lies to the east of Manatí, while Utuado lies southwest and is reached by winding, mountainous roads.

Fina—was the eldest of the sisters, and she had a big country house, so everybody gathered there.[6]

We'd drive up to the house and all the uncles and aunts would be there. My sister, brother, and I would open the car door, rush out, shout "Hello!" to the adults, and then go play with our cousins. There were usually about six to nine kids, a big group of children adventuring.

The house was on a hill, but behind the hill there was a mountain, so we'd all run to the mountain. Mountains are treasures. You can find anything and everything there. A beehive was a treasure for us. Often the beehives were so big that they were dripping honey, so we just had to put something below the hive to collect it. Then we'd get to have honey! Our parents always brought extra clothes for us when we went to Tití Fina's because they knew we were going to get really, really dirty.

We were always going on adventures, joking, playing, and inventing things because we were bright kids and a little bit hyperactive. I was also creative from a young age. I took art classes, and I've always enjoyed art as a way to release. I had a lot of fun as a child, but I also come from a family that was difficult, and art was a way of getting through that.

The domestic violence in my family is a part of who I am. When my mom and dad would fight, the abuse was more verbal than it was physical. Once or twice it turned physically violent, on both sides. Whenever I heard my parents fighting, I'd go to my room and hide in my closet so I couldn't hear them. Sometimes parents don't know when they do stupid things. You have to learn to forgive them because they didn't do it on purpose. My parents stayed together for twenty-five years. They divorced when I was going into college.

---

6. *Tití* means auntie.

I'VE BEEN BLIND AND I'VE BEEN PARALYZED

I met Cristián in 2004 at the Universidad Interamericana de Puerto Rico in San Juan. He was my college sweetheart. He's two years younger than me. When I saw him, I was like, *Oh my God!* My friend told me, "But he's still so young." But I replied, "Well, who doesn't like a piece of candy?" We've been together ever since—sixteen years now.

My favorite things about him are that he plays music and that he's smarter than I am. I come up with all these crazy ideas, but somehow he makes them better. He complements me. We've grown up together and have been through a lot of difficulties. We're in Puerto Rico during one of the worst economic recessions ever in history.[7] So it's not like we're floating in cash, but I can't complain. I've been through worse.

I have multiple sclerosis (MS), which is very difficult. I've been blind and I've been paralyzed. It's like the knee joints are rubber and you're trying to control them with your brain, but the body just won't respond. That's the best I can explain. But I'm managing it. I decided not to take the interferon treatments.[8] This is a personal choice. I don't want to say that the interferon treatment is unnecessary because it is good for most patients, but I did a holistic approach instead. I went vegan and gluten-free. I exercise. I go to a chiropractor and also a psychologist for stress management. I go to a neurologist and get a checkup with the doctor once or twice a year. The MS isn't progressing, so it means that what I'm doing is working for now.

---

7. Puerto Rico has been experiencing an economic decline since 2006, which culminated in the Puerto Rican government-debt crisis of 2014 and the archipelago filing for bankruptcy in 2017, just months before the hurricane. For more on the debt crisis and austerity measures, see "Economic Contexts" in the "Contexts" essay.

8. Our bodies naturally make interferons, which are proteins that help modulate our immune response. Interferon medications are human-made versions of these proteins that are used to treat a variety of conditions, including MS.

"YOU'RE A DIAMOND IN THE ROUGH"

In 2005, while I was still studying, I started working in tourism in Old San Juan. I grew up in the industry. Everybody knows me. At first, I worked in restaurants and then as a hotel concierge and tour operator. One day, in 2010, this guy came looking for me at the hotel and said, "I want to hire you." It turned out he was William Alicea, a Puerto Rican from the diaspora who fought in the civil rights movement in the 1960s and seventies in New York because Blacks and Latinos were being discriminated against. He's always been in love with the island, so he retired here, and he had a dream. He said, "I want to open up El Morro at night and do tours."[9] And I'm like, "Oh, I've dreamt of that, too."

Bill hired me to develop the Old San Juan Heritage Walking Tours company.[10] So, I was doing this candlelit production at night with people dressed in period clothing, and Disney heard about it. One day, I got a call from the economic development office of the government. They said, "Cancel everything you have. You have an appointment with the Disney people on Wednesday." I thought, *I guess I'm canceling everything I have!*

Disney was a great experience. In training, they told me, "You're a diamond in the rough, but we're going to polish you, girl." So, I worked with them and started the Disney program in 2011. I'd take people from Disney cruise ships on a six-hour tour of Old San Juan. I incorporated theater into the tour, writing scripts, designing costumes, and hiring people to play the characters.

---

9. The historical fortification Castillo San Felipe del Morro is generally called El Morro for short. It is part of the UNESCO World Heritage Site known as La Fortaleza and San Juan National Historic Site, which also includes Castillo San Cristóbal and a large section of the original wall that surrounded San Juan. The defensive structures, including a large portion of the wall, were built between the sixteenth and twentieth centuries. For more, see the timeline.

10. Old San Juan Heritage Walking Tours was incorporated in 2010.

We'd get to the cruise ship in the morning with a row of soldiers from 1797, which is the golden period for Old San Juan because it was the first time we got to use our defense system. That was when we fought Ralph Abercromby, who was a mofo for the English.[11] Abercromby defeated many other people, but he couldn't defeat us.

In our tour, we marched the visitors up the street with soldiers and then they'd meet Ponce de León and his wife, Leonor.[12] It was entertaining and funny because he was the conquistador who "built" the city, but there he was with Leonor, his Latina wife who brought him down to earth.

The program was intergenerational because the parents and grandma and grandpa are the ones who pay, so they have to be entertained, but we didn't want the children to be bored either. I had a mix of everything for everybody.

A "TABOO" COMMUNITY

Lorel was running the Disney program and Old San Juan Heritage Walking Tours, and Cristián also became a tour guide. Around 2014, William Alicea bought several buildings in La Perla, just steps away from where Lorel and Cristián were giving their tours. One of them was a three-story building, which William offered to let Lorel use as a workshop. Before she could use the building, it had to be cleaned. William organized the process, and over time Lorel, Cristián, and other volunteers took out thirty-seven truckloads of trash. They also had to remove two cars that were parked inside—one on top of the other. Eventually, the top floor became the workshop, which would later become the Colectivo PerlArte. The two lower floors were apartments, one of which

---

11. Ralph Abercromby was a Scottish soldier who became a lieutenant-general in the British Army.

12. Juan Ponce de León was a Spanish conquistador who became the first governor of the archipelago during the Spanish colonial period. For more on Ponce de León and colonialism, see "Spanish Colonization" in the "Contexts" essay.

Lorel and Cristián made their home. They have lived in La Perla for about six years.

La Perla is a historically significant neighborhood, which arose around the site of a nineteenth-century slaughterhouse. According to Spanish colonial law, slaughterhouses and cemeteries had to be built outside city limits. Therefore, the Cementerio Santa María Magdalena de Pazzis and a slaughterhouse were built outside the wall of San Juan. The slaughterhouse is now used as a community center, and the cemetery is considered a historical landmark and tourist attraction.

I love it here. It's magical. La Perla was built outside the historical wall of Old San Juan. It's a small community—just one street about a mile long that winds around in a circle like a merry-go-round. It's amazingly beautiful here. We're on the waterfront in between two historical fortifications. On one side we have the wall of Castillo San Felipe del Morro and on the other side we have the wall of Castillo San Cristóbal. In between those two castles there was actually a small fortress. It was built with limestone from here, which is white. When a ship was coming, they'd see this white structure that looked like a pearl. So that's the name they gave it—La Perla.

My first introduction to La Perla was when I was a teenager and my friends and I would come here to have a cheap beer, smoke a joint, and not be judged. But it's been a "taboo" community since the very beginning because the population here has always been poor.

Most people who lived here came down from the mountains and ended up in La Perla because it was cheap.[13] And they had jobs

---

13. In 1848, a Spanish government census documented eighteen shacks around the slaughterhouse located in La Perla. The population grew significantly in the 1900s when, as a result of the Great Depression and Puerto Rico's declining sugar cane industry, people from rural Puerto Rico migrated to San Juan. This led to the rise of what were considered to be some of the worst slums in the world at the time, including La Perla, which in 1940 reached a peak population of almost 4,500 people. See Yesmín Vega Valdivieso, "Service Provision in the Slums: The

in the city. They were servants. They cleaned houses. They worked in slaughterhouses or were low-rent soldiers.

Historically there was a lot of disregard for the lower class in Puerto Rico. People here were—and still are—discriminated against because they're poor. We're literally on the outside of the wall of Old San Juan, one of the biggest tourist areas in Puerto Rico and also a neighborhood where very affluent people live. I think we have one of the largest wealth disparities, if not the largest, in the US.[14] So that wall between the neighborhoods is literal, but it's also mental. I appreciate and love the historical wall, but I always wonder, *How can I tear down that mental wall?* Here and also in Puerta de Tierra, where my grandfather lived, are the communities where we've kept the poor.

About twelve hundred people live in La Perla right now. There are families that were born and raised here and they pride themselves on that, but this is mostly a place where people come and go. The community is extremely vulnerable. Our people have been systematically treated badly all our lives. Nobody is going to help our community because La Perla is also coveted now. This is prime real estate. In 2012, Donald Trump came here, and he wanted to buy the land to turn this into Santorini or another Greek island community.[15] If

Case of La Perla in San Juan, Puerto Rico" (master's thesis, Columbia University, 2015), https://doi.org/10.7916/D8PZ581J. For more on Puerto Rico's economy in the 1930s, see "The Great Depression" in the "Contexts" essay.

14. The estimated annual median household income of La Perla was $3,375 (in 2013 inflation-adjusted dollars). The annual median household income of San Juan at a similar time was $22,734 (in 2012 inflation-adjusted dollars). See Vega Valdivieso, "Service Provision in the Slums," and "Income in Puerto Rico Holds Steady after Recession," United States Census Bureau, 2014, www.census.gov/newsroom/press-releases/2014/cb14-17.html, respectively.

15. A 2016 *New York Times* article reports that residents of La Perla claim Donald Trump stood above their community (because his bodyguards wouldn't let him come down) and offered to buy them out for $11 million. See Mary Williams Walsh, "A Surreal Life on the Precipice in Puerto Rico," *New York Times*, August

no help comes here, people are hoping that it becomes abandoned, so they can just buy it up. That's what they want. That's why I say the lack of aid here is systemic—it is by design.[16]

As soon as I moved here, I started knocking on the tourism companies' doors to try to get the "X"—the stigma—removed from La Perla, trying to convince them to let us do tours. It took a couple of years, but we got them on board and everything was changing. I was doing tours and the Disney program until 2016.

That year, I stopped working to take a year off. It was the hundredth anniversary of the national parks, and they had their own activities planned, and I didn't want the bureaucratic process to kill me. Also, I was feeling bad about hiring 90 percent of my staff from off the island, and I wanted to see how I could change that. I talked to Bill and said, "This is unfair. The people here have been disadvantaged and not given any education or chances. We're making a lot of money with tourism and they deserve some of that money. We could be providing locals with skills."

That's when we decided to close down the for-profit company and open it up as the not-for-profit Old San Juan Heritage Foundation. Our mission was to include our vision of San Juan that has La Perla on the map. But when I was going to start all that, the hurricane came.

6, 2016, www.nytimes.com/2016/08/07/business/dealbook/life-in-the-miasma-of -puerto-ricos-debt.html.

16. "No issue better illustrated the intersection between tourism and the island's class structure than the continuous efforts to demolish the infamous slum dwellings of La Perla. . . . As early as 1949, government tourist planners recommended clearance of the area." See Dennis Merrill, *Negotiating Paradise: U.S. Tourism and Empire in Twentieth-Century Latin America* (Chapel Hill: University of North Carolina Press, 2009), 109.

MARÍA PARKED ON THE ISLAND

Cristián and I stayed here during Hurricane Irma.[17] I'd prepared for Irma. I'm an excellent prepper. I had water and everything we needed. But it was scary. The wind was howling through the windows. It sounded like it could tear everything away. In the middle of the hurricane, our door burst open. Cristián and I had to push the door shut, and we put furniture against it to keep it closed. But water came in on all floors of the building—each flooded with about a foot of water. It was a four-day cleanup process, pushing the water out with mops and brooms.

By this time, we'd heard María was coming, and I was thinking, *Shit just got real.* Two weeks before, we'd all bought out everything in the stores because of Irma. Then Irma hit Jacksonville, Florida—where the ports are—and devastated them.[18] No ships had come in to replenish the warehouses on the island. I thought, *Oh my God, this is a recipe for disaster.*

So Cristián and I packed up and went to his mom's house in Bayamón, which isn't far, usually like a twenty-five-minute drive.[19] When I was leaving my home, I was afraid that when I came back, nothing was going to be here. I was worried for my neighbors, but Irma was chaotic and traumatizing, and María was going to be even worse, so I didn't want to be here for María.

During María, I was with Cristián and his mom. Her name is Carmen, too, like my mom's. Carmen's house is concrete, so we felt

---

17. Hurricane Irma made landfall in Puerto Rico two weeks before Hurricane María. It killed three people, caused substantial damage, and left a million residents without power.

18. Hurricane Irma caused the worst flooding Jacksonville had experienced in over 150 years. Ninety percent of goods shipped to Puerto Rico from the States come from Jacksonville's port. For more on shipping restrictions in Puerto Rico, see "The Jones-Shafroth Act and the Merchant Marine Act" in the "Contexts" essay.

19. Bayamón is a metropolitan area municipality south of San Juan and approximately eleven miles away from La Perla.

very safe. The house was so safe that we opened up the balcony, and Cristián started playing the song "Temporal" on his harmonica.[20] He was sitting on the balcony with a lot of wind, a lot of water, and everything flying around. We saw a roof flying by, but there was Cristián, playing his music.

You have to keep in mind that we were inside for twenty-two hours. I didn't expect it to be that long. María parked on the island. She thought, *This is such a cool place,* and she decided to stay. I was scared for the people that I love here. I was feeling my people and I thought, *Oh my God, what are we going to do? This is too much.* I always knew the government that we had was unfit to run the island, and they proved me right. Nobody was prepared for the aftermath of María.

WE WATCHED THE SHIPS COME

Back at Lorel's home, everything was flooded again and there was a lot of water damage. She soon discovered that some of her neighbors had lost their homes, and like many people across Puerto Rico they would never receive federal aid. This is partly owing to Puerto Rico's history of informal construction and of property being passed down through generations without official documentation. Claimants would be deemed ineligible for housing assistance because of FEMA's strict guidelines for proof of ownership.[21]

Lorel was also worried about her mother, who lived in the mountains in Utuado. About a week after the hurricane, Lorel got a call from her sister in Florida. It was a surprise that the call even reached her

---

20. "Temporal" is a *plena* song, which is a type of Puerto Rican folk music. It is a song about a storm. Some of the lyrics can be translated as, "The sky is darkening. . . . What will happen to Puerto Rico, when the storm arrives? . . . Holy Mary, deliver us from all evil. Protect us, Lady, from the terrible storm."

21. As of May 2018, approximately 30 percent of the over 1.1 million households that had applied for FEMA grants were denied because they were deemed ineligible. For more on housing assistance, see "US Federal Aid" in the "Contexts" essay.

because hardly any calls were coming through at that time. Lorel's sister was crying and saying, "You have to go and get Mom." Their mother's house, which was made of wood, had been destroyed during the hurricane. Carmen had had to evacuate and drive about thirty-five miles to her ex-husband's home in Quebradillas. After the hurricane, Carmen did not have access to a working phone, so it would be two months before Lorel was able to speak with her.

I told my sister, "I can't go get Mom." There was no way I could go at the time. The roads were still too bad. Communications were down. I couldn't even talk to her. I was scared and didn't know what to do. I needed to focus on something that I could do here because there was nothing I could do for my mom or my family. I started helping others and that kept me sane.

In the days after the hurricane, I went to all the neighbors. It was complete devastation everywhere. So many wooden houses were just wiped out. The streets were littered with wood and metal roofs. So Cristián, I, and other neighbors worked together—we cleaned, we cooked, and we started rebuilding. We cut poles that had fallen and got them out of the way. We cut the tree that had fallen in front of the plaza and we started cooking with the wood, doing barbecues. We took all the food that we had and cooked it for a big dinner with the neighbors. Every day we cooked outside. We also started doing breakfast from the gallery space. We had a list of elders who couldn't come to the center and we took food to them. That was the priority—to bring food for the elders before anybody else would eat. At that time, all the work in this community was done by the community.

Cristián and I ran mostly on black coffee and crackers, because we had very little for ourselves. It was difficult. There was nothing in the supermarket. There was nothing coming from the government. Even in the first two weeks, we were seeing hundreds of ships come into the port with humanitarian aid. We're two minutes away from the pier where all the supplies are unloaded, so we watched the ships come. But we weren't getting the aid. It'd been fourteen days, and no officials had come here at all, for anything.

It's a governmental responsibility to take care of the poor. I started to question everything. *What's going on? How is this possible? We live next to the governor. If we weren't getting any aid, it must be even worse for the rest of the island. How about the people who are out of reach, in places like Las Marías or Utuado?* That's what was breaking me.

The first assistance to reach us from outside the community came after fourteen days, and only because we'd asked someone to post an SOS on the internet that we needed water and food. Someone saw that, and then local artists who were organizing aid came. Calle 13 came. Luis Fonsi came. I think Daddy Yankee sent some items.[22] We also got help from the diaspora. William Valentín, from Port Morris Distillery, was a lot of help. Artists, individuals, and the Catholic Church gave us water and basic necessities, especially in the first month.

FEMA came, but FEMA is a hoax. If you don't have land titles and if you're ultra-poor, they're not going to help you. That is a reality. And there's insurance that we pay for, but at the end of the day, insurance was also a hoax for Puerto Ricans. My 84-year-old neighbor, Ramón, lost his house in Irma and didn't get anything. Ramón has been living here all of his life. He had a two-bedroom wood house—it was the home that he'd shared with his late wife. The zinc roof fell. He had no roof. Water ruined most of what he owned. He lost all the things that had a memory of his wife—the bed they'd shared, pictures, everything. After Irma, he was living in a six-by-eight concrete room where he stored his tools—basically a tool shed.

Irma took his house, and María came and took the rest. When I saw Ramón after the hurricane, he was sitting on a bench in the

---

22. The band Calle 13 wrote and produced an award-winning single titled "La Perla" in 2009. Luis Fonsi and Daddy Yankee are Puerto Rican musicians. The video for their 2017 hit song "Despacito" was filmed in La Perla.

plaza with his head in his hands in despair. The first thing he said
to me was, "*Ay, Irma me afeitó, pero María me dejó calvo.*" Irma gave
him a close shave, but María left him bald.

WHERE PEOPLE COULD COME FOR A BREATH

I ended up getting a small generator, so we had a working fridge
here. I started storing insulin and other things for the neighbors in
the refrigerator. Running generators is very expensive, as I learned in
the hurricane. We were spending about $750 a month on gasoline.
I also had a landline that was working finally, so people could communicate. People were coming in and out all the time. And PerlArte
became a community center. This was the place where people could
come for a breath.

In late September or early October, I contacted La Fondita
de Jesús.[23] Alejandra Alicea Ríos, who does community education
for them, became a dear friend. I was already making breakfast
for neighbors and she would bring lunch. We'd go around the
neighborhood distributing the lunches.

We got water and electricity back around November 25. In
November, we also formed a partnership with Comedores Sociales
and Se Acabaron las Promesas, and we opened up the Pedro Albizu
Campos community kitchen.[24] So then we were feeding people dinner as well. It was a lot. We were feeding three meals to about four
hundred people a day for five months.

---

23. La Fondita de Jesús is a San Juan organization that was founded in 1985 and
provides services to the homeless.

24. Comedores Sociales and Se Acabaron las Promesas are mutual aid groups in
Puerto Rico. Comedor Comunitario Pedro Albizu Campos, a community kitchen
initiative, has expanded and is now known as Centro de Apoyo a Movimientos
Sociales y Activistas.

EVERYBODY SHOULD HAVE DIGNITY

I had wanted to teach the people here skills in customer service, English as a second language, and tourism education because those are my areas of expertise, but after the emergency passed, I was at a loss. Tourism was not happening, at least for a year. I had to redirect my efforts, but what could I do? I started educating myself, taking courses on grant writing with the EDA and HUD. I also did the cultural management program with Instituto de Cultura.[25]

All that took a couple of months. That's when my neighbors told me, "Let's get back to our art. We're all artists." I thought, *Yes, I am an artist.* I've always gotten through life with art. We decided to open up an art gallery. We'd be working, producing, and selling from here. Keyla Báez came up with the idea. I call her the honorary founder of PerlArte.

We have about eight artists working with us, including three children. There's Jaelys, who's twelve. She's talented, beautiful, and smart. Then there are Keyla's two girls. Yimaira is our champion. She's eleven and has been a judo champion in Puerto Rico for the past three years. And then we have Milenys. She paints and does mosaics. She created and ran her own doll workshop—at only eight years old! She's our diamond; she's not in the rough.

At PerlArte, we're not artists by profession or formally trained, but we translate arts and culture into something of value that can help sustain our community. We produce original, made-in-PR art and artisan work, including mosaics, kites, traditional masks, paintings, ceramics, jewelry, and serigraphs. Currently, the profit is divided 80 percent for the artist and 20 percent for the administration of the space.

---

25. The Economic Development Administration (EDA) provides grants and assistance to distressed communities. The Department of Housing and Urban Development (HUD) has programs that address community needs related to housing and other concerns. The Instituto de Cultura Puertorriqueña (ICP), known as the Institute of Puerto Rican Culture in English, has been working to preserve local culture since it was created in 1955.

Right now, we're doing a three-month program in which we're turning rum barrels into bomba instruments. Bomba is a folkloric dance. It's part of our African heritage. It's all rhythm. There are three instruments: the maracas; the sticks, which are called *cuá*; and the drums, which are called *barriles* because they're made of barrels. The special part about bomba is that there are two barrels, the *buleador* and the *primo*. The buleador keeps the rhythm. But the primo follows the dancer's movements and that's the beauty. It's a conversation between the dancer and the primo bomba barrel. Bomba is dynamic. It's dance, music, and art. In Puerto Rico, when we are losing so much, we have to go back to our roots and find what our core values are as people.

When we finish the bomba program, we're going to take the leftover wood and we're going to cook with it because it has the rum flavor and the smokiness. We'll do a barbecue for the whole neighborhood.

At PerlArte, there are people from La Perla and Puerta de Tierra, and also from Old San Juan. Ever since María, we've been integrating the three communities, trying to grow together. It's what binds us together that's important, not what separates us.

In some ways, it was María that helped break down these barriers because everyone was struggling with the same issues. We all didn't have water; we didn't have anywhere to shop for food. A lot of the neighbors from Old San Juan came down to our Campos kitchen to eat. And most of the elders that we took food to were in Old San Juan.

At that time, we were really living in the moment and we were learning from each other. Because there's the neighbor who knows how to use the machete, and then there's the neighbor who knows how to start a fire without a lighter, and then there's the neighbor who can cook for fifty people. After the hurricane people came together and your neighbors became your family—whether you liked it or not! And that's how we need to start rebuilding this country.

People across the island are still struggling every day. In our neighborhood there are still people who haven't had their homes rebuilt. Some people are living in the one room or a part of their house that survived the hurricane. Some are living in another person's house. And some have had to leave. My dream right now for our struggling communities would be that we could make money and rebuild our homes. For me, La Perla will thrive if it's not gentrified and if the people here can support themselves and have dignity. That's all we're asking for. Everybody should have dignity.

We spoke with Lorel again in July 2020. PerlArte had been closed to the public because of COVID-19 restrictions, but before that the gallery had continued to organize workshops, working with communities in need.

We're all okay here. We're taking precautions with the COVID-19 emergency. PerlArte is closed right now, but we're moving to an online platform with our workshops and also launching a community podcast.

The gallery is struggling, like many projects, but before COVID-19, I'd been working with people from the south who'd been affected by the earthquakes.[26] Most of these people, especially the younger ones, have never been to Old San Juan. So we gave them tours of Old San Juan and then we'd finish with an art workshop or storytelling.

The last group we had was in March. A teacher called me and said, "These kids are losing it. Everything's shaking constantly and most of them are sleeping in their cars with their families. I need to bring a few of them up there so that they can distract themselves." I said, "Of course! Come." A day later, about twenty-eight people

---

26. An ongoing earthquake swarm in Puerto Rico began on December 28, 2019. There have been thousands of earthquakes since then, the largest registering at 6.4. For months, thousands of people in the south were living in tent communities. For more on the earthquakes, see "Earthquake Swarm" in the "Contexts" essay.

showed up, most of them children. The kids had such a great day! They forgot about what they're going through, and they explored a new city. Then they did an art piece on canvas here at PerlArte.

One of the kids was Marcelo. He was a little hyperactive, and I identified with him because I used to be that kid. I worked with him because I knew he wasn't going to finish his piece unless I helped him. He actually did finish his piece, and he said, "Oh, I love this towel. I'm gonna dry myself every day with this towel." I said, "But Marcelo, that's not a towel." He asked, "Then what is this?" I said, "It's art that you hang in your room." And then he said, "But I don't have a room." My heart broke and I thought, *I knew this! I knew he'd lost his home in the earthquake.* But then I told him, "The past we leave behind; we cannot carry it with us. This picture is for your future."

He was so happy. He said, "Oh yes, this is for my next room. I'll hang it there. It's going to be perfect."

CARLOS BONILLA RODRÍGUEZ

BORN IN: 1966
LIVES IN: San Sebastián
Farmer

To get to the valley where Carlos Bonilla Rodríguez lives, we have to drive up one of the tallest mountains in San Sebastián and find a small road close to the top that is almost hidden between bushes.[1] As we drive along the road, on our left there is a view of brightly colored birds flying over a perfect sheet of green bushes and trees stretched out beneath us. Across the mountains, we can see parts of the cities of Las Marías, Maricao, and Mayagüez. On the right, a line of seven houses all in a row becomes visible. These are Carlos and his siblings' homes, built on their

---

1. San Sebastián is a mountainous municipality in the northwest with a population of approximately 35,000.

*parents' farm. In the middle of that line grows a massive mango tree with
a bench at its base—a tree that has sheltered countless family gatherings.*

*We meet Carlos in the garden next to the site of his new house,
sitting among the flowers and medicinal herbs that his wife, Miriam,
grows to help cure their family's ailments. This is the second time Carlos
has had to rebuild his home after a hurricane, but it is the first time that
he has been able to build any part in concrete. Carlos is a quiet man—
hesitant to talk about himself—but once Miriam sits down with us, he
starts to open up more. His sparkling eyes hint at his love of laughter,
though, and he sneaks jokes into our conversation whenever he can.*

WE NEEDED TO WORK

My parents had ten children—eight boys and two girls. I'm the
eighth child. Orlando, the youngest, was born with a variety of
medical conditions including muscular dystrophy and epilepsy. The
doctors said that he wasn't supposed to live past two years old. We
didn't have much money to live on, so there was almost no medical
equipment for Lando, as we called him, only a special bed that was
donated by the church. Even so, when he was taken for a checkup at
two years old, the doctors couldn't believe that Lando's cheeks were
pink and healthy and how well my mother took care of him. With
the care my mother gave Lando, he lived twenty-one years.

Growing up, the whole family lived in a rented house in Guacio
Barrio.[2] This wooden house was built in a valley among the coffee
trees and had three small bedrooms, a bathroom, a good-sized living room, and a kitchen. All the boys were in one room, the girls
in another, and our parents in the third bedroom. I loved living
in Guacio, down in that valley by the quebradas.[3] The water in a

---

2. Guacio Barrio is a town of approximately four hundred residents in the municipality of San Sebastián. It is known for its agriculture, especially coffee production.

3. A quebrada is a ravine that is sometimes dry but can fill with water after a heavy
rain.

quebrada is so cold that it makes a fog from meeting the air. There are quebradas on either side of the house and so fog comes from both sides to make everything very comfortable. It was all *tierra pura* there, nothing but pure land. Just a forest filled with birds.

When I was five, I started school. All us kids walked to school because there was no public transportation. We had to walk downhill through the fields to get to the road. We walked barefoot and when we got to the road, we'd wash our feet in a stream and put on our shoes. If it was raining, we carried the books in a plastic bag. I remember I had my own plastic bag.

We were all working to save up money so that we could have our own house and our own land. I've been working in agriculture since I was eleven years old. All my brothers and I left school because we needed to work. School took too much time that could be used for working and earning the money that we didn't have. So, I left school in the sixth grade and went to work. I picked coffee and oranges; planted yam, taro, beans, and plantains; and cleared land with a machete. I've done it all.

After four or five years of living in the rental with all of us working, *El Viejo*—that's what we call my father—was able to buy the house at the top of the hill, right across from the rental.[4] Along with the house, he bought all the land around it: three cuerdas, almost three acres of land, so that we could have our own *finca*, a farm for our family. When they bought the house, it was completely made of zinc—the walls, the ceiling, everything made of zinc. The zinc heats up from the sun during the day, but since we were always outside the house—working during the day and spending family time in the evening—we didn't suffer from the heat. During the night it was very cold, though, because of the quebradas. Over time, my father remodeled the house. He added wood panels, made the kitchen and floor out of cement, and built the balcony. The house ended up

---

4. *Viejo* is a term of endearment that means "the old man."

with wooden walls and a ceiling of zinc with two bedrooms and one bathroom.

WHAT I REMEMBER IS THE FOOTSTEPS

On one side of the road is the small zinc house that Carlos's parents rented while the children were growing up, and on the other is the farm that the whole family saved up to buy. Two of Carlos's brothers have moved to the mainland US, but all of his other siblings have built their houses together on that farm. In front of the farm and alongside the road are the homes that Carlos likes to call "roommate houses." Everyone has their own house, but they all share what they have and get together daily.

As they grew up, my brothers and sisters started to build their houses above *Los Viejos*, my parents, on our family land. My brother, Pity, the most serious family member—you can trust everything he says—has the house that's first in line. He knows construction and is an expert at *empañetando casas*.⁵ All the brothers framed out the walls with cinder blocks, mixed the cement, poured it, and put in the windows. We did it all, so that Pity only had to buy the materials. If it wasn't done like that, he couldn't have afforded to have a house. His house is the first one in line going from the bottom of the hill up to the top. It's strong, solid concrete, and, before the hurricane, had a beautiful garden growing around the house, with all kinds of flowers and herbs, some used for medicinal teas. His wife, Mercedes, knows which tea improves any health condition. If someone feels bad in the belly, she makes them a tea made from chamomile and spearmint boiled with ginger. After drinking it, you sleep well, too.

Cholo's house is next in the row. He's the oldest of the family and has dedicated his life to working the land, another farmer like me and El Viejo. He's also an adept maker of machetes. He sharpens

---

5. *Empañetando casas* is the process of pouring concrete over the cinder blocks and rebar frames to make walls. It is highly skilled work that is done by hand.

them all by hand and also makes the handles himself. There are always about a hundred of them at his house for sale. Maybe fifteen or twenty of the best ones are hung up on the walls for display. This house is wooden with three rooms and two bathrooms, but no garage. He was so eager to move in that he started living there without having bed frames, only mattresses on the floor. At first, Cholo's house had a wood floor, wood walls, and a roof made of zinc, but when Hurricane Georges hit the island in 1998 and destroyed his house, the financial help offered by FEMA was enough for him to pour a concrete floor. So, this house is now wood with a concrete floor and is very comfortable.

My brother Tito's house was the third up the hill after Cholo's. It was the first really fancy concrete house built in the area. Tito had a small shop where he'd sell tires and repair cars, so he had more money to build well. At the time, it was a mansion to the neighbors' eyes. It had the typical three bedrooms, but they were all really big. He had a big kitchen and living room, and a family room. They had a balcony on the back with a pool table. There was even a small laundry room and an office by the family room. He had an A/C in the main room. Can you believe that?

My sister, Mayi, bought that house from Tito. Her real name is Carmen, like our mom, and, like Mom, she's a strong woman with a strong character who talks loudly, even in a family that's used to yelling! When she divorced, she was living in a small wooden house on our family land—really a casita, a miniature house with two rooms and one bathroom—and Tito had this nice concrete one, but he wanted a bigger one. So, he sold his house to Mayi with her paying in part by trading her tiny house to him. He then demolished the casita and built the big concrete house on that land, which is next door to mine and closer to the valley. It's a two-story house, with a big living area on top, which has the usual three bedrooms and two bathrooms. And at the bottom is an oversized car garage that houses Tito's mechanic shop.

Tata, whose real name is Aida, is my other sister. She lives next to Mayi and beside the mango tree. She talks a lot and always makes everyone laugh. She organizes the parties because everything is an excuse for the family to throw a party. And any family gathering is a party! We all cook, bring some chips, and maybe a few beers. Tata's the soul of the party, though. She worked hard as a salesperson because she needed to take care of her four children. She's sold anything there is to sell, but recently, because her kids are more grown now, she works in a department store.

While my other brothers and sisters were building their houses, my brothers Tony and Raúl and I were still living with my parents on the other side of the mango tree. When my father first moved in, he brought that tree from Cabo Rojo.[6] It ended up growing so big and giving so much fruit that people who passed by would stop to take photos of that tree. We always hang out together under the shade of the mango tree.

While we were living there, I'd go visit my aunt who lived in Barrio Perchas.[7] They had a little store in that neighborhood where I liked to hang out. They sold beer and candy and stuff. That's where I first saw Miriam. She came in a few times. One day, there was a party in Perchas at Luis Durán's house and we both went. She came with her father and we talked a lot that day. We even left the party together and I walked her to her house, talking the whole time. From that day on, we've been together.

When we got married, I took Miriam back to my father's house, and then we moved into the house across the street that my dad had once rented. It was somewhat empty because we didn't have a lot of furniture or decorations to put around the house, but, since Los Viejos had lived there first, I liked living there. Me, Miriam, and

6. Cabo Rojo is in the southwestern corner of Puerto Rico, approximately twenty-nine miles from San Sebastián, and accessible via winding mountain roads.

7. Barrio Perchas, located in the municipality of San Sebastián, is a small neighborhood with fewer than a thousand residents.

our children, Cuyo and Lissette, were very happy there. Six family members have lived in that house at one time or another.

In time, we built the last house, the one for me, which was highest up in the row, the seventh and last in the line. So, my siblings' families each had separate spaces, but we were living all together. Mine was a really small house. It had two bedrooms: one with space for a queen-size bed frame and two small bureaus—one on each side of the bed—and a curved mirror. The second bedroom only had space for beds and a nightstand.

The kitchen was so small that only two people could fit in there at the same time. In the living room there was the usual setup of a couch, loveseat, and armchair. There was also a TV table that had a thirty-two-inch television on top. That television was the jewel of the house. It was our most expensive possession.

When I was growing up, before we moved into the house in Guacio, there was no TV. In Guacio, the television was in black and white and we usually watched whatever El Viejo decided we would watch. Now I have my own TV, but when my granddaughter comes and says she wants to watch a specific show, she goes ahead and changes the channel. It's okay. I just want to sit with her.

This house didn't have much, but it was all we had. When I think back on the twenty-five years that Miriam and I lived there, what I remember is the footsteps. The floor was raised and made of wood and so wobbly that any step you'd take would sound loud. So, whenever the kids were around, I would hear a vibrating *dun, dun, dun* sound made by the kids running. It was so loud and shook the house so much that sometimes it would even make the pictures fall off the wall onto the floor! When I think of my house, I see all the little kids running around—first nieces and nephews, then my children, and finally grandchildren—stopping only to eat the candy I bought for them. I bought mint balls because I liked them, and they did, too. There was also a yellow round one made of caramel that they didn't like so much, but whenever all the other candy was gone, they'd eat the *caramelos*.

I GIVE IT A *BENDICIÓN*

*Representatives from large industrial farms in the US regularly come to
Puerto Rico to recruit agricultural laborers.[8] Twice, once in 1995 and
again in 2003, Carlos went to work on these farms, which are known
collectively as Los Campos. When work was scarce, he and his brothers
would ask around in their neighborhood to see if anyone was forming un
grupo to go up to Los Campos with a recruiter. The group traveled and
lived together, picking strawberries, tomatoes, corn, and other crops, as
well as spreading fertilizer and turning over the fields at the end of the
season. The work lasted for a few months and then they were able to return to Puerto Rico, drawing unemployment benefits that are higher on
the mainland and oftentimes enough to support entire families. When
he was in the US, though, Carlos missed his family and the land that
they farmed together in Puerto Rico.*

My father worked in the sugarcane fields, but I never worked cutting
cane. I did carry the cut canes to the trucks, but I've spent most of
my life on coffee fincas. I've been with my current boss, Beltín, on
his farm for around twenty years. I'm pretty sure of this date because
when the Twin Towers were destroyed, I was picking coffee and I'd
already been working for Beltín for a few years when this happened.

Coffee only grows at high altitudes up in the mountains, and it
has to be fertilized to grow right. No one else fertilizes the coffee like
me. I have a trick. Most people start at the top of the area and fertilize
going down into the valleys, but you can only carry so much fertilizer
with you at one time. So, when you run out, you have to climb all the
way to the top to get more. I carry my fertilizer to the middle of the
hill and start there. I start from the middle, go down, back up to the
middle, and back down, and so on. This way, whenever I run out of

---

8. The National Puerto Rican Chamber of Commerce, for example, invites businesses in the US to come to the archipelago to recruit laborers as a way to avoid
dealing with the work visas—H-1B and H-2B—needed to employ foreign workers
on farms and in factories.

fertilizer, I am closer to the top where I have to go pick up fertilizer, and when I come back, I don't have to go all the way down to fertilize. Tricks like this make your life easier.

But you can't make everything easier. Sometimes farmers have accidents. I've fallen from trees; trees have fallen on me. Once I fell from an orange tree and landed on another tree. El Viejo cut that tree down right after I fell, saying that it had tried to kill me! I've cut myself with machetes so badly I still have a few scars on my knees and legs. I've gotten wasp and bee stings; whole beehives have swarmed at me a few times. I ran like a *caballo pelao* when that happened![9] The *abayardes*, red fire ants, have fallen down from the trees and bitten me; the *berracos*, big brown ants that live in the earth, have eaten my hands when I was pulling yams. The hospital? Why would I go to the hospital? It's far away and I'd just lose my time there. I just let everything heal. If I cut myself, my wife puts some *alcoholado* on it.[10] If my back hurts, Miriam adds salt and mashed ginger to the alcoholado and rubs it on. It feels cold and then you can feel it sinking in. If bees sting me, what can I do? My wife tries to get out the stinger and then I wait for it to heal. These are just things that happen to farmers every now and then. It's no big deal.

I farm not only for the income but because I love it. Every time I plant something, I give it a *bendición*, a blessing. I hold the seed or seedling to my lips, and I whisper, "May God give you many blossoms so that there are enough *frutos* for me to eat and to sell." Everything I plant, I plant with love.

"KEEP DOING MY WORK"

When Hurricane Georges came twenty years ago, I was working the piece of land that my father bought with the first of the seven

---

9. Like a "broke horse," one that needs to win the race to get the prize money.

10. Alcoholado is a homemade salve made from bay rum and other herbs. For more, see the glossary.

houses. I had that piece of land planted full of crops—mostly coffee that my wife and I picked—and paid my dad a fee for using it, but when Georges came, I lost everything. We lost the coffee, lost the plantains, everything I had planted. And so, I left that field. I just lost interest when I saw the destruction. And, since that hurricane also affected my house, I had other work to do. Georges destroyed the whole ceiling of my house and we lost everything inside. FEMA gave us less than $5,000, which was not enough to really do anything. So, we had to fix it using wood only. I was so sad, disgusted; I didn't want to do anything anymore.

But my father planted a few coffee trees on that land after the cleanup from Georges, and I helped him because I was always the one around. I helped him plant, kept the surrounding area clean with my machete, sprayed pesticides, and spent most evenings after work helping him. When he started getting sick in his legs with the diabetes, he would get tired really fast and had to take a chair with him to the fields so that he could sit and rest. He didn't suffer from asthma but used asthma therapies to cope with how tired he was after working. Finally, he had to leave that piece of land alone and told me, "Carlos, you have to take this land for me and keep doing my work."

I told him no because I didn't want to farm at that time. It was too hard to see the crops go down in the hurricane. He insisted that the land was ready. "We just cleared it! It's for you!" Eventually, I said yes and selected a portion of the land for myself, bought the coffee seedlings, and started planting them. I had coffee *del país* and the robusta.[11] Café del país has a lot of varieties—Limani, Caturra, there are a few of them—but when you say "del país," it means from here, from our soil. You can always tell when the coffee tree is del país because it has more branches and more coffee than the other trees.

---

11. *Del país* literally translates to "of the country" and is used here to refer to indigenous plants.

I planted a lot of coffee trees, acerola cherry, purple yam, and taro. Natural sour lemons from here, and orange trees, too. Pity took one of the other portions of the land that was unused and started planting it. And Cholo took the last piece and maintained it. We replanted it together.

THE ROOF WAS STOLEN

When we heard that Hurricane María was coming, my wife and I took shelter with Yinda, a neighbor who lives uphill from us in a cement house. I thought that if only a little wind came, maybe my house would still be standing, but I didn't want to take any chances, and Yinda is older and was all alone. She asked us to stay with her and it was a good place for us to go because you can clearly see my house from hers, and I wanted to watch over it. During the storm we stood in her kitchen looking down on my house.

We were standing in the kitchen when we felt the big wind hit and saw María peel back the whole zinc roof. She took the whole top of the house. Even from where we were staying up the hill, Miriam and I could hear the explosions as the cables that held the roof were ripped apart. All the zinc was nailed to the wooden beams that made the ceiling, and the wind just lifted all of it! It was incredible how the storm didn't break the ceiling apart piece by piece but ripped it off completely as one piece.

At first, María played with it. She picked up that whole roof—zinc, wood, everything—and blew it from here to there, up and down. The whole roof was just dancing around in the front of the house. It was still in one piece, just not on the house any longer. Then María got tired of playing; she threw the roof at the house across the street from mine! Thankfully, it got stuck in between the neighbor's water cistern and their house and didn't damage anything else. But that's what killed my house.

After the roof was stolen, there was a burst of wind and the rain grew so terrible that we couldn't see what was happening anymore. When it stopped, we saw that María had taken the walls too. In just seconds, the side of the house was torn off and we could see right into our house. I remember standing still for one moment while I watched the doors of the refrigerator blow open and the food fly out everywhere. Furniture rolled across the lawn. Framed photos were yanked off the wall and hurled around. And when everything was taken by the wind, all blown away, and I knew we had nothing, the only thing to do was cry.

"THAT COULD BE FIXED"

Just like after Georges, I submitted the FEMA applications. I went to the Luis Aymat Coliseum in San Sebastián with Cholo to file the papers. There were a lot of people there and it was a really long line. They eventually started handing out numbers, but they only went up to five hundred. Lots of people who were waiting couldn't get a number. It was brutal. I don't want to remember that.

When I went back to check on the report, I was told that there were some papers missing and I had to bring them down to Aguadilla, to the Cascadas Water Park. I filed the case again. The FEMA person who helped us had a computer and recorded everything, but at that moment they didn't give us an estimate of how much the damage was worth; neither did they ask. It was just information on what was lost, what was the condition of the house now, and those kinds of things. They needed the deeds and house papers, to know if the house was concrete in any part, and what things inside the house were lost.

The inspector came, verified the damage on my report, and took measurements of everything: measured from here to there and from there to here. In the end, he said, "Well, the house has some walls missing, but, you know, that could be fixed." María had thrown down the walls and taken the roof, but he thought the house could be repaired.

After the hurricane, then, we didn't have a house anymore and had to rebuild. We ended up staying at Mayi's house. When you have nothing, anything is like a twelve-star hotel. We've been really comfortable here. She gave us a room with a bathroom right next to the room, and no one else used it. So, we even had privacy. Can you believe it? Thank God for Mayi.

Every night at 7:00 p.m., Mayi prepares the after-dinner coffee for us, and all my brothers and sisters come down to her house to drink it and spend time with us. The family changed with Hurricane María, and some of the changes were for good. I've been working on my house's construction every single day—seven days a week, working and getting help from everyone. Thanks to the work we've put into rebuilding, it's going fast. We've been at Mayi's for just over a year with me building every minute I can. My brother Tony helped me a lot in the construction. Pity and my son, Cuyo, did the cement work. Even my sixteen-year-old grandson, Steven, who has Crohn's disease, came to help. A lot of my friends have come on Saturdays when they're not working to put in cinder blocks, make cement, and do anything I need.

A lot of people have helped me. My boss, Beltín, gifted me some cinder blocks. My brothers and sisters have all helped me. Not one hasn't. One helps me on this, the other on the other thing. For example, Juny, another of my brothers, bought me a lot of blocks, and the old man who lives a few meters past my house gave me some windows. He was going to sell me the windows, and when I went to pay for them, he said, "Take the money and go buy those blocks that you need." I was even able to gather up a lot of old nails and straighten them out, you know, so I didn't have to buy new ones.

Some churches, Catholic and Adventist, came here to help. Some pastors from Oklahoma also came. It was a Thursday when they arrived, and by Saturday they invited us up to a meeting. There they gave a few of us who had been really affected some food, along with a few other things. They prayed for us and gave me an envelope with $700 in it. $700! The next day I went and bought the steel rods, the last ones needed for the construction of the house.

Even though María was bad, there were a few good things that wouldn't have happened if it weren't for the hurricane. María hurt me, but, at the same time, I'm building a concrete house, which I never thought I could. Everyone's help has motivated me to keep pushing forward to finally finish the house.

After this destruction, I've cleaned a little bit of the land, sprayed some pesticides, and I'm going to seed it with robusta coffee, a type of coffee really well suited to Puerto Rico. I want to see if I can get it back up like it was before Hurricane Georges.

NOT EVEN A NAIL

After the hurricane, we got nothing from Puerto Rico's government. I've received nothing from the town or the mayor. They haven't given me even a little help, not even a nail. I've gotten a lot of help from the people, but not from the government of Puerto Rico. We haven't even seen the mayor.

Being part of the United States has always been of value for me because it has helped Puerto Rico. If the United States hadn't helped us, we wouldn't have anything. After both hurricanes, Georges and María, FEMA did help me, even if it wasn't much. FEMA has given me, in all, $14,000, and with that I'm building a concrete house. Well, part of the house will be built with the FEMA money because $14,000 is too little for the whole house. I can do a concrete foundation with it, though. That includes the concrete columns under the foundation, the floor, and the blocks.[12] This money won't cover the tiles to go on the floor, just the concrete alone.

---

12. The "concrete columns" referred to here are stilts. Houses on stilts are common in Puerto Rico. This type of construction can be used in the mountains to facilitate building on a sloped site and can also protect against flooding.

I had an estimate to replace the zinc roof, and it was $4,000. A concrete roof was $6,000, and since more hurricanes are likely to happen, I had to choose the concrete roof. Between the money FEMA gave me, what I had saved, the help from my family, the many people in San Sebastián, and the people and churches in the US, I'll manage to build most of the house in concrete. I'm glad because I don't want to lose my house a third time.

I believe people have helped me because I've always been good with others. I'm crazy and happy, and I'll do anything for others. So, people are good with me. Kids, teenagers, old people, they all like me. I joke with everyone.

I DON'T LIKE BEING STILL

I've been working all my life. *Hasta el sol de hoy*, until today's sunrise, I've never—from the age of eleven to fifty-two—taken a vacation. If I got really, really sick, then I skipped work for one or two days because I had to. But I've never been able to take vacations, only those one or two days. Because I had to, not because I wanted to.

Unfortunately, though, whenever I finish the concrete ceiling, my house's construction stops because I'm having an operation to treat my back and it will take six months to a year for me to recuperate. I can't do anything after the operation. I may even have to stop working altogether after that. Hopefully, if I can't work anymore after the operation, I can fight my way through the paperwork and get social security to have some income to survive. I would prefer not to reach that point, though. I prefer being healthy and able to work. I don't like being still.

ISRAEL AND SANDRA GONZÁLEZ

<small>BORN IN:</small> 1940 and 1943
<small>LIVE IN:</small> Adjuntas
Farmers

We meet Israel and Sandra González in March 2019 at their coffee farm in Adjuntas, which is reached by driving up narrow, winding mountain roads.[1] Sandra Farms produces coffee, citrus, and cacao using eco-friendly methods of growing and processing. We sit together on their balcony, sipping tiny cups of coffee brewed from their own beans. The patio of their house has a spectacular view of the surrounding cloud forest, and when there is a pause in the conversation, the only sounds that can be heard are the birds chirping and the wind in the trees.

---

1. Adjuntas is a central mountainous municipality with a population of approximately 17,000. Elevations in the region range from two thousand to four thousand feet above sea level. One nickname for the region is the "Switzerland of Puerto Rico."

Israel and Sandra have been married for more than fifty years.
They share many life experiences—working in the Peace Corps, rais-
ing children, and running the farm. They have even lived through two
hurricanes together. Over time, their individual narratives have become
interwoven, so now—as they sit with us—they once again come together
to tell their story of farming in Puerto Rico, before and after Hurricane
María.

TO CHANGE THE WORLD

SANDRA: I was born in Enid, Oklahoma. I lived in the same house
for my whole childhood. I walked a block to grade school and eleven
blocks to junior high. I drove three miles to high school. Then I went
to college across the street. So, I was very well acquainted with that
neighborhood—and very happy to leave it.

I left when I was twenty-three years old to join the Peace Corps.
That's when I met Israel, during training in Albuquerque in '65.
Then we went to Bolivia and we were teamed up. They wanted a boy
and girl, or a man and a woman—whatever we were back then! So
Israel and I were assigned to rural communities on the Altiplano,
thirteen thousand feet above sea level.[2]

I stayed in a room in a family's adobe house. The family didn't
like it because it was drafty. It had a straw roof, and the birds came
in. The walls were papered with newspapers from the time of the
Chaco War, which was fought between Bolivia and Paraguay in the
1930s. We didn't have electricity. We had camp stoves and a ker-
osene lantern, which we used to read by. The Peace Corps gave us
perspective. We learned that everyone didn't live like we did in the
States. One of the first projects we did on the Altiplano was building
school desks. We had very good intentions to change the world.

---

2. The Altiplano is a high plateau of the Andes, mainly situated in Bolivia, but also
reaching into parts of Peru, Chile, and Argentina.

ISRAEL: We were trained not to impose our ideas on the people of the community we were working in. The Peace Corps had learned from the failures of other aid programs, which, in the past, would go to places and tell the people what to do. "Here, plant this potato. Make bigger potatoes." But the locals wouldn't eat the potatoes. Why? Because they didn't taste the same. The locals knew potatoes better than we ever could know potatoes. So we didn't go around telling people what to do.

SANDRA: The Peace Corps also tried to teach us volunteers Spanish, but the people of the Altiplano didn't speak Spanish that much, they spoke Aymara.[3] Israel learned Aymara more easily because he already spoke Spanish.

Israel was born in Guantánamo, Cuba. His mother was Cuban and his father was Puerto Rican. In 1885, Israel's father, Andrés, was born in Lares, which is about three hills over from our farm.[4] Andrés was a farmer there, but in 1917, Israel's father, grandparents, aunts, uncles, cousins—about thirty people—moved to Cuba. Why? No one ever explained. But in 1898, there was the Spanish-American War. We know what happened there. Puerto Ricans were not unhappy to see the Spanish leave, but some weren't happy to see Americans come either. Then in 1917, Puerto Ricans became US citizens, but they were given citizenship without the right to vote for the president or to vote for representatives in Congress.[5] It was second-rate citizenship and it still is. This meant that in 1917 people from Puerto

---

3. Aymara, an Indigenous language that predates the Spanish colonial period, is one of Bolivia's official languages, along with Spanish and Quechua.

4. Lares is a mountainous municipality west of Adjuntas with a population of approximately 24,000.

5. The Jones-Shafroth Act, signed by the US Congress in March 1917, extended US citizenship to Puerto Ricans, but it came with limitations. For more on Puerto Rican citizenship, see "Unincorporated Territory Status" and "The Jones-Shafroth Act and the Merchant Marine Act" in the "Contexts" essay.

Rico were volunteering for the US Army in World War I, but they also could be drafted.[6] These may have been some of the reasons Israel's family moved.

ISRAEL: My father met my mother, Ezequiela, shortly after he moved there. They never officially married, but together, they homesteaded an abandoned sugar mill plantation in Guantánamo that was huge, and they ended up with forty-four acres. We produced everything we ate. My father would pick up seeds wherever he went. Sometimes he didn't even know what they were for. We had a mango tree that we called the "no-name mango" because we didn't know what kind it was. We grew everything. Nothing fancy, just mangos, citrus, corn, beans, and plantains. The only things my mother would buy were a little salt and sugar. We also had pigs and chickens and some cows, but we wouldn't eat the cows because they were too precious. We needed them for milk and even for plowing. Coffee was our cash crop. We didn't even drink the good coffee we grew. That was saved to sell. Instead, we'd pick up the coffee that'd fallen on the ground to roast for ourselves.

I'm number twelve of thirteen kids born on that coffee farm in Guantánamo. We children were to be seen but not heard. My mother told me many times that she had to protect us from my father, who was using the belt buckle, beating up my siblings. My father was quite a bit older than my mother. He passed in 1942 when I was two. So I don't remember him.

After my father passed, my mother and the older boys were in charge of the farm. I helped them, but I was young. I remember once—I must have been five or six—and I had this urge to plant something. So I asked my brothers, "Can I work a little piece of land?" They laughed at me and said, "Yeah, go ahead." So I planted corn.

---

6. In May 1917, Congress passed the Selective Service Act, which authorized the federal government to draft soldiers. Almost 18,000 Puerto Ricans were drafted to serve in World War I.

I didn't get much of anything. I failed at my first farm. I was sad I didn't get a good crop of corn. Probably I planted at the wrong time of the year. I have no idea why it failed, but I still wanted to farm.

When I was twelve, my older cousin came from New York to Cuba and asked me, "Do you want to go with me to New York?" I said, "Yes!" But my mother said, "No, you're too young."

SANDRA: His cousin wanted to take the younger two kids and put them in school in New York so they could have more opportunities. The other kids were considered too old to go. Israel's oldest brother was already in his thirties. He was kind of the head of the family at that point. Israel's cousin told his mother, "For heaven's sake, the boys aren't educated." Israel's mother had sent them to school. They could read, write, add, and subtract. But after several years in school, it seemed to be the third grade over and over. We think the teacher only had a third-grade schooling, so it was a poor education.

ISRAEL: Eventually my mother let me go to New York when I was fourteen.

SANDRA: He moved to New York in January 1955. Israel's mother found him some shoes, and she made him his first pair of underwear.

ISRAEL: I remember on the flight to New York there was a stopover in Florida. We went to eat something at the airport. I didn't know what my cousin ordered. I saw this bowl with milk and cabbage. I said, "I'm not eating that." Now I love coleslaw. But then I didn't know. I'd never eaten that stuff.

It was bitter cold when we got to New York. Someone had loaned me a heavy woolen coat, and my cousin had bought me a hat with earmuffs. Thank God, because man, it was cold!

SANDRA: The boys were enrolled in a Spanish Harlem Christian Brothers school called Commander John J. Shea Memorial. They'd never heard or seen English before. Every time they said something in Spanish in school, they had to put their hand out and get hit with a rubber hose. Israel learned English in one year. However, he stopped going to mass. He decided they weren't very Christian.

Long story short, Israel went to Morris High School in the Bronx, Bronx Community College, the City College of New York, and then in 1965 he joined the Peace Corps, and went to Bolivia. This is where I come in. We got married fifty-two years ago in Bolivia, in 1966.

ISRAEL: Fifty-two years, and it only feels like five minutes. Sandra likes to say it feels like five minutes . . . underwater!

SANDRA: I love that joke, but it has to come from me! We did work well together in Bolivia. We agreed on what needed to be done, and we cooperated. We're a good team. Everything is together, you know?

After Bolivia, we went back and worked that summer in Ohio, training new Peace Corps volunteers. Then we went to New York because Israel had a semester of college to finish. In order to work there, I had to get a New York City teaching license. To do that, I had to teach a class in front of a guy from the New York City Board of Education. At the end, he said, "González? You don't look or sound like a González." I wasn't really thinking, so I said, "I'm from Oklahoma—I have a little accent."

But I got the license. And in 1967 I got a job, teaching at Evander Childs High School in the Bronx. At that time, it was very difficult for somebody with a name like González to find work in the school system. When Israel wanted to become a Spanish teacher at City College, they said, "You'll have to lose your accent. We'll have to send you to language therapy." He said, "Well, I'm not doing that."

Instead, he went to graduate school at Columbia. He went there from 1968 to 1970. I was working as a substitute teacher and then I got pregnant with our first daughter, Lara. Israel was busy taking finals while I was having a baby!

GEORGES DOWNSIZED US

After Israel finished his graduate degree, he became a school social work-er and counselor. Israel and Sandra continued to live in the Bronx until 1974, when they moved to New Jersey. They had two more children, Carla and Robert. Sandra stayed home until their youngest child was out of kindergarten. She then returned to teaching and eventually be-came a principal. Israel and Sandra were still living in New Jersey when Israel proposed a change. He told Sandra he wanted to buy a farm.

SANDRA: By this time, he's almost fifty years old. It was around 1989, and he says to me, "I always wanted my own farm." I thought, *Hello? Then why did you become a school social worker?* But, in 1992, we started looking for farms.

At first, we looked into Costa Rica, but that seemed too far away. The kids were getting ready to get married, and have their own kids—we didn't want to be far from our grandchildren. So then we thought, Mexico? Dominican Republic? You could buy a lot of land in the Dominican Republic, but there's not much infrastructure. And when we visited there, Israel's friend picked us up at the airport and had a pistol stuck in his belt. I was like, "Oh, that's kind of bad."

People at Israel's work kept saying, go to Puerto Rico, but he said, "It's too expensive." But that's because he used to visit his cousin in San Juan, so he only knew beachfront property, which really isn't cheap.

Our farm was $96,000 for three houses and 225 acres. We got it for a very reasonable price. Not what you'd expect. But this house had been abandoned for ten years. It was totally covered with vines, and it was full of rats. And people generally thought we were fools for buying that much land. It's not big for Texas or Oklahoma, but for here it's big.

Israel said he knew I liked it because of my body language as we were walking up the driveway. He says my body shook. My body did not shake, but he could tell I liked it. It's just so "the hills are alive!" I think I'm in the Alps because it's just green all around.

ISRAEL: When people started coming here to taste our coffee, they were like, "Oh, this place is amazing." And I realized, *Oh, this* is *amazing.* I took it for granted. I was born in the hills. To me nature is beautiful everywhere. But the microclimate here is very unique. And the views are quite special.

We can always see the sun rising right behind those mountains. And the sunsets are magnificent also. On a clear day, we can see the ocean. Some days, I can see the big ships going to San Juan. Right now, the mountains are all green. In different seasons the shade of green changes a little bit, but it's always green up here. Except for after hurricanes.

SANDRA: We bought the land in '94, but moved here in '97, the year before Hurricane Georges.[7] Back in the States, I had become a school principal by then and was overwhelmed, and Israel was burned out with the social work thing. I had a picture on my desk of the farm and the mountains. And it was just torture. I said, "What are we doing here?" So we moved. We had downsized before we moved here, and then Georges downsized us more.

The hurricane destroyed our house. Georges took the roof to the Dominican Republic and it never came back. There was a huge landslide on the road by the house. I lost a shoe in the mud and I never found it. We couldn't get a Jeep out for five days. When we got

---

7. On September 21, 1998, Hurricane Georges made landfall in Puerto Rico as a Category 3 hurricane, leaving approximately 80 percent of the archipelago's population without water and electricity.

out, I went to the post office. Adjuntas Plaza looked like a war zone. There were big army trucks of water and the National Guard and sirens. People were standing around crying. It was horrible.

But the post office was open. I sent an overnight letter. I think it cost me $30, but at least our children heard from us. My daughter had called the Red Cross and about thirty days later they came looking for us—to see if we needed any water! The joke around here is if you die, the police will find you from the smell. They don't know where you live.

Our first crop was just coming in. They were young plants. The hurricane twisted them this way, and then it twisted them that way, and then they were dead. We had to pay eight people just to clean up the debris. Everything turned brown after Georges. That was depressing. I cooked for the men who were working to clean up the farm, and sometimes they'd have a beer after work. When Israel and the men would look at all the coffee trees blown down, they'd all cry because it was so dark and desolate.

ISRAEL: Everything was dull, torn, brown. It looked like a desert, really. It's true. I used to cry every time I had a beer.

SANDRA: Hurricane Georges was emotional. My blood pressure went up after Georges, and it never came back down.

THE WHOLE THING STARTS WITH A FLOWER

SANDRA: After Georges, we said, "What do we do now?" We'd sold the house in New Jersey and I said, "I'm not going back to work in the school system." So we decided to stay, and we replanted. We did a little bit, and a little bit more, and we started producing very good coffee.

ISRAEL: The whole thing starts with a flower. If the flower is pollinated, we get a cherry. The bees come out; they do a beautiful job pollinating. There are swarms of bees in hollow trees all over the area.

And we have all kinds of butterflies—large ones, little bitty ones—
they are pollinators as well. So, some of the flowers get pollinated and
from each dried flower a little bean will develop. Eventually it will get
quite large—I mean, large for a bean! The beans begin to get yellow,
and then become red, and then deep red. And then they begin to turn
a purple color. After the purple, they get a little dark, a little black,
which means the sugar has begun to ferment, so they should be picked
at the right time. In the industry, when the coffee ferments, they call it
overripe. It can happen on the tree if the cherry doesn't fall down or it
can happen if you pick ripe coffee cherries and don't process them that
day. On the tree, you have a window of time of about a week to pick
the cherry. But once you pick it, it begins to ferment immediately. So,
if you leave it in a bag overnight, it's not good because the sugars will
continue to ferment, and the organic matter creates heat, and there
goes your coffee. We have to process and dry it every day.

Basically, you get coffee from new growth. The old growth gives
you less coffee, so you need the new branches to replace the stems
that are not productive. With fertilizer we get all of the new branches. Fertilizer is so important. I'll give you an example. One of our
trees was attacked by coffee leaf rust.[8] One of our workers said, "Let's
burn it," because that's what you do. But then I noticed trees right by
the tree with coffee leaf rust, and they were fine. I thought, *Why does
this tree have the rust and the others do not?* I said, "Put some fertilizer
on it." And, you know what? It dropped all the sick leaves and grew
brand new leaves, *no problema*. Its resistance was built up through
nutrition. After that, I went online and saw that the rust is an oppor-
tunistic disease, and the literature says to keep your trees well fed so
the disease doesn't attack them—so that's what we're doing.

SANDRA: That's all part of being specialty coffee. We sell to people
who appreciate fine coffee and are used to paying a little bit more

---

8. Coffee leaf rust is a disease that is caused by the fungus *Hemileia vastatrix* and
can be devastating to coffee plantations.

than four or five dollars a bag. That would be US tourists. And that would be Rincón. So, that's where we started. We worked with Thanh-Thanh Dang, the Banana Dang coffee shop lady. She owned and ran that café in Rincón with her husband.[9] She was good at marketing. She'd come up with descriptions of our coffee. One time she said something like, "Tall, dark, and handsome." She always added something a little sexy to the marketing. We'd deliver coffee and chocolates to her and to twelve other small businesses.

ISRAEL: We do everything independently. We plant the coffee, take care of it, harvest it, process it, roast it, grind it, and we put it in bags and market it.

EVERYTHING IS A MONOPOLY

SANDRA: In Puerto Rico, the government controls coffee. Because the government controls the price of coffee, everything is artificially low, so farmers are kind of locked into paying the pickers a low wage—around $5 for twenty-eight pounds.[10]

ISRAEL: If I'm a worker, I'll go to Orlando and work at Disney World and make three times as much as I'd make here!

SANDRA: If you paid workers significantly more they'd probably show up, which is what we did.

---

9. Rincón is approximately fifty miles from Adjuntas. It is known locally and internationally for its beaches and for surfing. It has a substantial tourist trade and a significant expatriate community.

10. Typically, pickers get paid a flat rate per every twenty-eight pounds of coffee cherries collected and often earn less than the federal minimum wage. See "News Release: Puerto Rico Coffee Roasters Owes Nearly $68K in Back Wages, Damages and Penalties after US Labor Department Investigation," US Department of Labor, August 18, 2015, https://www.dol.gov/newsroom/releases/whd/whd20150818-0.

ISRAEL: We are paying pickers fifty cents per pound of coffee, $14 for twenty-eight pounds, which in Puerto Rico is unheard of.

SANDRA: One of the problems with paying pickers a low flat rate is that it affects the quality of what is picked. The pickers can't possibly make enough money just picking ripe coffee, so they take everything—green coffee, leaves, everything. And the government guarantees that they will buy any coffee anybody brings, so good, ripe coffee gets mixed with green or fermented or rotten or robusta coffee, which some people like but is bitter. We tell our pickers we don't want you to strip the tree just because it means more money. We pay more per pound because we don't want our coffee green or overripe.

ISRAEL: The lack of quality control is a real shame for Puerto Rico, which has phenomenal potential for producing great coffee. Puerto Rico is 110 miles long and 35 miles wide. In the 1890s, Puerto Rico was the sixth-largest exporter of coffee in the world. That's a lot of coffee to come from a relatively small island! Today we are losing coffee farms in Puerto Rico. Why?

SANDRA: People don't want to be farmers anymore. With government controls, businesses can't thrive. That's why we went "specialty." If you're specialty coffee, you're not restricted to the government price.

ISRAEL: The government controls the price of coffee and also has a monopoly on the importation of coffee.

SANDRA: It's illegal for anybody else to import coffee in Puerto Rico. That's supposed to protect the coffee farmers here. But we're only producing 10 percent of what Puerto Rico drinks. So the government is importing coffee from Mexico and the Dominican Republic.[11]

---

11. The Puerto Rican government lacks autonomy in the global trade market. Among other decrees, the Foraker Act of 1900 states that US laws and regulations

ISRAEL: The government goes to other places and buys coffee cheap and then brings it back here to resell to the big roasters, the big brands. It's a real coffee dictatorship here. In Puerto Rico everything is a monopoly—importation, the power and water companies, the banking industry. Puerto Rico is not self-governing. It's controlled by the US. I call the US a not-so-good steward because it has allowed these monopolies to exist in Puerto Rico. The US has anti-monopoly laws. Why don't they apply in Puerto Rico? Monopolies are exclusive institutions.[12] When there's a monopoly there cannot be other competitive institutions that do things differently or better. We don't have a free market here. To me, that's what keeps Puerto Rico poor. I'm not talking against the people of the island. We have intelligent, hardworking people here. Puerto Rico will never become wealthy because we have the wrong institutions. It's not going to work. What's the proof that it doesn't work? Puerto Rico is bankrupt. To me it's a shame. We already had junk before María. María just turned the junk into worse junk.

THE TREES WERE GONE

Israel and Sandra waited out the hurricane in their house with Israel's eighty-two-year-old cousin, Ray, who lives nearby, and their friend Carmelo, who has worked for them on the farm for many years.

---

dictate Puerto Rico's coastal transportation. The Merchant Marine Act of 1920 imposes further shipping restrictions. For more on these federal laws, see "Unincorporated Territory Status" and "The Jones-Shafroth Act and the Merchant Marine Act" in the "Contexts" essay.

12. "Exclusive institutions" can refer to institutions that are discriminatory or do not provide equal opportunity. It can also refer to a ruling party that favors itself, instead of the needs of the nation. One of the major negative impacts of exclusive institutions is poverty.

ISRAEL: We spent most of the hurricane in the office. It's more protected there. Where Ray was living, the roof was gone. Just, *psh,* disappeared. So he was glad to be here.

SANDRA: Thank goodness we had a concrete house when María came.

ISRAEL: I was hoping that the windows wouldn't break and that the house would hold. I was worried because I'd made a mistake. I'd put plywood up only on the eastern side of the house, but the hurricane came right over us. So the western side got it too. These windows were supposed to withstand 200-mile-an-hour winds, and they did! In a way, it was good that we could see what was happening out there. Leaves flying, rain going horizontally, terrible winds. And we heard a lot of noise, monstrous noise, incredible noise. The drains on the balcony got clogged with leaves. So, it became like a tsunami in the dining and living room. It kept trying to come in, oh my God. So, we put towels and blankets everywhere we could. It was too dangerous to go outside to clear the drain.

SANDRA: The hurricane sandblasted the front of the house. It tried to lift the roof. The farm was a big mess. I remember it was like two o'clock in the morning, and the wind was howling. I was leaning against the wall, and I felt a tremor, and then I heard a *whooosh* sound. I didn't think anything of it, until the next day. I looked outside to the place where I always sit to drink my morning coffee and watch the birds, and I saw that the trees were gone. There had been a landslide. All the bamboo and the trees standing across the road there and that whole coffee field came down and got pushed across the road into the lower coffee field. It also covered the spring we were using for water. It was devastation.

ISRAEL: The next day, I had to go out there because the propane line had broken, and I had to turn off the propane. The wind was still powerful. Sandra and I went out together, and I said, "Watch me in case the wind takes me." It was still very dangerous. Everything was destroyed. The pergola was blown apart; its pieces were everywhere. It was just gone. There were no leaves on the trees. The canopy was down. The fronds of the royal palms were gone, leaving only the trunks standing bare. Everything was totally changed.

SANDRA: I said, "Where are we?" It wasn't recognizable.

ISRAEL: The following day, Carmelo and I walked over the top of the mountain to get to our neighbors. Usually we drive there, but the roads were all blocked by landslides. We said, "We can't go that way." So, we went over the ridge. It was raining. We took machetes. There were thousands of trees down. You jump over one tree, and there's another one, and another one, and vines. It was just endless. It was incredible, really. From here it's only about a mile away, but it took about half a day to get to the neighbors.

We finally got to the neighbors and they said, "Look, we are okay. But there's a couple way down there; we don't know about them." We wanted to check on them, but there was a landslide, and we couldn't get through. Carmelo and I didn't talk much on the way back. It was tiring. We just said, "Be careful," or "This way." We were able to get back here before dark. I don't know where I got the energy.

NOBODY COULD GET THROUGH TO US

SANDRA: We couldn't leave for three weeks, and nobody could get through to us either.

ISRAEL: Here's how it works. A Caterpillar plow will come to clear the mud of the landslide. But they will not go in until fallen branches and trees are removed because it's too dangerous. So, we had to do all that. Carmelo, me, neighbors, and everybody with chainsaws cleared the trees. And only then could the Caterpillar come in.

The municipalities had no money to pay for this, so the understanding was that FEMA would cover the cost of the Caterpillar. The Caterpillar owner didn't get as much as he expected. But we'd still be stuck here if it weren't for that help from FEMA.

SANDRA: We started getting FEMA people coming for our farm tours on their days off. How do you give a tour when you don't even have coffee growing? You just keep talking. And serve them chocolate.

ISRAEL: The military came when they were working on that humongous landslide there—almost three weeks to a month after the hurricane. They started bringing military rations and water.

SANDRA: I told them, "We don't need anything. We have food. Give it to somebody who needs it."

ISRAEL: I said, "Look, we have water. We've fixed the spring we use." We have a lot of springs on our land. Two of them are higher than the house, so the water can flow here by gravity. After the landslide, we had to dig out the mud that was left in the spring we use for water. We couldn't clear it all, but at least we had some water we could treat to use.

SANDRA: We had water, but we had no communication, no power. After the hurricane, we didn't have electricity for ten months. Luckily, the month before María, we'd finally bought a generator that we had needed for twenty years. So, during that ten months, we kept our frozen stuff frozen by turning that on for three hours every night. Now, we have solar panels. But, you know, one of the things you learn in the Peace Corps is to be flexible. We didn't have electricity for two years when we were in Bolivia.

ISRAEL: Still there was no reason for people to be ten months in Puerto Rico without power. In the States, how long do people go without power? Come on.

SANDRA: At least the kids knew we were all right. I wrote them a letter. The post office was open. And finally, over a month after the hurricane, I called them. We were going to Rincón, past the Subway shop in the little strip mall there, and my cell phone beeped. I said, "Ohhh. Stop, stop. Let's go in there." We sat in the Subway and chatted with the kids. They asked us, "When are you going to get out of there?" They sent us one-way tickets to Colorado for Christmas.

THE MOST BEAUTIFUL TREES

In December 2017, Israel and Sandra went to the States to visit with their kids. It was not long, though, before they returned to their farm.

ISRAEL: After about fifteen days there, Sandra says, "Let's go home." For months, I wouldn't say a word to Sandra about the farm because I thought she wasn't going to want to do it again. We got back here to the farm, and she says, "Most of the coffee trees are alive—they're not destroyed. Let's hire some people." So, that's how we restarted.

SANDRA: That was the biggest worry. We had to make a decision. Are we going to do this again? It's not the money; it's the way of life. It's something that you love, or you don't. If you love it, you'd rather spend your whole time doing that. It's therapeutic. Sit and dig in the dirt a while, and you sweat, and then you go inside and take a shower, and you feel really good.

But it was a humongous job. We had to dig the farm roads out. The debris was just terrible. The fields have to be clear for people to pick coffee. They have to be able to walk through.

ISRAEL: After María, we hired one guy, then two, and that's it. We went from five workers to two workers because that's all we could afford. We had no money. We lost the coffee harvest. We lost the citrus harvest. We had no income from the farm.

SANDRA: We usually sell our coffee and chocolate online. But at the top of our website, it says we are out of coffee until further notice.

ISRAEL: We were not going to go hungry. We borrowed $10,000, just to get started. FEMA doesn't help with farms. It only helps with housing. We also had our social security benefits, but we were running the farm with that. We spent it on two workers who are miraculous. Eventually, almost a year later, we finally got money from the crop insurance. But it was very little.

Nobody really knew what would happen to the trees after the hurricane. They were stripped down. Many people thought the trees were going to die. We weren't sure what would happen. It was a new experience for us. In '98 with Hurricane Georges, we lost five thousand coffee trees. But they were small—they had a thin stem with a bushy top—so the hurricane came and destroyed them. But these guys—well, they are girls actually—these trees that we have now are older and have a very powerful root system, so they survived a little better. They were still hurt, but they survived.

Many months after the hurricane I began to see the trees struggling back a little. We said, "We'll take care of them and see what happens." Now, two years later, the trees are dark green; the leaves are shiny and that shows health. They're putting on new growth and the flowering is magnificent. The branches have clusters of small flowers. They're very aromatic and they're stark white. In March, when we had the big flowering, it looked like snow had fallen on the trees. We have the most beautiful trees I've ever seen in my life. So apparently, they're healing. You know, it just takes time.

We called Israel and Sandra in June 2020 to catch up. Israel answered his phone even though he was out working on the farm.

Harvests are never the same. Before María, there was one time that we picked almost 25,000 pounds. So the harvest typically ranges from 5,000 to 25,000 pounds. After María, the trees were so hurt that in 2017 and 2018 we only had minor crops—600 pounds. The trees were not healed enough. But we had committed. We kept the faith, and in 2019, we managed about 5,500 pounds of coffee. Under the circumstances, that's decent. The thing is, the trees were so hurt that they're still healing three years after the hurricane. We'll take good care of them, and we'll see what happens.

BELLE MARIE
TORRES VELÁZQUEZ

BORN IN: 1981
LIVES ON: Culebra
Medical Doctor

The archipelago of Puerto Rico includes two island municipalities off the eastern coast of the main island, Culebra and Vieques, both of which are reached by an airplane or an unreliable public ferry. These islands receive their water and electricity through underwater pipes and cables from the main island. On Culebra, there are no freshwater sources and only a few small family farms. Every necessity has to be brought in by boat, airplane, or helicopter.

We are nervous about making the trip to Culebra because there have been so many problems with the ferry since the hurricane that we are not actually convinced that we will be able to make our meeting

207

with Belle Marie—Culebra's only doctor—until the boat pulls away from the shore. It is a relief to finally dock on Culebra and make our way over to the island's clinic.

Two weeks before Hurricane María struck, the clinic was destroyed when Hurricane Irma damaged its zinc roof. Culebra has an extremely fragile health care system that has been severely impacted by the shortage of medical professionals. This situation has only been exacerbated by the austerity measures put in place by the Financial Oversight and Management Board, and this rebuilt clinic—with a concrete roof—has been made possible only through private grants and individual donations.[1]

As we sit in a row of shiny green plastic chairs waiting for Belle Marie to finish up with a patient, one of the nurses explains to us that the day we have arrived—eighteen months after the hurricane—is the day that the last of the industrial generators has been unhooked and power has been restored to the whole island. "It's a time for celebration," she tells us.

She brings us back to Belle Marie's office and we sit and listen to the doctor's strong, metered voice describe the destruction of her clinic and the efforts of the whole community to build a new one. Throughout the interview, Belle Marie's voice stays steady, even when she describes delivering a premature baby in the middle of a storm almost two months after the hurricane, long before electricity and telecommunications were restored. We were able to also talk with the new mother who delivered her baby under these circumstances, Neysha Irizarry Ortiz. Her narrative follows Belle Marie's, giving us two perspectives on surviving Hurricanes Irma and María on Culebra.

---

1. In 2016, President Obama signed PROMESA into law, creating a US federal government–appointed Financial Oversight and Management Board (FOMB) to oversee bankruptcy and debt management in Puerto Rico. The FOMB has employed drastic austerity measures that have undermined health care throughout the archipelago. For more on the FOMB and austerity measures, see "Economic Contexts" in the "Contexts" essay.

THE ISLAND'S ONLY DOCTOR

My father is a doctor in San Juan. My mother was a pharmacist, but with four children, having a family and a separate job was a handful. When I was five years old, she decided to join my father's clinic. So, we kids started going to the office to be with them every day after school. They had a cozy room just for us with a little kitchenette for snacks, but whenever my father could, he'd show us something interesting or ask us to assist him. He'd call and we'd run shouting, "It's my turn to help!" Today, my sister, Rina, and I are both doctors. Our training started there.

I've worked for the health department of Puerto Rico for many years. For most of that time, I was assigned to different urgent care centers around the main island. My husband and I lived in the town of Carolina, but I had to travel to wherever they needed a doctor.[2] It was a very hectic life for me. Six years ago, when I was pregnant with my second child, we had the opportunity to move to Culebra.[3] Here you're surrounded by nature: everything is green with trees and mangroves. There's no place in Culebra where you don't see the ocean. And there are only eighteen hundred people who live on this island full time. Everybody knows each other here—maybe not by name, but you know who they are, where they live, where they work, or what they do. I really wanted a quieter, more stable place for us.

After we moved here, though, I got divorced. Suddenly I was a single mother of two and the island's only doctor. I knew going back to the main island would mean relying on somebody else to help me take care of my children while I was at work, and I didn't want that. I do have people here that help me, because I need to be in the clinic a lot, but it's different because I live only ten steps from the

2. Carolina is a small municipality just east of San Juan and is the location of the Luis Muñoz Marín International Airport.

3. Culebra is approximately seventeen miles east of the main island and can be reached by ferry or airplane.

clinic. The kids are so close to me that I can just walk two minutes and stop in to say hi.

Culebra is not for everyone, though. Sometimes other doctors fly in from the main island to relieve me, and sometimes they fly out before their time is done and don't tell anyone! If the other doctor leaves, the nurse has to run to my house and knock on my window. Sometimes I wake up in the middle of the night, hearing, "Come quick! The other doctor left, and now there's an emergency!"

Our clinic is very small, and we're not equipped to admit patients. We don't have a birthing unit and we can't provide long-term care. Usually all of our emergency patients are evacuated to the main island. If we hear that there might be tropical storms or hurricane weather, we take precautions and evacuate all patients who need special care, along with the pregnant women who are near their due date. We're not prepared to care for women if they go into labor here. For the past twelve years, no baby has been born on Culebra.

For us, Hurricane Irma was worse than María.[4] It became completely silent and still before Irma arrived—there wasn't even a breeze—and then all of a sudden, the winds were roaring. Like something was in the walls howling at us. When I peeked out at the storm through a small part of the window that wasn't covered with a shutter, I could see the ocean covering the ferry docks and the ticket booths, coming up into the street. It arrived as a Category Five hurricane and took down all of our trees and most of our houses, which were mainly wooden and went down easily.

After Irma, we did have some help from the government because Irma didn't impact the whole of Puerto Rico as much, but the ferries weren't running so they couldn't get the equipment over to clear the roads. Some people here had tractors, though, and neighbors were helping neighbors. They were gathering up all these broken house pieces, appliances, furniture, trees, debris, or just plain garbage and

---

4. Hurricane Irma made landfall on the eastern side of the main island and Culebra and Vieques on September 6, 2017, two weeks before Hurricane María.

piling it all up for eventual removal.[5] It took about one full week after Irma for us to regain contact with the main island, and, by that time, they were starting to talk about María. So, when she finally came there wasn't much left to destroy!

The emergency room of the clinic was also severely damaged in Irma—a projectile broke the zinc roof—which was very worrisome because it's the only urgent care on this island. The emergency room generator also broke down during Irma and nobody could turn it back on. Everyone tried—staff, police, fire, well-meaning friends— but it was dead. There was another generator on the clinic side that was working, and we were running extension cords from the clinic to the cardiac area of urgent care so that we could at least have the resuscitation equipment available for emergencies.

After five days of the emergency machines being run by extension cords, the mayor let us move into another building nearby— that's what we're using now and where we're sitting today. This was an office building with small rooms, but we had no other choice, so we marked off some of the offices to be a makeshift emergency room. It was better than nothing, but we kept having to go back and forth across the parking lot to the old urgent care for supplies. When María came, we still didn't have electricity and we were working around the clock with the one generator. As I'm speaking, I have goosebumps on my arm. All those same feelings of desperation are inside me still.

For a long time after the hurricane, there was no electricity, the public schools were closed, transportation was next to impossible, and there was no communication.[6] There is no potable water on Culebra, and we have only a few family farms, so all our supplies had to be flown in, too. In those days, we kept one nurse with me on each

---

5. The Puerto Rico Solid Waste Authority estimated that Hurricane María "created 6.2 million cubic yards of waste and debris." For more on the conditions after the Hurricane María, see "Aftermaths" in the "Contexts" essay.

6. Culebra was the last municipality of Puerto Rico to be reconnected to the main electric grid.

shift. We couldn't do more because there were so many problems everywhere you turned and because everyone had so much to attend to in their own lives.

I FELT A BEATING HEART

After two months like this—with one generator for the whole clinic, no electricity, no water, and me as the only doctor working with just one nurse—the nurse came to tell me, "There's a pregnant woman here and she has pelvic pain. What do you want to do?" I know that this pain could be anything. So, when I went out to the waiting room to talk to the woman, I wasn't too worried at first. I have a list of the pregnant women on Culebra for evacuation purposes. And we had evacuated all the people who were at least eight months pregnant, near their due date. I called each of these women personally and we provided transportation to the main island for them and their families. But this person, Neysha, was not called because she was only seven months pregnant and showed no signs of any high risk. She was nowhere near her due date and not having any problems.

We met and she began to describe her pain, but while she was talking, she kept pausing, putting her hands to her side with a distressed look on her face, and it looked like she might be having contractions. And what she was describing sounded a lot like labor pain. I started thinking to myself, *Dear God, this cannot be possible.*

I was growing concerned because I knew there was absolutely no possibility for me to evacuate her. But when I brought her back to our makeshift exam room and proceeded to examine her, I found that she was ready. I finally stopped talking and said, "Enough. We need to get the stretcher." I needed to get her off the exam table and in position for the birth. But the stretcher wasn't even a stretcher for giving birth. It was a regular one that couldn't accommodate our needs, so it was harder for her and for us. And the room we were in is not that big. If I'm being generous, that space was about seven feet by eight feet, and in it we had the stretcher and an oxygen tank and there was a crash cart behind my back. So, it's a small room with a lot of equipment, the mom, me, and the nurse. We didn't really have the space to move, let alone deliver a baby.

Honestly, I was hoping that she wasn't giving birth. The circumstances were too grim. But that wasn't the reality. This baby was coming, and it was coming *now*. It wanted out! There was nothing I could do. I just kept praying in my mind because I'm a general practitioner, not an obstetrician. This was my first birth since medical school. When you're a student, you need to assist in a certain number of deliveries in order to graduate, but I didn't go into that specialty, so this was my first birth in years. This baby was coming under very poor conditions—with no access to special equipment, no transportation, and no possible communication with an obstetrician.

We didn't have a way to communicate other than satellite phone. In order to use it, you have to go outside, point it at the right angle to pick up a signal, and then hope that there are no clouds to interrupt the signal. So, there was no way to use the phone *and* deliver the baby. No way that someone could guide me through the birth.

When the baby started to come, what we saw were toes and not a head. This baby was coming breech, which means that the legs are coming first and not the head. This is not typical. Usually when a baby is carried to term, it turns on its own so that the head is downside and the first thing that will come through the vaginal canal will be the face. This happens because of the baby's need for oxygen. It's also better that way for the umbilical cord. If the baby comes out headfirst and the cord is around the neck, you can untangle it and help the baby, but you can't do that when the baby is breech.

Under this circumstance, many OB/GYNs will just do a C-section.[7] If they know by a sonogram that the baby's breech, they don't

---

7. OB/GYN is short for obstetrician-gynecologist. A C-section, also known as a Caesarean section, is a surgical procedure during which a baby is delivered through the mother's abdomen.

do the vaginal delivery. But in our case, we didn't have a sonogram or any type of imaging. We didn't know the position of the cord or anything at all. There was no way we could know if the baby was even still alive. We didn't have any equipment! The nurse and I looked at each other; we were communicating our concern with our eyes, knowing that this birth would be chancy. We looked at those teeny feet and we were scared, but we had no choice and just had to proceed.

In the beginning, Neysha was doing fine. Most of the baby was out—we could see it was a boy—and she was pushing. She didn't seem to be feeling pain despite us not having an epidural for her. She was relaxed, but very tired and just wanted to sleep. But the baby wasn't out yet. He was stuck at the shoulders and his head was still inside of her, and we were worried. I thought about God and asked him to use my hands. Neysha looked at me and asked, "Is everything all right?" I met her eyes and told her, "Everything's fine, but you need to push a little bit harder. Can you push one last time? Really hard." But the nurse motioned to me and her eyes were very large. She shook her head, no. She was giving me the sign that she thought the baby was dead. It was cyanotic. The baby was blue. He wasn't breathing.

I reached over and put my hands on the baby's tiny shoulders. With my right hand, I searched his little body and prayed to God, until I felt a beating heart. "This baby is alive, and it's coming!" I cried. I told Neysha again that everything would be fine. She still had work to do and needed to be calm. "The baby is fine, and you are going to birth him *now*." So, I really pressed her belly and told her, "Push as hard as you can!" And we got the baby. He came out all at once in a rush, smoothly. And he was alive. He cried right away, as soon as he was free. His coloration quickly came back to normal and everything was perfect after all. We placed the baby in an incubator that we powered by generator. He was two months early, but he was alive!

And then I started to try to find help to transfer Neysha and her newborn to the main island. By protocol, both needed to be in the hospital. But it was almost impossible to contact any planes or hospitals.

I was using the mayor's satellite phone, as, at that time, he was the only one on the island who had one. The health department had given us a satellite phone maybe five years before I even arrived on Culebra, but no one on the staff was told how to maintain it. It has a chip in it that expires yearly. So, we thought we had a satellite phone for emergencies, but it was just for show; it didn't work.

When I was finally able to get through to the hospital, I learned that transportation by their helicopter was out of the question. The air ambulance has many specifications for flying. If there's wind or if it's too cloudy, they cannot come and pick up a patient. It was raining hard, so the conditions were too dangerous. We sent a driver to the police station with a handwritten note that said, "Please contact the police on the main island for a rescue helicopter! We have a newborn baby that needs to go to the hospital immediately!" And the police were finally able to give us that assistance.

HELP STOPPED COMING

After María, so many doctors left Puerto Rico that they had none left to send to Culebra. Help stopped coming. Since I was the only doctor on the island throughout that whole time, all patients were my responsibility twenty-four hours a day. We had injuries from the hurricane that were never tended to and then new injuries from the cleanup. We saw so many skin infections in those days. And that was all on top of the regular things like refilling prescriptions and tending to our patients with chronic conditions. It was hard to be on duty for so many consecutive hours. I don't remember how many "Dear Fathers" I threw out during those days, but I kept saying, "Please, God, use my hands to help others."

And, finally, my own father came to our rescue. He's seventy-four now, but still has his own clinic in San Juan. He doesn't have a generator there, though, so it remained closed for a long time after the hurricane. At first, the police boat would bring him from San Juan to work with me in the clinic, then he used the ferry when it started running again. It was twenty-one days after María before transport between Culebra and the main island was even partially restored. And, even now, he's still coming to help.

Today, the clinic is rebuilt, and it even has a permanent roof. The first clinic was opened over thirty years ago and, since then, the staff had to move out of the building and set up a temporary care site whenever there was a storm warning because the zinc roof wasn't safe. After Irma and María, that was unacceptable. And I told that to everyone from the government who came to inspect our clinic. "It's a shame you haven't paid for the roof," I'd say. And they'd answer, "Keep holding on. Maybe one day." But some nonprofit organizations, a foundation, and even individuals came together to help us with the money, and I finally have a cement roof. Of everything we've done to rebuild, I think I'm most proud of that roof.

NEYSHA IRIZARRY ORTIZ

BORN IN: 1989
LIVES ON: Culebra
Seasonal Hotel Worker

We meet Neysha at Posada la Hamaca guesthouse in Culebra, a few minutes' walk from the ferry dock. Her husband, Ricky, works there and he offers us a seat outside on the deck where we can sit and talk while looking at the water. We are seated at a picnic table with an umbrella sheltering us from first the hot sun and then a light rain that falls all around us. Ricky interrupts us once to offer cool bottles of water, and, refreshed, we talk for hours.

Neysha had wanted to be a nurse so that she could help others, but she had to drop out of nursing school. Since then, she has been struggling to get medical care for herself and her children, something that is more challenging on Culebra since it is an island off the coast of Puerto Rico

217

that does not have a full hospital and is dependent upon an unreliable ferry for all goods. As she talks, it becomes apparent that Neysha knows all too well about these limitations as she went into labor on Culebra in the aftermath of the hurricane, long before electricity and communications were restored. Her story is connected to Belle Marie's, the previous narrative in this volume, as the two experienced the birth together as mother and doctor.

I WAS REALLY LUCKY

Growing up on Culebra is really special. We don't have movie theaters or fast-food restaurants, and our hospital is really small. Pregnant women have to leave the island to give birth. When it was her time, my mother went to the main island and I was born in Hato Rey, not on Culebra.[1] Medications and things like that tend to get a little delayed, too, because they have to come from the main island. But those are small things. We have other things that aren't common in any other places. Our plants and animals are really unique. For example, we have a rock forest and when you climb up it, you will find very rare purple orchids growing out from among the rocks. Our beaches are incredible. Everyone in the world comes here for the beaches! And then there is the turtle nesting.

I was really lucky because when I was in high school, I had a teacher who was a volunteer for the US Fish and Wildlife Service. He was in charge of monitoring the leatherback turtle population on Culebra, and every week during nesting season—April to August— he would gather together high schoolers to help monitor the process. We had to get our parents' permission first, though, because we spent the whole night on Brava Beach, camping there until four in the morning. We'd sit up near the trees, on the beach but away from the water, watching for the turtles. The mama leatherback turtle seems

---

1. Hato Rey comprises three barrios, or wards, in the northern section of the city of San Juan.

like she's as big as a car, like a Volkswagen Beetle. It's something to see her emerge from the sea.

When the mama turtle comes out of the ocean, it takes some time until she finds the spot in the sand that she likes. We have to wait calmly until she starts digging. They dig holes four or five feet large for their nests. When she stops digging, she puts her head up a little and it looks like she's breathing hard. That's when the mama turtle is starting to lay her eggs. She lays somewhere around one hundred eggs. She goes into a trance and you can come next to her and watch her laying the eggs without disturbing her. And this is when Fish and Wildlife does most of its work. Volunteers measure her, check to see if she has a tag and, if so, what the numbers are on the tag. If she's not registered, they have to tag her right there. They also count the eggs and measure them, too. They do all this before she finishes, covers the nest with sand, and then heads back into the ocean.

After the birth, we have to wait almost three months for the hatching. This is where the students get to help. We protect the nests that whole time. The hatching never happens at night. It's almost always very early in the morning at sunrise, but sometimes at five or six in the afternoon, at sundown. And you can't touch those little turtles. They're only three inches long or even less, but you can't help them get to the water. They have to get there their own way, or they won't be strong enough to survive. It's hard to see some of the babies taken by predators, but it's part of life. We try hard to help how we can, though, keeping the birds and crabs from eating them, so most of the babies can survive.

I can't describe how beautiful it feels to watch this process, to see the mother come out of the water so large and then the babies returning to the sea at just a few inches long. Knowing they start their lives so small and end so large is very emotional. When it's all done, the volunteers turn to each other with tears and hugs.

"THIS DOESN'T LOOK GOOD"

In high school, Neysha began working at Mamacita's Guesthouse, a popular hotel near the ferry dock. That is where she met her first husband, Bryan. They were both still working there when she had her son, Ryan, but divorced when she was twenty. Neysha remarried and decided to continue her education with the support of her second husband, Ricky. There are no colleges on Culebra, so students have to either move to the main island or travel back and forth each day by ferry. Neysha used the ferry to save money and stay with her family, but she never stopped working at Mamacita's, as she loved the people and made good money to pay for tuition and some of her family's other bills.

I started nursing school in 2010, but I didn't finish. In the middle of the program, with almost two years left, I noticed a bump on my neck. It started growing so I went to see Dr. Venturo at the Culebra clinic. He ordered a CT scan and when he read the results, he immediately ordered a biopsy of the lump. I had to take the ferry to Fajardo with my mom for the test.[2] The surgeon who did the biopsy told me, "I think you need an oncologist."

There was an oncology office in his building, so I went right upstairs to it. Because I didn't have an appointment, we had to sit there and wait all day until they took care of all their scheduled patients. My mom got nervous and impatient, but I kept telling her, "Keep calm. The doctor will see us, and everything will be okay." But when we finally saw the oncologist and she read my results, she said, "This doesn't look good." At the age of twenty-three, I was diagnosed with Hodgkin's lymphoma stage 3, type B. Cancer.[3] My mom was cry-

---

2. Until October 2018 the terminal for the ferry between Puerto Rico and the island municipalities of Culebra and Vieques was located in the town of Fajardo, a small city on the northeastern coast of Puerto Rico that is approximately thirteen miles from El Yunque rain forest. The ferry ride was approximately one hour each way.

3. Culebra residents have significantly higher-than-average cancer rates. For more on potential causes for this health concern, see "Military Bases" in the "Contexts" essay.

ing, and we had a lot of questions, but we had to leave to catch the seven o'clock ferry. It was the last one of the day and if we didn't go, we'd be stuck on the main island. What was very clear, though, was that I had to leave school to begin treatment immediately.

That appointment was in November and less than a month later, I began my chemotherapy. The PET scan had revealed that the cancer wasn't just in my neck, but under my arm and in my chest very near my heart and my trachea.[4] The doctors started with one kind of treatment first, but it wasn't working, so they switched to something more aggressive. With the first treatment I had to be on the main island for the radiation only one day per week, but with the second, it changed to one week per month that I had to be in Fajardo. With the first treatment I didn't lose my hair, but with the second one I did.

At first, my husband, Ricky, couldn't go to the one-day-a-week treatment with me. My ex-husband, Bryan, could get the time off, though, and he accompanied me. Some people might think it's strange, but my husband is the cousin of my ex-husband, and we're all family. It's funny how life works out, but we're happy. Bryan and I also have a son together, Ryan, and I am very grateful that he not only helped me with the treatments, but also took good care of our son while I was sick. When the treatments were switched to one week per month, Ricky came with me and stayed in the hospital. He'd tell jokes to make me and the nurses laugh.

In that one-week treatment per month, I'd have up to six bags of chemo. I have a port, but it never worked right, so I often took the chemo right through the veins.[5] I'd made up my mind to stay

---

4. A positron emission tomography (PET) scan uses radioactive drugs to search the body for the early stages of medical problems that do not show up in other tests.

5. A chemotherapy port is a small device that is implanted under the skin, usually in the chest, and is a semipermanent receptacle for the chemo fluids. It is intended to eliminate the need for continual needle pricks during the chemotherapy process and to prevent fluid leaks that can damage skin and other tissues.

positive. I had my cry, but then I made my peace with it and said to myself, *Have faith.* At the time I was diagnosed, I was working at Mamacita's Guesthouse, one of the hotels up the street from where the ferry docks. I'd been working there since I was fourteen years old and I really developed a family there. The owners especially support-ed me. They let me continue working throughout the treatment so that I could keep my mind off things and pay my expenses, but they were also very understanding when I wasn't feeling well or if I had to leave early. Sometimes I'd come home from treatment in Fajardo on a Friday and then you'd find me at the hotel on Saturday morning.

I tried not to slow down, and I never stopped fighting. I had to fight because of Ryan, my little boy. So, every day I said to myself, *Look, you're young. You can get through this.* I was in treatment for three years. A lot of it was hard, but the worst part was when I found out that I was pregnant. Because of the radiation I was receiving, it was not a viable pregnancy and we had to end it. Losing that baby hurt, but we knew that we had to be grateful that the cancer went into remission.

A FORCED "VACATION"

After Hurricanes Irma and María, I was left without a job for a long time. The hotels laid us all off because there was no electricity, no water, and obviously no clients. It was like a forced "vacation." Both my husband and I work in hotels, so it was very hard for us financially. Thank God we had savings. I actually had a piggybank at my house that I was going to use for travel, and it was mostly full. We survived with that money. We didn't have a bank open on the island at that time because the electric system was down, and they didn't reopen for more than a month. But between the piggybank and help from the local government, we were okay. The town brought food and drinking water to the mayor's office every so often, and everyone on the island who was able to do so lined up for supplies. I think the hardest part, though, was not having running water.[6] I can live without electricity, but not having water with a little kid—that was hard.

After María, we had no running water for two and a half months. We had electricity for part of the day from the town generators—usually from six in the evening until six in the morning. So, we had some electricity but no running water because the water pumps run on electricity and there wasn't enough fuel for both power and water.[7] Three or four times in those days they announced we would have running water for a short time. There was one day when we were waiting with the faucets open. We heard the water coming through the pipes and were ready to refill every container we had. We only had water for thirty minutes that day. My husband got in the shower and then my son. I was finishing filling up all the bottles—and our fifty-gallon drum—but when I went to the shower, there was no more water. So, I had to shower with a bucket of water I'd just saved. This was especially hard because it was extremely hot, there was no electricity, no water, and I was pregnant again! I was worried then, but not to the point of freaking out.

I HAVE A LITTLE PAIN

On November 7, 2017, my husband left the house to help a neighbor, and I stayed home with Ryan. I was seven months pregnant and had been feeling a little discomfort. Ricky got home around six o'clock at night. He found me lying on the couch. "Are you okay?" he asked me. "I have a little pain," I said. "But I'm okay." He finally went to bed, but I stayed on the couch and the pain just kept coming. I

---

6. There are no natural sources for freshwater on Culebra, so all water for cooking, cleaning, and drinking has to be pumped in from the main island.

7. In December 2017, FEMA brought additional generators to Culebra and people were finally able to have regular electricity and running water.

turned on my left side and tried to relax, to just let go of the pain. At one point, though, it was unbearable. I went to the bathroom and when I pulled down my pants, I saw blood. That's when I started to freak out. I thought, *No! This can't be! Not our baby.* And I screamed, "Ricky! Ricky, wake up!"

He burst into the bathroom, "What happened? What happened!?" And I told him, "I'm bleeding, and I'm in pain. This baby has to come now! Help me get my stuff and get me to the car." I grabbed my bag, but it was only halfway prepared. I thought I still had two months to go and had only started a few days before that to prepare the bag.

When we got to the clinic, the nurse asked me if I was okay, and I said, "No! I'm in labor!" And she said, "Are you sure?" They were surprised because on Culebra, you have to tell the clinic when it's close to your time to have the baby. They don't have a delivery room, so they need to make a plan with the hospital on the main island to send the helicopter to come and get you when it's your time. And I knew what we all knew. The emergency room had been destroyed by Irma and hadn't gotten any better in María. They weren't ready for me!

The doctor, Belle Marie, brought me into one of the tiny rooms that was being used as an emergency room, got me lying down, and started an IV of antibiotics to prevent infection. Then she said she was going outside to try to use the satellite phone to call the air ambulance. In the meantime, I told the nurse that the baby was breech. And I know that this is a very dangerous way to give birth. A lot of things can go wrong. Usually when that happens there's a C-section, but here on Culebra we don't have that kind of equipment. We don't even have an OB/GYN. Just the regular doctor, Belle Marie.

My water broke with my pants on. I felt the pressure and then it popped like a balloon and then I could feel that the baby's legs were a little bit outside. Then the pain got worse and worse and the contractions weren't that far apart. When the nurse saw the baby was coming out, she got really pale and her eyes opened up wide. I think she was pretty freaked out but trying to keep calm. But I know the face of freaking out!

MY LEGS OUT THE DOOR

It was such a small room that they had to reposition the bed with my legs out the door so that there'd be room for them to work. The baby got out safely—until the head. The hands and feet were out, but not the head. That was the tricky part.

The doctor worked really quickly. She got absorbing pads under me and the baby and told me, "The baby's head is still inside, so when I tell you, you're going to have to push. You push, and we'll maneuver the head."

I started pushing and pushing and pushing, and she worked away. I remained conscious throughout, and I saw them lift the baby from me. I just lay there and watched Belle Marie sit down with the baby. She was kind of massaging him. There were a few minutes that I didn't hear him cry. I could hear her saying, "Come on, baby. Come on." And then, I heard him crying. Just a small thing, but he was there.

He was two months early and only weighed three pounds. He came into a world with no electricity or running water—and no painkillers for mom—but he was okay, and I was okay. And I had my beautiful boy.

EVERYBODY WAS SHOCKED

It was almost eleven o'clock at night when I gave birth. They had to get Ricky, me, and the baby into the ambulance and take us to the airport, and from there we had to take an air ambulance to San Juan. It was still pouring rain and cold outside. There was no thermal blanket or anything else to keep the baby warm. So, they wrapped him the best they could, got me ready to go, and then waited for the rain to die down a little. When it did, they gave me the baby and rushed me to the ambulance. I had to sit with my premature newborn son wrapped in this giant blanket and take him to the hospital for care. *Oh, my God*, I thought. *I am so scared.*

When we got to San Juan, there was another ambulance waiting for us. I told the EMTs, "Watch out for the baby," and they were shocked to see him. "How come you had a baby on Culebra?" they wanted to know. Even when we got the hospital, the nurse asked me, "What are you doing here with a baby? Why are you taking a baby out in this weather? What's the matter with you?" The worst part, though, was her face. Her eyes were big and wouldn't leave the baby in my arms, but her mouth was small and tight. That look asked, *Where do you come from that you'd take a baby out on a night like this?*

A lot of people came to ask me questions then. That nurse, the emergency room doctor, the maternity room doctor. Then the EMTs came back to ask me more questions, too. And, oh God, there were insurance questions. I was just so tired. I didn't know what was going on, but Ricky had all the necessary paperwork. Finally, the first nurse came back and said, "Look, I'm really sorry for what I said when you arrived and for the expression on my face. I was angry because we didn't know that a baby was coming. We just were so shocked to see him in your arms."

"THE CULEBRA BABY!"

Neysha and Ricky's newborn son, Nathan, had to spend weeks in the neonatal intensive care unit until he was strong enough to go home with them. Since the ferry to Culebra was still not operational, they stayed with Neysha's aunt in Carolina so that Neysha could return to the hospital every day to breastfeed and visit with her son.[8] At that time, her aunt's house had running water but no electricity, which made the

---

8. Carolina is a northern municipality located approximately twenty-five miles west of Fajardo.

house extremely hot and difficult to sleep in. A neighbor let them run
an extension cord from his generator to the house so that Neysha could
turn on a fan, but the generator died after a couple of nights. When the
power came back on, three weeks later, she could hear the whole block
screaming "Wepa!"[9]

I spent Thanksgiving at the hospital and at my aunt's house. Nathan
spent almost the first month of his life in the hospital. The nurses
from the NICU and nursery ward were great. They were so, so help-
ful. They were very lively women. My kid was so active. He actually
kept turning himself around in the incubator, and the nurses joked,
"What did you give birth to? An athlete?"

The incubator has two holes for your hands. And he turned
himself and put a leg through one of those holes. The nurses aren't
supposed to take pictures of the babies, but one of the nurses knows
me and took one for me. "If I tell you and Ricky what's going on,"
she said, "you're not going to believe me. I have to show you what
your baby was doing." And when she showed me the picture, one of
his legs was sticking out of that hole completely. And she told me,
"He's ready to get out of there and start walking."

I would go to the breastfeeding room to pump milk. It was private and relaxed, and I made friends there. A lot of mommies came
in there to breastfeed their children. I actually stayed in contact with
two of them. Every day, we were all telling stories about the experience with María and Irma, you know, just how their town is and how
the people are. And at first, every time new people heard I was from
Culebra they were so surprised. "What? Really?" they would ask. But
then word got around and they would say, "Oh! The Culebra baby!"
It seemed like everybody knew about Nathan and the circumstances.

---

9. An enthusiastic exclamation akin to "Hooray!"

RESPIRATORY ARREST

The nurses were so proud of Nathan and everything that he could do. They kept telling me, "If he's here for a month, we'll have a party! We'll have cupcakes and a banner to celebrate his first month." But we left two days before he got to one month old. Everybody was happy to see him go, though, because he was going home.

We didn't go right back to Culebra, though. Instead we went back to my aunt's house in Carolina. Nathan needed to have some checkups with the pediatrician in San Juan. We needed to have his eyes checked a few times to make sure that they were developing correctly, and he had a little cough. So, I decided to stay. Plus, my aunt's house had electricity again and there was still no power on Culebra.

The pediatrician is Ryan's doctor and was mine, too, when I was a kid. We got a good report, there was no fluid in Nathan's lungs; so we just got a little medication for congestion, and then we were able to finally return home. We got home on a Tuesday morning, but on Wednesday night, the baby started making a weird noise. My husband was working. Nathan wasn't breathing well. And actually, he was getting pale. So, we rushed back to the clinic here. At the clinic, they checked his oxygen levels and saw that they were way too low. So, they put him on a respirator to give him oxygen. He was in respiratory arrest.

Again, we all got into the air ambulance and flew from Culebra to San Juan and then went to San Jorge Children's Hospital. What I don't understand, though, is why he wasn't given any oxygen in either of the ambulances. When we got to the emergency room in the children's hospital, the doctor who saw us was very mad. He scolded the EMTs pretty badly.

I saw so many people rushing to Nathan—nurses, doctors. They were working and working, and I was so worried. I just started to cry. Ricky was crying, and kept saying, "Oh, my God. What if we'd waited just a little longer? What would have happened if we waited?" And I was praying over and over again, *Please don't let him die.* We saw that Nathan couldn't breathe, and we knew that he was premature and only a month old, and there were just so many people working on him.

When they got him stabilized, a nurse grabbed me and took me to one side of the room, and another grabbed Ricky and pulled him to the other side. "Okay," the nurse said to me. "What happened?" I started to explain about the premature birth, and the cough, the medication. Everything. They told us that he had pneumonia and wanted to know how we let a baby get to the point of respiratory arrest. They thought that we had ignored his symptoms, neglected him.

But it wasn't our neglect. Before Nathan was discharged from the neonatal ward after his birth, he was given a vaccine for pneumonia and we were told that he would need extra boosters to prevent lung infections because he was a preemie.[10] But we couldn't get them all because the deliveries weren't coming to Culebra. After the third one, we gave up. And the pediatrician told me not to worry, that it wasn't necessary, just a precaution.

We had to be in the hospital ten days that time and wound up spending Christmas inside San Jorge Children's Hospital. We got visits from lots of famous people, people from TV. Someone was passing out presents, and Nathan got one. Some of the nurses working in that hospital were even people I studied with in college. We were able to return to Culebra on December 31, 2017. We couldn't go out because the baby still didn't have all the vaccines, but I got to spend New Year's Eve in my house with my husband and both of my children.

When we spoke with Neysha in 2020, she described Nathan as healthy, active, and fun-loving. The numerous pictures she has shared show a little boy with soft, cascading curls, a wide smile, and big, bright eyes.

---

10. According to the CDC, pneumococcal conjugate vaccines protect babies from the serious infection known as invasive pneumococcal disease.

While the owners of La Hamaca were able to rehire Ricky after the hurricane when the tourists returned to Culebra, Neysha struggled to find work. For a little while, she volunteered at Ryan's elementary school and was hired part-time as a teacher's aide. Unfortunately, because of COVID-19, work opportunities have been sporadic at both the hotel and the school, and she and Ricky struggle to take care of their small family.

CARLOS FIGUEROA VÁZQUEZ

BORN IN: 1978
LIVES IN: Juana Díaz
Electric Lineworker

Carlos Figueroa Vázquez has been a lineworker with the Puerto Rico Electric Power Authority (PREPA) for more than sixteen years.[1] He works in Juana Díaz, a municipality in the south of the main island.[2] His job is to install and maintain outdoor electrical lines. Climbing posts, hauling heavy cables, and working in severe weather are some of the physically demanding and life-threatening tasks he takes on each

---

1. The Puerto Rico Electric Power Authority (PREPA) is the English translation of Puerto Rico's Autoridad de Energía Eléctrica (AEE), the agency responsible for electricity generation, power distribution, and power transmission across the archipelago.

2. Juana Díaz has a population of almost 45,000.

day. When we first meet with Carlos in September 2018, it is almost
exactly a year after María made landfall, and he is wearing the safety
uniform that PREPA provides, which has not been replaced since the
hurricane and shows obvious signs of wear and tear.

PREPA IS GOING THROUGH SOME TOUGH TIMES

I got my lineman certification when I was twenty-two. I learned how
to operate a truck with a basket that goes up to seventy feet, to work
wearing spurs on a sixty-foot-tall post for more than an hour, to
work on a post that had rotted out, and to avoid lines that might be
live to prevent electrocution. You have to know these things or you
could die.[3] I work with live electricity all day. My job is to connect
and disconnect services and install electricity meters. I also do repairs and construct the lines. The lineman does everything you can
think of when you look at electrical lines. We do it all.

Before Hurricane María, we prepared as much as we could. PREPA
had a contingency plan, but it was weak. At the time of the emergency
there was too little of everything. PREPA's director stopped buying
supplies and gas for our trucks and tanks, so when the hurricane arrived, we didn't have enough.[4] But with what little we had, we filled the
vehicles with gas and arranged bases that had gas tanks, diesel, and oil.
We prepared a separate "homemade" vehicle: we took a pickup truck
and stocked it with supplies that weren't being used on the other trucks.
If not for that vehicle, we wouldn't have been able to do as much as we
did. It's still in service now. We did everything we could with what we

---

3. Electrical powerline installer and repairer was the eleventh most dangerous job
in the US according to a list compiled in 2020 by the website 24/7 Wall St., which
based its rankings on workplace fatality rates in 2018.

4. In response to the financial crisis of 2014, Governor Alejandro García Padilla's
administration hired a US consulting firm, AlixPartners, to restructure PREPA to
cut costs, so the director at this time was appointed by AlixPartners. For more on
this controversial contract, see "Economic Contexts" in the "Contexts" essay.

had. Honestly, I think the agency could've done much better. But that would take money, and PREPA says it has no money.

PREPA is going through some tough times because of the economic situation.[5] All the agency gives linemen nowadays is an adjustable wrench, a hammer, pliers, a flat screwdriver, and a manual stapler. We have no battery-powered tools. We aren't given powered staplers, even though we use them all the time to attach cables to posts. Some cables are aluminum and are soft, but some are copper and require more pressure to properly attach. If they aren't properly attached, the cable might fall. If it's a live cable and there's someone below, they might get killed. So the stapling has to be done right. To attach a cable fifteen or twenty times a day with a manual stapler is nothing, but when you have to do a hundred staplings a day, like we do, it can cause injuries, like the small fracture I had in one of my elbows. Working like this is exhausting. Imagine fixing five to eight posts daily with hand tools. Imagine working with an adjustable wrench during the time after the hurricane when everything was down. We're doing a job where being tired or physically burned out is dangerous. If we make a mistake or if our hands fail us because of tiredness, we can lose a limb or die. Even before the hurricane, I and many of my coworkers had to equip ourselves and buy tools that helped us prevent injuries and stay safe. After the hurricane it was even worse.

I LEARNED TO SLEEP ANYWHERE

Four days after the hurricane, I went back to work, repairing lines and restoring electricity in Juana Díaz. The town was destroyed. It

---

5. Puerto Rico has been experiencing an economic decline since 2006, which culminated in the Puerto Rican government-debt crisis of 2014 and the archipelago filing for bankruptcy in 2017, just months before the hurricane. Austerity measures have been imposed on the archipelago, affecting public works, including the electric utility PREPA. For more on the debt crisis and austerity measures, see "Economic Contexts" in the "Contexts" essay.

truly was astounding. In the plaza, which is one of the prettiest and most visited places in town, the trees were all blown down. We saw houses with no roofs, without walls, where only the floors remained. You'd say, "*Ay, Dios*, there used to be a house here!"[6] People were walking the streets and crying. It was like a horror movie. The roads were brutal, completely blocked with fallen trees. The community tried to cut and clear the trees, but sometimes it was impossible. I'm talking about giant trees. When my coworkers and I saw the electrical lines, just by looking at them, we knew how bad it was. We said, "We're going to be without electricity for a really long time."

The first four or five months, I started at six in the morning and finished around midnight. Those were some really, really exhausting months. I learned to sleep anywhere. I remember being so tired that I'd lie on the ground during my break to try and get some rest, and sleep would overtake me. Before the hurricane, I never drank coffee; now I drink coffee. My wife, son, and stepson told me they were worried, always thinking, *Please let him arrive home safely.*

If we didn't have enough materials before the hurricane, then you can imagine how it was after. Sometimes what we needed was as simple as a roll of tape, which we always keep in our truck. It only costs $1.50 or $2, but even that wasn't supplied for us. Each paycheck we would set aside some money to buy something we needed for work. We said, "This week when we get paid, we'll buy this. Next time we get paid, we'll get this." Sometimes, it was cordless power tools like drills, impact guns, and reciprocating saws.[7] But we also had to buy things like LED lights for our helmets for working in the dark. At night in the mountains, we couldn't see to drive, so we bought and installed LED lights on the vehicles. We also bought inverters for charging batteries and mounted those on the trucks. All of this is expensive; it's not like

---

6. "Ay, Dios" means "Oh, Lord."

7. An impact gun, also known as an impact wrench, is a socket wrench power tool. It requires little exertion to use. A reciprocating saw is a handheld power tool that can cut various materials, including metal and wood.

it's just $100. After the hurricane, I went to Home Depot and spent around $700. Overall, I've spent over $1,000 of my own money. None of that money is reimbursed. But seeing all those people without electricity was really sad. My coworkers and I bought materials and equipment because we felt the need to provide electricity for the people. If we hadn't, the process would've dragged on even longer.

The problem wasn't only the tools; it was also the vehicles. We don't have good vehicles. We try to take care of them, but they're from 1998 or 1999. The maintenance of the vehicles is supposed to be done by PREPA, but the smallest repair can take two to three weeks. Mechanics have been leaving Puerto Rico and there are no mechanic supervisors. Also, PREPA sometimes doesn't pay the supplier, so they don't release the parts. Many times, I've paid to fix my work vehicle from my own pocket. Or we collect money among ourselves. Sometimes it's a part that only costs $60 or $70, so we say, "Let's buy it." Some local mechanics have also lent us a hand so we can repair the vehicles more quickly and avoid sending them to PREPA repair shops. Those shops are like Neverland—if a vehicle goes there, it disappears.

After the hurricane, people were impatient and didn't understand that restoring electricity was a step-by-step process and that we had to wait for materials. The delays weren't our fault. Here, where I work, at the Técnica de Juana Díaz, people came to picket PREPA.[8] One day, a man who ran a center for the elderly was really riled up and wanted to fight with everybody. We had to call the police and ended up having to ask for a police car at the Técnica every morning because people were hysterical. People would insult us. Some wanted to fight with us just because we worked at PREPA. Someone actually hit a coworker of mine. There were serious problems. We'd say, "Look, we don't even have power in our own homes."

---

8. Carlos works at PREPA's station in Juana Díaz, which is called the Unidad Técnica de la Autoridad de Energía Eléctrica (AEE) en Juana Díaz, or "Técnica de Juana Díaz" for short.

THE WORK SHOULD'VE BEEN BETTER

I wasn't able to do anything about the lack of electricity in my own home—couldn't even help myself and my family—because our area administrator had assigned my neighborhood to a US company and I had to wait for them to do the work! My coworkers and I were all worried about our families not having power. Every time we'd leave work, we'd say the same thing to each other: "Will there be electricity at home? Have the Americans finally got us our power back?"

PREPA hired many American electricity companies, and thank God they came to help, but there were problems. At PREPA, my coworkers and I would sometimes take more time to restore power because if we didn't have the proper materials that we needed to do the job, we wouldn't do it. But some of the outside companies didn't wait for proper materials. They'd do some crazy quick fix and be on their way.

Even now, there are cables falling and cracked electrical posts. There are still places being reported where those companies left live cables lying on top of houses or on people's lawns. Almost a year after the hurricane, there was a complaint in the town of Villalba.[9] A company had left a live cable dangling from a post. There was a dog tied to the post and it died. Some girls tried to remove the dog and they almost died, too. The investigation as to why that happened is still ongoing. But whatever happens, PREPA has to repair all the problems left behind by those outside power companies. Soon we'll be in almost the same shape as we were after the hurricane because of the job they did.

The work should've been better considering how much money was spent. These companies made millions of dollars, yet there are millions of deficiencies in their work.[10] There's no excuse. The outside workers

---

9. Villalba is located in the central region, approximately seven miles north of Juana Díaz.

10. In October 2017, a Montana-based company, Whitefish Energy Holdings, was awarded a controversial contract for $300 million. Later that month, the contract was canceled, and eventually the US Army Corps of Engineers oversaw the power

were treated better than us. They were being paid double or triple the wages we're paid here in Puerto Rico. They had more materials and better equipment than us. They had new vehicles. Their living conditions were better than many of us local workers. They stayed at hotels where there was water and electricity, and where they had no problem finding something to eat. For months, I'd go home after working long hours to no water and no electricity. At my house, we were without water for around six months and without power for five and a half months.

But the situation wasn't all bad. Some people treated us really well. People did prayer circles for us. I met a child who had autism and he made a strong impression. He was around nine years old. We were still working in Juana Díaz then, and I used to see him on the balcony of his house with a notebook and a pencil, watching what we were doing. His father told us that he was drawing our vehicle with me working up in the basket and my coworkers on the ground. He got really happy when he saw us getting closer to his home as we worked. His father brought him out and we got him up on the truck. He stole our hearts. Later, around Christmas, we went back to his neighborhood and brought him a little truck as a present. Another time we were working and a couple of little kids approached us with their crayon drawings. The pictures were of little people with a lot of hearts all over the page. At the bottom of one drawing, it said *Gracias*. That message of thanks meant a lot to us. We were doing everything we could to provide electricity for the people. We were also risking our lives. I don't know if people understand how dangerous the job is. We have death after us daily.

The most dangerous experience I had while working after the hurricane was when I had to get out of the basket to work on the posts. The arm of the truck only went up forty feet, so sometimes the basket wouldn't reach the lines. So with my security belt on, I had to go out onto the post to be able to connect the electricity. That's

restoration. For more on this and other controversial contracts, see "Aftermaths" in the "Contexts" essay.

always our highest risk, making a line live. Sometimes we were up on those posts for four hours or more. Our feet were hurting. It was hot. It was a pretty hard experience, but we were able to do it.

WITHOUT POWER FOR NINE OR TEN MONTHS

From May to July we were working in Orocovis, which is in the central mountain region, about an hour's drive from Juana Díaz.[11] There were still many places in Juana Díaz that didn't have electricity, but since the American companies were working in our town, PREPA sent our crew to Orocovis. There, people had been without power for nine or ten months. PREPA didn't even provide us with a place to work from. They just said, "Go ahead." That was an experience! We set up a camp on a piece of land that a local lent us. We'd leave the big vehicles there and every morning we'd all travel together from Juana Díaz in four-doored vans. We still went in at six in the morning and worked until at least nine at night, often later. Materials were still taking too long to arrive. We'd go into the mountains and stop where towers and posts were lying on the ground and dismantle those in order to recover materials.

In Orocovis, people had been without power for so long, but never once did anyone disrespect us. They were calm and helped a lot. They'd prepare lunch for us and bring us snacks. If they had ten bottles of water at their house, they wanted to give us eight, and we'd be like, "No, look, we have water."

IF YOU HAVE AN ACCIDENT, YOU'RE SCREWED

On April 19, 2018, the Financial Oversight and Management Board of Puerto Rico (FOMB) released a fiscal plan that would affect employees

---

11. The rural municipality of Orocovis has a population of approximately 20,000. Orocovis suffered extensive damage, and because it is in a harder-to-reach mountain location, its recovery after the hurricane was especially slow.

of PREPA like Carlos. The new plan called for expenditure reforms for government employees that involved cutting employee health care benefits and sick and vacation days, as well as the elimination of the Bono de Navidad—the Christmas bonus—for all public employees. Negotiations between the FOMB and Puerto Rico's government are ongoing and the fiscal plan continues to be amended.

You know, PREPA worked very professionally, especially compared to the way some of the outside companies worked. It's not fair what's happening to us at PREPA. Before, during, and after the hurricane we've been taking blows from the government. They took away our State Insurance Fund benefits.[12] Right now, if you have an accident, you're screwed. If you don't have sick days saved up, then you're out. What's called the "risk bonus" has been taken away from us. They took our holiday bonus away. And yesterday the news came out that they're taking away our medical plan because of the fiscal plan. Who will work for a company like PREPA, risking their lives daily, if they don't have a medical plan?

Our union, UTIER, is trying to fight for our medical plan and safeguard the linemen's work.[13] But right now, I don't really see a lot of results from the negotiations between the union and the government. I don't see anything happening that will better our circumstances. The government is trying to sell PREPA, so they're just stalling for time and we're in limbo, waiting to see what will happen.

Right now, PREPA isn't prepared for anything. PREPA isn't buying vehicles, tools, or equipment, and it's not following safety guidelines. PREPA is supposed to provide linemen with uniforms

---

12. The State Insurance Fund Corporation is owned and operated by the Puerto Rican government and is responsible for providing worker's compensation in the archipelago. The cuts are a result of current austerity measures. For more on austerity measures, see "Economic Contexts" in the "Contexts" essay.

13. Unión de Trabajadores de la Industria Eléctrica y Riego (UTIER) is the Electrical Industry and Irrigation Workers Union.

that we have to wear daily. They're supposed to be fire-retardant, and the lifespan of the uniforms is limited. We haven't received new uniforms in two years. Mine have holes in them. Look, that's three holes on my sleeve alone. It's a violation of safety guidelines.

PREPA is also buying less gas. If they keep on buying such little amounts of gas, an emergency doesn't even have to happen—there will be blackouts. But if there is an emergency, like an earthquake or a tsunami, and petroleum barges can't come in, Puerto Rico will be powerless again.[14] If a hurricane were to strike today, we're as unprepared as when María hit.

---

14. An ongoing earthquake swarm in Puerto Rico began on December 28, 2019. There have been thousands of earthquakes since then, the largest registering at 6.4. The archipelago's frail power grid has never been completely restored after Hurricane María. For more on the earthquakes, see "Earthquake Swarm" in the "Contexts" essay.

LUIS G. FLORES LÓPEZ

BORN IN: 1970
LIVES IN: Juncos
Salesperson

Luis Flores López lives in a large two-story house near the top of a mountain in rural Juncos.[1] To the left of the house is the mountainside and to the right is an external staircase leading to the second floor where his parents live. Further to the right is a tamarind tree and, under its shade, a small covered patio built for his family to gather together and find a breeze, share a meal, and play dominoes.

Luis followed in his father's footsteps by becoming a salesperson. He works long hours and his work can be precarious. After the hurricane,

---

1. Juncos is a small town on the eastern side of the main island approximately twenty-six miles south of San Juan. It has a population of approximately 38,000, close to 51 percent of whom live below the federal poverty line.

both his job and his family were impacted by the combination of downed trees and mudslides that left the roads impassable for weeks and by the prolonged lack of electricity that left his family in the dark for months.

THE ONLY ONE WHO SURVIVED

When I was fifteen days old, the doctors told my mother that I would need open-heart surgery. She said that when I cried, I'd run out of breath and turn purple. Dr. Valdés, the cardiologist at Hospital Pavía in Santurce, diagnosed me with pulmonary stenosis, a heart valve that wasn't opened.[2] I needed an operation to open the valve so that the blood could flow, but the doctors said they needed to wait until I was nine years old. The doctors were waiting for me to be stronger so that I'd be able to survive such an intense surgery.

My dad's health plan didn't cover the operation—and it cost $15,000—but he didn't ask for a cent from anyone. Dad saved up money little by little until he had all $15,000. I know it was a sacrifice, but I never heard him complain. He owned two small businesses in Juncos that everyone in our family worked in, a cafeteria and a clothing store. The store was named Nandy's Fashion, after me. My full name is Luis Germán and, when I was born, my abuela wanted my older brother, Ángel, to call me that. But he couldn't say *Germán*. It came out *Nan-Nan*. And that name stuck. Eventually, everyone just called me Nandy, and so that was the name of the store.

Everyone in Juncos knew that I was going to get operated on. In a town that small, a little boy who was going to have open-heart surgery was news. I didn't know that surgery was something serious and didn't really give it much thought until we were three months away from the operation. Then I started to think, *Damn, I'm going to have open-heart surgery!* But at that age, I didn't believe that anything catastrophic could happen to me.

---

2. Santurce is the most populated neighborhood in San Juan and is situated on the northeast coast of the city.

In 1979, they didn't do that type of operation anywhere in Puerto Rico, so we had to go to Buffalo, New York, to receive care. We went all together as a family: my parents, me, and my two brothers, Ángel and Hector. There were two other children, René and Oscar, who also needed care that you couldn't find on the island, and they traveled from San Juan to New York City with their families on the same plane as us. Oscar had problems with his kidneys and René had complications from Down syndrome.

My family stopped at my aunt's house in the Bronx before going to the hospital, and my brothers stayed there with Tía Alejita, Dad's sister, throughout the entire process. My parents brought me on another plane to Buffalo, and on May 30, I entered Oishei Children's Hospital five days before the surgery was scheduled so that the doctors could do electrocardiograms, blood exams, and check my hemoglobin levels.

On the ninth floor of the hospital there was a game room with an ice cream truck where you could pick any flavor you wanted. They had a puppet theater where the puppets would show the different operations so that kids wouldn't be scared, and I even got a coloring book showing what my surgery would look like. What I remember most, though, is that the nurses were really pretty. When they came into my room, I would ask them for a kiss on the cheek and they would always give it to me.

Throughout this time, we were still with René and Oscar and their families, all going through similar processes. Of the three children who flew from Puerto Rico to New York for their surgeries, though, I was the only one who survived.

I FELL IN LOVE WITH BASEBALL

I loved sports and the operation couldn't stop me from playing. My recuperation was slow, but it was doable. I spent two months in my bedroom until I finally snuck out to my garage to play ping-pong. I got in serious trouble with the doctor for that one. Soon after that, though, I got to go to the basketball court to see my friends. All the guys from our barrio crowded around excitedly because they had thought that I was going to die. "Damn, Nandy," they said, "you look so white!" I'd lost so much hemoglobin that my skin color looked different.

Even with the surgery, I remember my childhood as being beautiful and fun. I did everything with those friends from my barrio and from the whole town. Juncos is a small town, so we all knew each other and played together. Everyone came together—kids that lived in government apartments, kids from fancy neighborhoods, and kids like me, in the middle. After school we would all meet up and go play sports or play at each other's houses.

Lots of Sundays my dad would take us to the baseball park in Juncos to see the AA games, and I just fell in love.[3] I loved to watch with him and have him explain the game to me. I started playing on a baseball team when I was five years old. I had to take time off for my surgery, but the year after my recovery, I played in every junior league that I could. I won many awards as a young person thanks to my abilities in both offense and defense. I still hold the batting record for our league. Our team won the regional eastern championship, and no one could beat us. We were the number four team in Puerto Rico and even played against a New York team. I even played against guys who made it into the major league. When I was twelve years old, I played against Ramser Correa. He was signed by the Milwaukee Brewers in 1987 when he was only sixteen years old and I scored against him!

Sports marked me in a very significant way. I learned that every achievement is made through sacrifice. To get to the parks where the team played, I had to take public transportation from one town to

---

3. Double-A (AA) baseball is the second highest level of Minor League Baseball in the US. In his youth, renowned baseball player Roberto Clemente played for Juncos's competitive amateur team, Ferdinand Juncos.

another.[4] I often went to Gurabo and Caguas to play.[5] It cost me between fifty to seventy-five cents each time. My dad worked six days a week and didn't have time to take me, and my mom didn't drive. I think I could have gone a lot further with sports because I had the ability and talent, but my family couldn't afford it.

At sixteen, I had to work with my father on many of the days that I had games, and I just couldn't do both. So, I decided to keep playing sports, but not on a team or league because I had to help my father with the businesses. When I stopped playing baseball, a lot of people in my town were surprised. Many people asked me, "Why did you stop playing, Nandy? You have the talent to get far!" I wanted to study in the United States and sign a professional baseball contract, but I had to work and couldn't do both. I saw that my family needed me, and I wanted to help.

My dad was a great businessman, but he didn't get to go to school. He had fourteen siblings and there wasn't enough for all of them. So, he doesn't have a high school diploma, but he was smart with his businesses. We were never in need of anything. We didn't have luxuries, but we always had what we needed: food and clothes and things like that. He grew food for us and kept some cows, too. My dad came from nothing, and with no education he provided for my mother and our whole family.

He worked from Monday to Saturday, from eight in the morning to six at night, but he was with us all day on Sunday. On that day, he'd always have an activity for us. Sometimes it was the baseball games, but other times, he'd tell us, "Hey, let's go fishing in the river. Let's go visit the family. Let's go to the field and see what's growing. Let's go to the pasture to work with the cows." My dad doesn't have anything that he thinks of as his. Everything he owns

---

4. The public transportation that Luis refers to here is in the form of privately owned cars and vans that do not operate on a regular schedule.

5. Gurabo is approximately five miles west of Juncos, and Caguas is another five and a half miles to the west.

he offers to those who need it, no matter the circumstances. He's a good man. So, even though I was very disappointed not to continue on with my baseball career, I understood.

MARRIAGE IS COMPOSED OF THREE

I had wanted to study to be an emergency room technician, but in those years, you had to first get a bachelor's degree in nursing and then later study to be an EMT. But in my family, we didn't have a car for me to use and we couldn't afford to get one. Regrettably, what I wanted to study was only available in the San Juan metropolitan area and I had to go to a school closer to home. I couldn't afford a long-distance commute. So, I started working at the Álmacenes department store in 1988 and studied business administration at the Universidad Ana G. Méndez in Gurabo, a degree that I use to this day.

After Hurricane Hugo hit in 1989, there were some FEMA programs across the island. One of the people working on the program was Brenda I. Santiago. After her program finished, she came to work at Álmacenes, the same store where I was working as a salesman. I was only nineteen years old and she was older than me by one year. She had been studying at the University of Puerto Rico at Río Piedras in San Juan and was doing a semester in New York. She was there for quite some time but came back to help after Hugo. When she came back, she transferred to the UPR campus in Humacao.[6] I actually knew her in childhood because she had also lived in Juncos, but I didn't remember her. And our relationship blossomed.

We had been dating for one year and eight months when I purchased a ring. She didn't know I was going to propose, but she knew something funny was going on. She thought it was something bad and she was very upset, jealous. When I picked her up, she got in the car, but she said to me, "I am not going anywhere with you!" She

---

6. Humacao is a small municipality on the east coast.

was reaching for the door handle, but I reached for her other hand, "Come here, Brenda, give me your hand." And I took out the ring and put it on her finger. "Look, I want to propose to you!" Then she stopped and threw herself at me, crying. She said yes.

I have learned from my wife that marriage is composed of three: you, your partner, and God. So, if one of those three is not a part of that union, then it is really easy to break it. The Bible says that "a rope of three knots is not easily broken," and I believe that these words are at the base of every lesson I've learned in my life: you can go nowhere without your family and God by your side.

So, even though I would've liked to study something related to health care, this career is what has helped me take my family forward. When my dad was close to retiring, I was already married and had to search for some work on the side. I needed to continue helping him with his business while looking for another job with benefits like health insurance for my family. I kept working with my dad, and started a part-time job with Gerber. I worked there for a year and then when my dad retired, I went to work with Méndez and Company for another year, also selling baby food and baby products.

During that time, I learned of a job opening at V. Suárez and Company, the number-one distributor in the Caribbean. I got that job twenty-three years ago, and it has been a blessing that I've been with that company ever since. Brenda and I have now been married for twenty-six years and have three children: Lilyvette, Brendita, and Luis Samuel. My job lets me take care of them. I'm a sales representative in the beverage division, in charge of fourteen towns on the east coast, including the islands of Vieques and Culebra.[7]

A normal day for me is waking up early in the morning and planning out the route for the fourteen towns I visit every day. When I go out there, I entrust myself to God and try to give my best. It's a risky job since I have cash at hand every time. I take money from

---

7. Vieques and Culebra are island municipalities off the east coast of the main island that are accessed by ferry or airplane.

my clients when I do the sales, and then in the afternoon go to my house to square the money and deposit it in the bank. I always leave myself in God's hands when I do this work.

ASSAULTED AT GUNPOINT

One time, in 2005, I was on the road and stopped to gas up my car. And when I came back from paying, three men were waiting for me at my car. Two were tall and one was short, but all three were skinny and all of them had guns. They pushed me into the driver's seat, got in around me, and told me to drive.

I think that they had been watching me and knew that I'm a salesman. That I go to my clients, take their orders, and pick up the money. That's what I do. And it's all in cash. People pay the storekeepers in cash and that's the money they give me. They must've known because once we were in the car, they knew right where to look for the money. They pointed to my work briefcase and said, "Give us the money."

They were talking really slowly, like their tongues were weighted down with something. The words came out slurred. Their eyes were mostly closed, and it seemed like they were having a hard time keeping them open. And they kept playing with those guns. They had guns pointed at me and they were clearly on drugs. If one of their hands had slipped, they would have shot me dead.

"You can have it. Take it all," I said, and just gave them the whole case. They wouldn't let me go, though. They gave me directions and we drove around for about thirty-five minutes. The whole time they kept playing with the triggers on those guns, and I kept praying. I couldn't help thinking, *I am going to die here in this car.* I was worried about Brenda and our children, about my parents. *What will they do without me? Who will take care of them?* That's a feeling I will carry for the rest of my life.

I was worried about how these men were going to respond to the words coming out of my mouth, so I was thinking and overthinking every move so as not to provoke them. But I told them about Brenda and our three little children. "Please let me go home to them," I begged. They had me stop at an abandoned house and they got out of the car. They took the keys, but then one of the tall ones threw the keys back at me as they ran away. They decided to let me live. I picked up those keys and drove as fast as I could back to the gas station where it had all begun.

The ironic thing is that I had permission to carry a gun, too. I had asked for one after a coworker had been assaulted at gunpoint. And that day I decided to leave it at home. Maybe it was for the best. After this I was even more careful with my route. I changed my routine for each client. And then I gave up my license to carry a gun because it didn't feel safe.

SO HIGH UP IN THE MOUNTAINS

Luis worked hard for many years to support his family and help them to be financially secure. His three children are all in college now. Luis Samuel is studying in the US on a baseball scholarship, while Brendita and Lilyvette are studying in Puerto Rico. All of them were at their home in Juncos during the hurricane.

We prepared for the hurricane. We have some metal storm shutters, *tormenteras*, but we had to divide them between our house and my parents'. Ángel had come over earlier to help put them up, but there weren't enough to cover all the windows and doors upstairs and downstairs. He put most of them upstairs to protect our parents, so downstairs we had more of a mixture of the steel panels held in place with screws and the plywood boards nailed together. Even though it was less protected, we thought it would probably be okay.

Since our house is so high up in the mountains, you can really feel the winds. I always say, "The higher you are, the more you feel the wind." When María started, that's what I noticed, how strong and constant the winds were. I started to realize that this hurricane was going to be really bad and began to worry about how long the hurricane was going to actually be in Puerto Rico and how powerful, since the first bursts of wind were already so strong. I said to myself, *Damn. If this is how the hurricane is going to start, how's it going to be once it's actually in Puerto Rico?* That's when I started to worry about those tormenteras.

After three or four hours of blowing in all directions without stopping, the wind began to take from us. The wooden planks we'd nailed over the doors and the steel tormenteras over our windows went flying away. It's a desperate thing to see these panels of steel and wood—the only barrier that we had between us and María—ripped off like they were no heavier than sheets of paper. And without them, the wind started pushing the doors inward.

Both Brenda and Brendita stood pressed against doors for almost eight hours. For all of those hours they used their bodies to hold those doors in place while we were praying that they would hold up against the wind. My wife was crying while holding the side door with all of her strength, but Brendita, who was doing the same thing with the front door, kept a smile on her face and made jokes to stop her mother from crying.

I was so upset because I was the one who was supposed to be holding the doors shut tight. Not my daughter. Not my wife. But water was pouring into the house without stopping and I had to help Luis Samuel and Lilyvette keep the water out of the house.

I had to start reinforcing the windows and doors. I put emptied drawers and heavy posters in front of the windows that were no longer protected by tormenteras. As a salesman, I have lots of heavy cardboard posters laying around the house, promotions for the things I sell—like Coors Light beer, Tito's Vodka, and even food brands like Old El Paso, Lipton, Ocean Spray, and Brookfield. So, I was using those to cover the windows from the inside. I used anything I had to try to stop the water from getting inside: mops, towels, even our comforters and blankets. I used the towels to mop up the water, squeezed the water into a large cooler, and then drained that water in the kitchen sink. Over and over again.

I kept quiet about it, though—no complaining, no worrying out loud—so that the family wouldn't think about anything other than the task they were doing. I was trying to get the water out as quickly as I could, but time slowed down for me then: eight hours felt like twenty-four. All I could think was, *Lord, when will this stop?*

I was afraid for us, but I was terrified for my parents. They were only a flight of stairs away, but I couldn't get to them through the wind and rain and didn't know what was going on up there. I could only imagine that what was happening inside my house might be worse upstairs. And they're in no kind of physical condition to do the work that we were doing downstairs. I kept thinking, *Ángel is all alone trying to do the same things we're doing downstairs. He's trying to survive, and to keep our parents alive.* I had my whole family by my side, working together, but he was doing it all by himself while taking care of our parents.

I got mad. I remember thinking, *If they had just stayed downstairs with us!* I told them, "Stay with us. It's safer if we're all together." But they are really proud people and they wanted to be in their home. They wanted to take care of it. We did what we could, until there was nothing that we could do.

The first thing I did when the hurricane finally stopped was go check on my parents. Their apartment had gotten really badly hit—the front door and their windows burst open, too. I thank God that Ángel stayed with them the whole time, taking care of them, and that our house is cement, so it was still standing.

Once I saw that they were safe, I went out into Juncos. I love my town, and it was really hard to go in and around the plaza where we used to play and see that the baseball and basketball courts were destroyed, buildings were knocked down, and trees lay broken on the ground. It's hard to see everything that has taken a town years to build disappear.

BLOCKED BY FEMA

Twelve days after the hurricane, the Suárez company reopened, and the streets were cleared enough for us to go back to work. Before that, it was too dangerous for the truckers that deliver products and the salespeople who take the orders to go out on the road. I work on commission and the biggest percentage of my salary comes from sales. And with the roads closed there were no sales. For two weeks after the hurricane, I didn't have a job. And I worried. *Will I still have a job when this is all over?* I thought.

I have 114 clients that I couldn't serve at this time. I couldn't go out to check what merchandise the clients were asking for or what their needs were. When I was able to go out again, I saw that there were clients who'd lost their whole store, everything. They didn't know what to do. And I couldn't help them. Ninety percent of our products are imported from the US. Canned beans, corn, beets, and chicken, soap, hand sanitizer, toilet paper, baby formula, milk, juice—it's all imported![8] And my employer is one of the biggest suppliers of these goods in Puerto Rico.

But the ports were prioritizing FEMA products over ours. If a delivery of ours came to Puerto Rico, FEMA would confiscate our products, pay the supplier, and then give them away. When the shipping container was empty, they would send it back to the States so that it could be filled with FEMA products. They did that with every delivery that came from the US and we couldn't ask for any merchandise. We were being blocked by FEMA.

When you see a store owner not getting their products and that store not having products for a community in need of food and emergency supplies, it breaks you. The east coast was the most affected by Hurricane María. It really impacted Yabucoa and those towns on the

---

8. The USDA estimates that over 85 percent of all the food sold in Puerto Rico over the last decade was imported, a number that, according to multiple news sources, contributed to massive food shortages after the hurricane. For more on food aid, see "Aftermaths" in the "Contexts" essay.

coast that are on my route.[9] And FEMA wasn't there! The people had no other way to get food than in the stores we supplied. It was heartbreaking knowing we weren't going to be able to deliver food when people were hungry. The government wasn't involved. It got covered up in the press; they were saying that everything was all right, but it wasn't.

I did my best to help out my clients. These were people I knew, friends that I'd made through the years. It was hard to see that destruction—all their losses—and then have to head back to my own house and face the situation we were living in, without electricity and running water. We have a neighbor who has a pool and he let me get water for the toilets. When it came to potable water, it was a bit harder. I had saved some before the storm and bought more when we could, but we were struggling for some time. Finally, when goods started moving again, the Suárez company was able to give employees water and even food.

When it came to gasoline, it was even harder. To get gas we had to wait for four to five hours in a line, and sometimes when you got to the front there wasn't any left. Then we had to wait for the truck to go and get more gasoline. Even though there are a lot of gas stations where I live, it was hard because there was enforced rationing. There was a desperation in the crowd because gas was not only for cars, but also for generators. It was hard to see my children, wife, and parents suffering so much.

I COULD SEE HIM GET PALER

It wasn't just my job that worried us. My father has been a smoker since he was twelve years old. Because of this, he has some health

---

9. Yabucoa is on the southeast corner of the main island, approximately twenty miles south of Juncos. The eye of Hurricane María passed directly over it, causing multiple mudslides and destroying numerous houses. Six months after the hurricane, 61 percent of Yabucoa's residents were still without electricity. The continued lack of electricity was detrimental to the majority elderly population and led to many deaths.

problems. One is that his blood gets clogged with toxins that don't get out through his urinary tract system. He needs to have dialysis every other day. Without his treatment, he can't live. After the hurricane, I had no work and no income, but in addition to that there was no gas, water, or electricity. And no way to get the dialysis. The center where he goes for treatment stayed closed after the hurricane, and we didn't know when it was going to open again. There was no official information, no plan. We just heard that desperate people had stolen the diesel fuel out of the center's generator, so it couldn't work.

For five days he went without getting his dialysis. He missed three treatments. Every day I could see him get paler right in front of me. His eyes were getting cloudier. Those five days after the hurricane were so hot, but dialysis patients can't drink a lot of fluids. I knew that drinking water would up the chances of him dying, but he was so hot and all he wanted to do was drink. He was so thirsty. "Dad! No!" I would say. "Try to hang on a little longer." And then I'd take the glass out of his hands. Can you imagine taking a glass of water out of your father's hands?

We spent those five days on the patio, hoping for a breeze. It was so hot after the hurricane and there was no electricity to start the fans. And on the fifth day, Brenda screeched up to the house in our car, slammed on the brakes, and jumped out. "Now!" she screamed. "You have to go now! The dialysis center has reopened, and you can take him for the treatment now, if you hurry. They only have a few spaces, so you have to go!" I shot up from my seat and tried to run in more than one direction at once. "Get your clothes. Get dressed! We're going for your dialysis!" I shouted at my dad.

Brenda had taken our daughter to her friend Katherine's house to play board games as a distraction. Katherine's father also needed dialysis, so they were trying to keep each other's spirits up. When they got there, Katherine was out running errands, so they were playing with her husband and children. All of a sudden, Katherine ran in breathlessly, crying, "Go home! The dialysis center is opening for a short time. I'm here for my father so that he can get his treatment. Go home and tell Nandy! There's room for one more," she said. Brenda left our daughter and raced to bring me the car.

When he got his treatment, the bag of rocks on my shoulders was lifted. This is the man who saved every one of his pennies for my heart surgery. He gave me the opportunity to live a long life, and I could then give him hope. But I keep thinking how fragile hope is. If Brenda hadn't gone to her friend's house, we would never have learned that the center opened up that day, and we wouldn't have taken my father in for his treatment. I don't think my dad would be here today.

WHEN IT HURTS THE MOST

I don't believe that any family in Puerto Rico was prepared for María because of the magnitude of the hurricane. It just wasn't what you could have pictured beforehand. You never thought that you were going to be without electricity or water or the other resources that you need to survive for so many months. We got our electricity back in January, four months after the storm. While we waited, I had to watch my family and everyone around us get desperate. I always wondered, *How many other people had sicknesses that required electricity in order to survive? How many weren't as lucky as we were?* I kept my job and was able to support my family. And, by the grace of God, my father is alive today.

That's when it hurts the most, realizing that the government is also handicapped, standing with their hands tied. We saw them trying to do things but not being able to do them, not having the equipment or the specific knowledge to make things happen. In the town where I live, for example, water ran out quickly after Hurricane María. To see our mayor have to spend so much money on generators for the pumps so that we could at least have water was heartbreaking. The town didn't have the money, so he had to beg. He humbled himself looking for money because no one would help with something as basic as drinking water. And then later they found all those bottles of water and warehouses of supplies.[10] It was devastating to know that the government had made us beg like that when there were supplies available. The aftermath of the hurricane was an experience no one should ever have to go through.

The devastation also helped the community come together, though. Neighbors were helping each other and that was something beautiful. I have a new neighbor who lives a little farther away, but he was the first to take out his chainsaw and help. Sometimes we must go through catastrophe to come together. We are human beings, not machines that are programmed to work and then go straight home. Yes, there were times when I was desperate and resentful—I saw the condition of my town and other towns that were even worse—and it brought me low, but I kept going. And we are still here.

When we talked with Luis in spring 2020, he told us that his family—including his children and his parents—were currently out of their two-family home and divided up among relatives because the house had been without running water for days. Both of his parents had recently been in the hospital and he was worried about their health and safety, especially as cases of COVID-19 were on the rise in Puerto Rico. There was no internet connectivity in the countryside where Luis was staying, so we talked across crackling phone lines, calling each other back again and again as the signal was repeatedly dropped.

A few days into the quarantine, my father got sick and then my mother. My father's blood pressure went up and he started vomiting

---

10. Almost 1.5 million cases of water were found at an abandoned airfield in Ceiba approximately one year after the hurricane. Likewise, a fully stocked warehouse of relief goods was found in Ponce over two years after the hurricane. For more on supply distribution issues, see "Aftermaths" in the "Contexts" essay.

so hard that it lacerated his stomach and he threw up blood. We got to the hospital at 5 p.m. and got out at 1 a.m. I had to stay outside of the hospital and my dad was all by himself inside the emergency room. Then weeks passed and the doctor found that my mother's white blood cell count was much too high. She had to stay in the hospital for a week and a half. She took it really badly that no one could stay with her. And we just couldn't help thinking that being at a hospital during COVID increases the risks of getting infected. They're old—it's not the time for them to be in the hospital. It's been difficult on top of difficult. COVID is like María. It reminds you who you're making the sacrifices for.

MILIANA IVELISSE
MONTAÑEZ LEÓN

BORN IN: 1989
LIVES IN: Caguas
Customer Service Representative and Doula

Miliana Ivelisse Montañez León works full time in customer service at Walgreens, and is also a doula and a certified infant-feeding specialist. She lives in Caguas in a two-story house divided into two separate units, one on the top floor, one on the lower floor.[1] Miliana, her husband, and their two young children live on the top floor. Her mother, stepfather, and two younger siblings live on the ground floor.

---

1. Caguas is a municipality in the central mountain region with a population of almost 125,000.

When we speak with Miliana in her home in the fall of 2018, she tells us that during the hurricane, the wind was so powerful that the entire house was vibrating, the windows on the top floor broke, and water flooded in, forcing Miliana to flee with her husband and children to the lower floor. Miliana recalls the fear on her son's face as she took his hand and they started running, shouting "Open up!" to their family below. They waited out the rest of the hurricane downstairs. Miliana says, "María lasted for what felt like an eternity."

She also talks about how—just before the hurricane hit—she had told her husband, "This is going to change everyone's lives." What she could not know then was the devastating impact María would have on her own life and family. Two months after the hurricane, Miliana's mother died unexpectedly. And because of inefficiencies in the health care system and postmortem process, she still does not know why.

EVERYBODY CAME TO BUY WATER

After the hurricane, it was apocalyptic. Local supermarkets were closed; some had a lot of damage. Walmart, Costco, and Sam's Club also had damage. There was no food. Everybody was going to San Juan, where some stores were open.[2] But even in the capital, ATMs didn't work. Banks were closed. There was no cell service. You could spend twelve to sixteen hours in line for gasoline. One day we waited from 5 a.m. to 7 p.m. Sometimes, you'd stand in line for a whole day and end up with nothing. You lived and breathed chaos.

It usually takes me about an hour to drive to the Walgreens store where I work in San Juan, so I couldn't go to work for two weeks partly because I couldn't get gas. When I was finally able to return to work, I saw that the store had lost a large portion of its ceiling and had been flooded. Merchandise was lost, and we also lost our AC units. It was really hot and humid. Black mold started growing on

---

2. San Juan is approximately twenty miles away from Miliana's home in Caguas.

the walls. Because of those conditions many people got sick; the mold gave people symptoms that were similar to having a cold.

For some time after the hurricane, we were only selling canned stuff, paper towels, nuts, housewares—nothing fresh. Still, people came from all over. And not just for supplies. We had a generator, so mothers were coming to give their children respiratory therapy, and elderly people were storing their insulin here. We provided storage for medicine in an employee fridge. It's not something we usually do. In a way, we were doing the government's job.

Since there was no potable running water, everybody came to buy water. We'd receive water every three or four days. When the shipment arrived, the company set some aside so the employees could buy it, and then the rest was put out for sale. We rationed it, but even then it would only last one or two hours.

One day a family with three children came from Aguadilla. Post-María, that journey could take two hours or more.[3] They must have used at least a quarter tank of gas. When gasoline is being rationed, that's big. This family made the trip because they couldn't find water in Aguadilla and somebody had posted on Facebook that we had some.

We told the family that we were out of water and they burst into tears. I said, "Look, go to the back door, and I'll give you water." Then I gave them my two packs of water. It was very difficult to see people without water, especially the elderly. Someone would arrive completely sweaty and say, "I just need water because I haven't had any all day."

Because people didn't have water, they started to go to the creeks, rivers, and lakes. When my family used up the water we had stored, we were getting it from springs and rivers. But then we had a

---

3. Aguadilla is a town on the northwest coast. It is approximately eighty miles away from San Juan. It usually takes under two hours to drive from Aguadilla to San Juan, but after the hurricane many traffic lights were dysfunctional and roads were in disrepair, so driving times were often longer than usual.

leptospirosis outbreak on the island. Leptospirosis is a disease caused by bacteria in the urine of rats. It's carried by water. Humans in contact with rat urine can get symptoms of vomiting and diarrhea—like a strong flu or virus. It can end in organ failure and can be fatal if it isn't discovered in time.

Rats were going crazy after the hurricane. We could see them everywhere—on our patio, in our house, in the streets. So a lot of people here had leptospirosis. My family eventually received a water filter from an aid brigade, so then we had a way to have clean water. But the government confirmed, I think, forty cases of leptospirosis during the first month after the hurricane. Later, people in the health industry found the number of cases was way higher.[4]

MOM WENT TO THE HOSPITAL

While I was going to work, my mom, Ivette, had been helping out in the neighborhood. For years my mom had been a community leader. When I was young, her passion was scouting. She went with me to meetings when I was a Girl Scout, and she was a troop leader when my brother was a Boy Scout. She'd also been a social worker in Pueblo del Niño during the '80s and '90s.[5] It didn't matter who needed help, my mom was going to find a way.

---

4. In 2019, the Yale School of Medicine reported that fifty-seven cases of leptospirosis were confirmed as being a result of the hurricane. Doctors acknowledge that the number of deaths caused by leptospirosis are often underestimated because of misdiagnosis. From September 2017 to June 2018, septic shock was listed as the cause of death for 507 people. In these cases, leptospirosis cannot be ruled out as a cause of death without tests. See "A Deadly Bacteria Has Killed People in Puerto Rico, and Health Officials Didn't Detect It," Centro de Periodismo Investigativo, June 5, 2019, https://periodismoinvestigativo.com/2019/06/a-deadly-bacteria-has-killed-people-in-puerto-rico-and-health-officials-didnt-detect-it. For more on leptospirosis, see the glossary.

5. Pueblo del Niño is a transition home for minors in foster care, located between the municipalities of Río Grande and Canóvanas.

So after the hurricane, Mom started to have little meetings with the neighbors. We've lived here almost twenty years. The neighbors are like family. So we all started cooking together, and Mom even organized a Halloween street party for the kids.

But in November, two months after María, my mom got sick. She had fibromyalgia and circulation problems in her legs that forced her to use a walker and wear compression socks, but she didn't have a life-threatening condition. Mom went to the hospital because she'd been vomiting and had diarrhea. Her symptoms were intense; she even had anal bleeding. Despite this, the hospital staff sent her home, saying it was a virus.

I wasn't at home when she called me after she was discharged. Even on the phone I could hear that she was still very ill. I asked, "How can you be discharged if you're so sick?" She admitted that she didn't feel well, but just said, "Oh well." She asked me to pick up a small can of mixed fruits for her. I bought the canned fruit at the supermarket and went home. We had a little chat, but since she was feeling ill, I let her rest and went up to the second floor to take care of the kids and to sleep.

My stepfather, Marcos, called in the morning. Marcos has been with us since I was four years old; he's like a father to me. I call him "Dad." He said, "Come down. Mom is not okay." I ran downstairs and went to a door we have on the patio, but it was locked. I moved to the other door on the patio, which was also locked, but from there I could see what was happening in Mom's bedroom. Even now, I still have this image. I see my dad at the side of the bed and I can see my mom's arms hugging him. My dad looked at me and signaled for me to go around the house to the other door. And that's when I knew. If he can't leave Mom for two minutes to open the door, this is serious. I ran to the front of the house, yelling to my husband, "Luis, *baja*. Come down!"

I got in the house and went to my mom's room. My dad was holding my mom because she couldn't breathe. She looked at me with terrified eyes. She was saying, "I can't breathe. Help me. *Ayú-dame.*" My dad was on the phone and said, "911 isn't working. The call isn't connecting." Over two months after María, telecommunications were still poor. I stayed with my mom while my dad went out to the street to try to get a signal.

I held my mom and kissed her forehead. My husband came down, and we were telling her, "Please breathe." She said, "I can't breathe. I can't breathe." She was gasping for air. I started to tell her that I was sorry and that I loved her. Suddenly, she said, "I'm seeing little stars." I told her, "Just breathe. Please." She took a deep breath, and then she was gone. She had her last breaths in my arms.

Dad came back and we started CPR. I remember screaming, "Help! Someone help!" A neighbor heard me and came. Another neighbor came. Everyone was yelling and trying to call for help. But none of the phones were connecting to 911. It was the most chaotic twenty minutes—so frustrating. A person is dying in front of you, and you can't do something as basic as connect to the emergency number.

An ambulance did come. I can't remember exactly when, but it wasn't fast because the streets were crowded and the traffic lights still weren't working. When the paramedics arrived, I remember I was crying in the living room because I knew it was too late—my mom was already dead.

MANY CORPSES DIDN'T RECEIVE AUTOPSIES

Instituto de Ciencias Forenses de Puerto Rico (ICF, known as the Institute of Forensic Sciences in English) is located in San Juan and is Puerto Rico's sole medical examiner's office. Even before María, the ICF had operational problems and backlogged cases, due in part to chronic understaffing. ICF's restrictive budget is a hindrance to the hiring of more pathologists. Adequate staffing is also difficult because qualified pathologists often leave the island for better pay. In addition, in 2017, the

ICF and other departments were consolidated into a new Department of Public Security of Puerto Rico, which resulted in a lack of fiscal and operational autonomy for the ICF that reduced the institute's efficiency. The problem of backlogged cases was exacerbated after María. In July 2018, in response to complaints, legislators investigated the ICF and reported that 335 bodies were being stored at the institute, some dating back to 2012.[6]

Normally, when people pass away there's a protocol. An autopsy can be done when it's not clear why a person died. So the day after my mother died, my dad, brother, sister, and I went to the Forensic Sciences office.

It was a pure nightmare. Less than twenty-four hours after my mom had died in my arms, we had to fight the system for an autopsy. You're broken inside, completely shattered, and people are receiving you like it's another day at the office.

We first had to talk to security. "Why are you here?" the officer said—with attitude. My dad started to explain, and his voice broke. He is one of the strongest people I know, and seeing him break just by talking about what happened—well, everybody started crying.

The officer sent us to this little office. There, they told us, "Wait here." The office was ten by twenty feet. And full. All the chairs were taken. There were around fifteen people, all trying to make arrangements for their family members who'd died. As we waited, we spoke with people who were sitting near us. One woman was there for the sixth time that week to ask for the body of her son. He'd died of a headshot wound. They knew the cause of death and even who'd killed him, but they wouldn't give her the body. She'd been waiting a month. One family was waiting for the personal things

---

6. See Melanie Ortiz, "The Forensics of Death in Puerto Rico," *Metric*, July 13, 2018, https://themetric.org/articles/the-forensics-of-death-in-puerto-rico, and Danica Coto, "Puerto Rico Probes Forensic Institute as Bodies Pile Up," Associated Press, July 20, 2018, https://apnews.com/b5578b971a134ec5a13271216911b41d.

of their family member who had died three weeks before. Another person was waiting for an autopsy on someone who had died two months before.

We waited a long time and kept repeating our story to various people in different offices until somebody had the honesty to tell us that Forensic Sciences didn't have any obligation to do an autopsy. In my mother's case they decided not to, even though they knew she'd been in the hospital the night before. Many corpses didn't receive autopsies because Forensic Sciences didn't have enough personnel to handle all the cases after María. They were only doing autopsies for cases of suspected murder or if the court ordered it.

I knew an autopsy wasn't going to bring my mom back, but to understand what had happened would help with closure. So then we wanted to request a private autopsy. Someone finally told my dad, "You have to go to this other place." So we drove there, and they said, "You have to go to this other office." At the last office, my dad said, "Are you the person who's finally going to explain to me the process? Because I don't want to repeat myself again." The hardest part of it all was explaining what had happened over and over again. Finally, they said, "If you want a private autopsy, you should call these people." And they gave a list of numbers that covered both sides of four pages.

We started calling. The list was outdated. Some offices had been closed forever. Some people weren't on the island. When we finally got advice about the process, we learned that it might take months, which meant my mom's body would be in a fridge all that time. And after so many months, it would probably be an unclear report that wouldn't give us closure anyway. So, in the end, it wasn't even worth it.

My mom was fifty-four years old when she died. No known preexisting conditions could have caused her death. According to the hospital she only had a virus. The death certificate says my mom died of natural causes. We think that she may have had leptospirosis, or maybe a massive heart attack, but since an autopsy wasn't done, we won't ever know.

PEOPLE PAID WITH THEIR LIVES

For months after the hurricane the government's official count of deaths caused by María was sixty-four. In August 2018, the official death toll was revised to 2,975 people, making María among the deadliest hurricanes in US history.[7]

Our case wasn't isolated. Even months after María, autopsies weren't done. Before the hurricane I was aware of the problems Puerto Rico faced, but we're not talking about what we normally think of as a poor county. We're talking about a US colony in 2018. I say "colony," because colonies exist to be exploited. And we've seen that since the years of *las guácaras*, the times of old. Just one example was the unethical testing of birth control pills on Puerto Rican women.[8] The government isn't there for us; it's there for its own interests.

After the hurricane, both the federal and local governments did a horrible job, especially in their response to health issues. Medical services weren't working. People paid with their lives. The navy did bring in a hospital ship, but it was difficult to access. Doctors left the island. Medical offices were closed or destroyed. Many hospitals were flooded, or had shattered windows or damage to their infrastructure. There are photos of doctors doing surgery with cell-phone

---

7. Research shows that even the revised number for the death toll may be greatly underestimated. For more on the death toll, see "Aftermaths" in the "Contexts" essay.

8. In the 1950s, biologists from the US mainland who were developing the birth control pill conducted clinical trials in Puerto Rico. Women given the drug were not informed of the potential side effects or even that the drug was experimental. These clinical trials were done in tandem with a government-endorsed sterilization program that left approximately one third of the female population sterilized, the highest rate in the world. For more on these trials, see "Sterilization and Birth Control" in the "Contexts" essay.

lights.[9] It's like asking someone to fish with their hands! People had to make do, they had to *hacer de tripas corazones*, as we say.[10]

For us, the chaos started with problems in the health system, when my mom was released from the hospital even though she was still obviously sick.[11] Everything after was just painful. María completely changed my life. Nobody should have to experience what we did. It's been a roller coaster. Especially the grieving. I'm still coping with it every day. When my mom died, everything was so chaotic. The neighbors were there, trying to help. It was such an intense way to die, but maybe if she had died in a hospital by herself, it would've been worse. At least when she died here, she was surrounded by people who loved her.

---

9. The US Navy ship *Comfort* arrived in San Juan on October 3, 2017. During the fifty-three days it stayed in San Juan, many of its 250 hospital beds remained empty. Local doctors reported that the bureaucratic process to admit patients to the ship was unclear. Meanwhile, many local hospitals lacked power and working generators, forcing doctors to examine patients by flashlights or cell phone lights. Photos of surgeons operating by the light of cell phones were also circulated on Twitter and posted by the media.

10. The Puerto Rican expression *hacer de tripas corazones* translates literally to "turn guts into hearts."

11. Even before the hurricane, Puerto Rico's health care system had been struggling for a variety of reasons, including the economic instability of the archipelago, the migration of health care professionals, obstacles facing block grant–funded programs like Medicaid, and austerity measures. For more on the debt crisis, block grants, and austerity measures, see "Economic Contexts" in the "Contexts" essay.

TEN THINGS YOU CAN DO

1. Hurricane María is one of several cataclysmic weather events of the past few years that are part of our current climate emergency. You can act against climate change by participating in a climate strike, voting for candidates who will protect the environment, and participating in community-level projects that help protect waterways, combat industrial pollution, employ alternative energy, and so on.

2. In the autumn of 2020, watchdog reports were published decrying the FEMA response to Hurricane María, stating that—among other things—it took an average of more than two months for food and water to reach Puerto Rico and that FEMA lost track of close to 40 percent of the relief goods. As catastrophic climatological events become more commonplace, FEMA must change its operating procedures to accommodate all areas of the US. FEMA is overseen by the US Department of Homeland Security (DHS) and you can contact the online DHS Idea Community to share your thoughts on improving disaster readiness and providing unbiased relief efforts for all.

3. Even though the people of Puerto Rico have been US citizens for over a hundred years, it is a second-class citizenship, and the people therefore exist in a colonial state in which they have neither autonomy over relevant financial and political decisions nor voting representation in Congress. Call or

write to your congressperson to demand self-determination for Puerto Rico.

4. The Financial Oversight and Management Board (FOMB) created under the PROMESA law is implementing unjust austerity measures that are creating a humanitarian crisis in Puerto Rico. The US House Committee on Natural Resources oversees the FOMB and all issues pertaining to Puerto Rico. Contact the committee through its webpage to call for an end to these detrimental austerity measures.

5. The austerity measures enacted by the FOMB have been so severe that there are widespread shortages of food, medicine, sanitary supplies, and baby care items. Organize a fund drive or collect goods to donate to families in need. The Family Church of Rincón from Pastor Jose's narrative is still caring for families on the west coast; Come Colegial at the University of Puerto Rico at Mayagüez is feeding the Mayagüez community; and the Puerto Rican Network of Mutual Aid Centers (Centros de Apoyo Mutuo) is helping communities throughout the archipelago. You can find these organizations and others online through their websites and Facebook pages.

6. There are numerous opportunities to help out through volunteering. The Comisión Voluntariado y Servicio Comunitario de Puerto Rico website maintains a list of opportunities in the archipelago. Sandra Farms—from Israel and Sandra's narrative—accepts volunteers. Larger organizations such as the Hispanic Federation, Fundación de Surfrider, Habitat for Humanity, and World Central Kitchen are also looking for help in Puerto Rico and in your neighborhood.

7. Puerto Rico has a unique ecosystem and is rich in culture and history. In accordance with any posted guidelines or restrictions, plan a visit to see what makes it such a special place. Find out about socially responsible tourism from the

Old San Juan Heritage Foundation, discussed in Lorel's narrative.

8. The public university system of Puerto Rico has eleven campuses. If you're a student, you can attend as part of a semester-long exchange, take summer courses, or participate in an alternate spring break program.

9. If you don't already know Spanish, take a course at school, online, or at a community center. Practice your new Spanish skills by starting a pen pal program with a school in Puerto Rico. There are several established pen pal programs that you can find online.

10. Many schools, libraries, and community centers are looking for people to tutor others in English, both in conversational English and the language skills needed to fill out important forms. You can help some of the people who have been displaced from their homes by disasters through tutoring. All you need to start is fluency in English and a commitment to helping others.

HISTORICAL TIMELINE
OF PUERTO RICO

This timeline focuses on events of economic and sociopolitical significance in the twentieth and twenty-first centuries. However, it also provides a glimpse into the very early history of the archipelago, since this history is present in the stories of our narrators as they contemplate their relationships to their homeland. The timeline draws largely upon *Surviving Spanish Conquest: Indian Fight, Flight, and Cultural Transformation in Hispaniola and Puerto Rico*, by Karen F. Anderson-Córdova; "Puerto Rico's History," by the editors of the site welcome.topuertorico.org; *Fantasy Island: Colonialism, Exploitation, and the Betrayal of Puerto Rico*, by Ed Morales; and "Puerto Rico in Crisis Timeline," by the Center for Puerto Rican Studies. When material is drawn from other sources or specific quotes are included, they are cited in the footnotes.

4000 BCE: Humans first arrive in the archipelago that is now known as Puerto Rico.

400 to 300 BCE: Arawak-speaking Taíno peoples travel by canoe from the Orinoco Delta of Venezuela to the Caribbean islands.

400 BCE–1492 CE: The Taínos establish agrarian communities throughout the Caribbean with large ceremonial sites in Puerto Rico.

1493: On his second voyage, Christopher Columbus lands on the west coast of Puerto Rico, claiming it for Spain.

c. 1500: King Ferdinand of Spain writes a letter to the Taíno peoples, claiming ownership of their lands and sovereignty over them.[1]

1508: Juan Ponce de León arrives in Puerto Rico to search for gold and establishes the first European settlement on the island, Caparra.

1509: Ponce de León is named governor of Puerto Rico and enforces the royally decreed *encomienda*, which enslaves Indigenous peoples and gives their land to Spanish subjects.

1511: The Taínos organized several rebellions to overthrow the Spanish colonizers; however, none was successful. The most notable of these uprisings, commonly known as the Spanish-Taíno War of Boríkén or the Taíno Rebellion, was led by Agüeybaná II and ended with Ponce de León executing some six thousand Indigenous people.

1517: The Spanish monarchy declares that landowners may purchase twelve enslaved Africans each.

1539: Construction begins on Castillo San Felipe del Morro, a six-level stone fortress that deters attackers and situates Puerto Rico as an essential strategic stronghold.

1779: Puerto Ricans fight on the settlers' side in the Revolutionary War under the command of Bernardo de Galvez, governor of Louisiana and general of the Spanish colonial army.[2]

---

1. "King Ferdinand's Letter to the Taíno-Arawak Indians," American History, www.let.rug.nl/usa/documents/before-1600/king-ferdinands-letter-to-the-taino-arawak-indians.php.

2. Shannon Collins, "Puerto Ricans Represented throughout U.S. Military History," US Department of Defense, October 14, 2016, www.defense.gov/Explore/News/

1821: Throughout the 1800s, there are numerous attempts by enslaved peoples and abolitionists to end human bondage in Puerto Rico. One of the most famous of these revolts is led by Marcos Xiorro in 1821. Although it is unsuccessful, Xiorro will become a hero whose legend spurs further rebellion and the eventual end to slavery in Puerto Rico. His story is prominent in Puerto Rican folklore.

1868: Hundreds of people rise up against Spanish colonial rule in El Grito de Lares.[3]

1873: Spain abolishes slavery in Puerto Rico with the caveat that enslaved peoples must raise the funds to purchase their freedom.[4]

1895: Cubans rise up against Spanish colonial rule and the US declares that it will take action if the fighting is not contained.

1897: Spain grants Puerto Rico a greater degree of autonomy by signing the "Autonomic Charters for Cuba and Puerto Rico."

1898: On February 9, the "Autonomic Charter" is enacted in Puerto Rico and six days later, the USS *Maine*, anchored off the coast of Cuba, is sunk by Spanish forces. The Spanish-American War breaks out.
- In July, US troops land in Guánica and Ponce.
- The Treaty of Paris is signed in December, ending the war. Spain cedes Cuba, Puerto Rico, Guam, and the Philippines to US control.

Article/Article/974518/puerto-ricans-represented-throughout-us-military-history.

3. Marisabel Brás, "The Changing of the Guard: Puerto Rico in 1898 – The World of 1898: The Spanish-American War," Library of Congress, Hispanic Division, www.loc.gov/rr/hispanic/1898/bras.html.

4. "Chronology of Puerto Rico in the Spanish-American War – The World of 1898: The Spanish-American War," Library of Congress, Hispanic Division, www.loc.gov/rr/hispanic/1898/chronpr.html.

1899: The 65th Infantry, better known as the Borinqueneers, is formed and later incorporated as a unit in the US Army that served in World War I, World War II, and the Korean War.[5]

1900: The Foraker Act is passed in the US, declaring Puerto Rico an unincorporated territory that is allowed one nonvoting representative to Congress.

1901: The US Supreme Court case *Downes v. Bidwell* decides that the US Constitution does not apply to unincorporated territories as they are determined to belong to, but not be a part of, the US.

1903: The University of Puerto Rico is founded.

1904: The US Supreme Court case *Gonzales v. Williams* (*sic*) declares that Puerto Ricans fall "somewhere between citizen and alien" and are therefore US "nationals."[6] This case paves the way for citizenship for Puerto Ricans.[7]

1909: The Olmsted Amendment to the Foraker Act is passed in the US, undermining Puerto Rican autonomy by placing control of economic and legal affairs under the jurisdiction of an external governing board.[8]

---

5. "The Borinqueneers: The Forgotten Heroes of a Forgotten War," CENTRO: Center for Puerto Rican Studies at Hunter, n.d., https://centropr.hunter.cuny.edu/centrovoices/chronicles/borinqueneers-forgotten-heroes-forgotten-war.

6. Sam Erman, *Almost Citizens: Puerto Rico, the U.S. Constitution, and Empire* (Cambridge: Cambridge University Press, 2019), 87.

7. "Gonzales v. Williams, 192 U.S. 1 (1904)," JUSTIA U.S. Supreme Court, https://supreme.justia.com/cases/federal/us/192/1/.

8. "Olmsted Amendment – The World of 1898: The Spanish-American War," Library of Congress, Hispanic Division, "Puerto Rico in Crisis Timeline."

1911: The Mayagüez campus of the University of Puerto Rico is founded, the only land grant institution in Puerto Rico.

1917: In March, President Woodrow Wilson signs the Jones-Shafroth Act, which extends US citizenship to Puerto Ricans while placing significant limits on self-governance and economic freedom.

- In April, the US enters World War I and 236,000 Puerto Ricans sign up for selective service and another 104,550 register for the draft.[9]

1920: The Merchant Marine Act—more commonly known as the Jones Act—is signed into law forcing all goods imported to Puerto Rico by sea to use US-owned and -operated vessels.[10]

1933–35: Two Great Depression–era programs, the Puerto Rico Emergency Relief Administration and Puerto Rico Reconstruction Administration, are created to provide relief and develop infrastructure.

1935: The Puerto Rican Nationalist Party becomes increasingly outspoken in favor of independence. The Puerto Rican government responds with force, killing four members of the Nationalist movement in the Río Piedras Massacre.[11]

---

9. Dr. Harry Franqui-Rivera and Monique Aviles, "World War I," CENTRO: Center for Puerto Rican Studies at Hunter, https://centropr.hunter.cuny.edu/digital-humanities/pr-military/world-war-i.

10. The Jones-Shafroth Act was introduced by Representative William Atkinson Jones of Virginia and the Merchant Marine Act was introduced by Senator Wesley Jones of Washington.

11. José Javier Colón Morera, *Puerto Rico under Colonial Rule: Political Persecution and the Quest for Human Rights* (Albany: SUNY Press, 2006), 71.

1937: Government attacks on the Nationalist movement continue, and nineteen people are killed and two hundred wounded by police at a Nationalist Party parade in Ponce.[12]

- The government of Puerto Rico passes a law allowing sterilization without consent. Beginning in the 1930s, over the next forty years about one-third of Puerto Rico's female population will be sterilized.[13]

1941: The US Navy establishes bases on Vieques where it conducts military training involving testing missiles and other live munitions.[14]

1947: The Industrial Incentive Act, better known as Operation Bootstrap, is passed in the Puerto Rican legislature. Intended to move the economy from the wealth disparity of plantation culture to industrialization, it highly incentivizes investment from the US.

1948: The US allows Puerto Rico to elect its own governor. Luis Muñoz Marín is elected and holds the office from 1949 to 1965.

1950: Public Law 600, drafted by the Puerto Rican Congress, is signed by President Harry S. Truman on July 4, allowing Puerto Rico to create its own constitution. However, the US Congress still retains ultimate control over the government.

---

12. Colón Morera, *Puerto Rico under Colonial Rule*, 72.

13. Katherine Andrews, "The Dark History of Forced Sterilization of Latina Women," Panoramas, www.panoramas.pitt.edu/health-and-society/dark-history-forced-sterilization-latina-women.

14. "Vieques, Puerto Rico Naval Training Range: Background and Issues for Congress," Naval History and Heritage Command, www.history.navy.mil/research/library/online-reading-room/title-list-alphabetically/v/vieques-puerto-rico-naval-training-range.html.

- On October 30, Nationalists attempt to assassinate Puerto Rican governor Muñoz Marín, and two days later they attempt to assassinate President Truman.

1950–60: Roughly 470,000 Puerto Ricans move to the continental US in what is known as the Great Migration.[15]

1952: A public referendum is held to validate a new constitution that establishes the Estado Libre Asociado or Commonwealth of Puerto Rico.

1954: Puerto Rican Nationalists attack the US House of Representatives in Washington, DC.

1956: Hurricane Betsy, known as Santa Clara in Puerto Rico, makes landfall, killing sixteen people and leaving over fifteen thousand homeless.

1967: The first plebiscite vote is held. This nonbinding referendum on the status of Puerto Rico determines that most Puerto Ricans are in favor of maintaining commonwealth status, as opposed to seeking US statehood or independence.

1976: Section 936 of the Internal Revenue Code is created by the US Congress, allowing US corporations to receive federal tax cuts on income generated in Puerto Rico.

1976: Filiberto Ojeda Ríos and others found the Ejército Popular Boricua (Boricua People's Army), also known as Los Macheteros or the Machete Wielders. The pro-independence group engages in

---

15. "Puerto Rican Emigration: Why the 1950s?" Lehman College, http://lcw.lehman.edu/lehman/depts/latinampuertorican/latinoweb/PuertoRico/1950s.htm.

civil disobedience and armed interruptive actions to fight against US colonialism.

1984: Revisions to the US tax code block Puerto Rico and Washington, DC, from declaring bankruptcy under Chapter 9.

1989: Hurricane Hugo makes landfall, causing billions of dollars' worth of damage and leaving thousands homeless.

1996: President Bill Clinton signs the Small Business Job Protection Act into law, which phases out Section 936 of the tax code, a provision that offered incentives to US corporations operating in Puerto Rico.[16]

1998: Hurricane Georges makes landfall, causing billions of dollars' worth of damage and leaving almost the entire island without electricity.

1999–2003: In 1999, during training exercises on Vieques, a bomb dropped in the wrong place causes the death of a civilian and sparks the Vieques Navy protests. This long-term, well-coordinated pressure campaign successfully forces the US government to end munitions testing on the island in 2003, pull out all troops, and turn over these grounds to the Department of the Interior.

2005: The FBI kills Filiberto Ojeda Ríos, leader of Los Macheteros.

2006: Puerto Rican Law 291 is passed, creating the Puerto Rico Urgent Interest Fund Corporation, or the Corporación del Fondo de Interés Apremiante (COFINA), which sells government bonds that allow debt to grow.

---

16. Sean Holton, "Puerto Rico Loses Business Tax Break," *Orlando Sentinel*, August 3, 1996, http://articles.orlandosentinel.com/1996-08-03/news/9608021051 _1_puerto-rico-ricans-section-936.

2006–16: More than 525,000 Puerto Ricans move to the continental US. By 2016, there are approximately 5.5 million Puerto Ricans in the US, compared with 3.4 million people in the archipelago.[17]

2009: Led by Governor Luis Fortuño, the Puerto Rican legislature passes Ley Siete, or Public Law 7, declaring a state of fiscal emergency.

2014: Puerto Rico reports a debt of $72 billion.

2015: In June, Governor Alejandro García Padilla announces that the commonwealth's debt is "not payable," and in August, the Puerto Rican government defaults on its monthly debt payment for the first time.

2016: In June, President Barack Obama signs the Puerto Rico Oversight, Management, and Economic Stability Act (PROMESA) into law, which facilitates the restructuring of the commonwealth's debt and establishes the Financial Oversight and Management Board (FOMB), a body with final say on all economic decisions.

2017: In May, Puerto Rico files for bankruptcy.
- On September 6, Hurricane Irma makes landfall, decimating the island municipalities of Vieques and Culebra, causing billions of dollars' worth of damage, leaving a million people without power, and killing three.
- On September 20, Hurricane María makes landfall, causing $90 billion in damage and the largest blackout in US

17. Marie T. Mora, Alberto Dávila, and Havidán Rodríguez, "Migration, Geographic Destinations, and Socioeconomic Outcomes of Puerto Ricans during La Crisis Boricua: Implications for Island and Stateside Communities Post-Maria," ProQuest, https://search.proquest.com/docview/2196367364?pqorigsite =gscholar&fromopenview=true.

history, leaving tens of thousands homeless, and killing thousands.

2019: In August, Governor Ricardo Rosselló resigns as a result of massive protests known as the Ricky Renuncia movement.
- In December, the archipelago is struck by the first of an ongoing swarm of earthquakes.

2020: On March 15, COVID-19 forces Puerto Rico into lockdown. All businesses are closed except for those providing essential services. Regulations are modified in later months, but remain restrictive, causing job loss and closure of businesses.
- In July, Tropical Storm Isaías makes landfall, causing millions of dollars' worth of damage, flash flooding, and widespread power outages.

2021: Under the leadership of the New Progressive Party (NPP) and Governor Pedro Pierluisi, Puerto Rico holds elections for a special delegation to the United States to advocate for statehood. Only 4.5 percent of eligible voters participate in this election, with disgraced former governor Ricardo Rosselló winning a spot through a write-in campaign. The cost of the special election is almost nine million dollars, an expenditure highly criticized as being wasteful during an ongoing budgetary crisis and new financial needs brought on by the COVID-19 pandemic. These actions push many toward activism in and outside of Puerto Rico in favor of self-determination.

THE CONTEXTS OF DISASTER

In July 2020, multiple news sources reported that directly after Hurricane María, President Trump explored the possibility of selling Puerto Rico. According to Elaine Duke, the acting secretary of the Department of Homeland Security at that time, the president asked if it was possible for the US to sell or "divest of that asset." Other reports reveal that in 2018 the president also floated the idea of trying to trade Puerto Rico to Denmark in exchange for Greenland because, in his words, Puerto Rico is "dirty" and "poor." While it is particularly onerous to picture the president attempting to barter away a place in which 3.4 million US citizens live—especially while they were experiencing unimaginable loss and destruction—it is not wholly surprising.

Puerto Rico is a twice-colonized place. In 1493, Christopher Columbus landed on its western shores on his second voyage and claimed all he saw for the monarchy of Spain. It remained under Spanish control until the United States took possession of the archipelago in 1898 at the conclusion of the Spanish-American War, transferring control from one global power to another. Fully understanding the failed government-led relief efforts in the aftermaths of Hurricane María, then, depends upon contextualizing this disaster within the ongoing trajectory of colonization, marginalization, and ingrained, systemic inequality that has stretched across hundreds of years since first contact between European colonizers and Indigenous peoples. Puerto Rico has consistently been treated as a possession that grants its overseers numerous benefits while they habitually shortchange its people. President Trump's attempt to leverage Puerto Rico for profit is but one link in a continuous chain of events leading up to Hurricane María and its long aftermaths. While by no means exhaustive, this essay is intended to provide an overview of some of the issues and events pertinent to understanding the contours of the narratives included in this volume.

I. Contact, Genocide, and Enslavement

SPANISH COLONIZATION

The Taíno—Arawak-speaking peoples who arrived in the Caribbean by canoe from the Orinoco Delta of Venezuela around 400 BCE—established permanent settlements on the islands that we now know as Puerto Rico, Hispanióla (which is divided into the present-day nations of Haiti and the Dominican Republic), Cuba, Jamaica, the Virgin Islands, and the Bahamas. The Taíno referred to Puerto Rico as Borikén, or Land of Great Lords.

When Columbus landed in the Caribbean on his first voyage in 1492, he was greeted by the Taíno. In his journal, he recounts how he "took possession of" their land for Spain and ultimately kidnapped seven men "to bring home." One year later, Columbus returned, landing on Puerto Rico's western shore and naming the island San Juan de Baptista.

In response to Columbus's observations from his voyages, King Ferdinand sent a "Letter to the Taino-Arawak Indians" (c. 1500), in which he refers to himself and his daughter, Juana, as "conquerors of barbarian nations," informing them that Pope Alexander VI and the Catholic Church awarded him mastery over them and their lands; in addition, they were to instantly convert to Christianity. Ferdinand concludes the letter with a series of threats: "Should you fail to comply [with this decree] . . . we shall enslave your persons . . . sell you . . . seize your possessions and harm you as much as we can."[1]

These decrees were enforced by Juan Ponce de León, who accompanied Columbus on his second voyage and returned to Puerto Rico in 1508 to search for gold.[2] Ponce de León was welcomed by Taíno chief Agüeybaná, but Ponce de León betrayed Agüeybaná when he implemented the royal decree of subjugation that enslaved the Indigenous peoples and gave their lands to wealthy Spaniards. Within fifty years most Taínos were thought dead from enslavement or the pestilence of diseases brought to the islands by conquistadors. Recent genetic studies conducted at the University of Puerto Rico at Mayagüez, however, have revealed that, despite the genocidal tactics of the Spanish colonizers, Taíno DNA is present in many contemporary Puerto Ricans. Some Indigenous peoples likely survived by escaping to the mountainous interior of the island where they were able to hide in the dense jungle, while others were forced into sexual relationships or intermarried with the Spanish.[3]

TRANSATLANTIC SLAVE TRADE

Many members of the elite class of Spaniards who were awarded lands by the crown converted them into sugar plantations. Economic

---

1. "King Ferdinand's Letter to the Taíno-Arawak Indians," American History, www.let.rug.nl/usa/documents/before-1600/king-ferdinands-letter-to-the-taino-arawak-indians.php.

2. Colin Schultz, "Setting Sail: The 50th Anniversary of Juan Ponce de Leon's Discovery of Florida," *Smithsonian Magazine*, March 27, 2013, www.smithsonianmag.com/smart-news/setting-sail-the-500th-anniversary-of-juan-ponce-de-leons-discovery-of-florida-10197205/.

3. Biology professor Juan C. Martínez Cruzado conducted a genetic study of the people of Puerto Rico, revealing that 61.1 percent of those tested had mitochondrial DNA of Indigenous origin. Robert M. Poole, "What Became of the Taíno?" *Smithsonian Magazine*, October 2011, www.smithsonianmag.com/travel/what-became-of-the-taino-73824867/.

success of colonial plantations depended upon the labor of enslaved peoples and, as the Taíno population was decimated, plantation owners relied upon the Transatlantic slave trade to produce forced labor. In 1517 the monarchy declared that landowners could purchase twelve enslaved Africans.[4] The first mill to refine sugarcane was established in 1523, and by the mid-nineteenth century there were 789 registered sugar plantations in Puerto Rico, all of which relied upon the work of enslaved West Africans—predominantly Yoruba and Igbo—and their descendants until slavery was abolished in 1873.[5] A caveat was added to this law, though, that enslaved peoples had to accumulate the wealth necessary to purchase their own freedom.

EL GRITO DE LARES

In 1868, Ramón Emeterio Betances and Segundo Ruiz Belvis incited a rebellion against Spanish colonial rule known as El Grito de Lares (the Cry of Lares). Hundreds of people gathered in the town of Lares to declare Puerto Rico an independent nation. This movement was marked by its inclusivity, as participants were landowners, merchants, peasants, and enslaved individuals. The enslaved peoples who participated in the insurrection were immediately proclaimed free citizens by the movement's leaders. The Spanish suppressed the revolt and sentenced its participants to death, although the sentences were later commuted.[6] It was not until February 9, 1898, when the "Autonomic Charters for Cuba and Puerto Rico" were implemented, that Spain granted Puerto Rico further rights of representation in

---

4. "World Directory of Minorities and Indigenous Peoples - Puerto Rico," RefWorld, UNHCR: The UN Refugee Agency, www.refworld.org/docid/4954ce5923.html.

5. "Puerto Rico Sugar Mills," Caribbean Trading, https://caribbeantrading.com /puerto-rico-history-sugar-mills/.

6. "The Grito de Lares," Library of Congress Digital Collections, www.loc.gov/collections/puerto-rico-books-and-pamphlets/articles-and-essays/nineteenth-century -puerto-rico/rebellion-of-1868/.

Parliament and control over taxation, providing a local budget not dependent on the whim of the monarchy.

II. US Annexation and Resistance

THE SPANISH-AMERICAN WAR

As early as 1823, the US explored purchasing or annexing Caribbean islands as military and economic strongholds.[7] When Cuba rose up against Spanish colonial rule in 1895, the US—aware of both Cuba's strategic military location and its lucrative sugar industry—supported independence.[8] On February 15, 1898, six days after the Autonomic Charter was implemented in Puerto Rico, Spanish forces sunk the USS *Maine* off the shores of Cuba, and in April the US Congress responded with a resolution calling for war.[9] On July 3, a naval battle ensued in the Bay of Santiago de Cuba in which the Spanish fleet was destroyed.[10] Weeks later, US troops invaded Puerto Rico, and on August 12, a ceasefire was signed in which Puerto Rico was ceded to the United States.[11]

UNINCORPORATED TERRITORY STATUS

The Foraker Act of 1900 assigned Puerto Rico unincorporated territory status, which afforded Puerto Ricans some legal rights for

---

7. "Mahan's *The Influence of Sea Power upon History*: Securing International Markets in the 1890s," US Department of State: Office of the Historian, https://history.state.gov/milestones/1866-1898/mahan.

8. "Chronology of Puerto Rico in the Spanish-American War," Library of Congress, Hispanic Division, www.loc.gov/rr/hispanic/1898/chronpr.html.

9. "Chronology of Puerto Rico."

10. "Documentary Histories: Spanish-American War," Naval History and Heritage Command, www.history.navy.mil/research/publications/documentary-histories/united-states-navy-s/the-battle-of-santia.html.

11. "Chronology of Puerto Rico."

autonomous governance but only allotted a single representative to Congress—the resident commissioner—who does not have voting privileges.[12] This law ultimately maintained colonial status for Puerto Rico by simply transferring power from Spain to the United States. In 1901, the US Supreme Court case *Downes v. Bidwell* declared that the US Constitution does not apply to unincorporated territories as they belong to, but are not part of, the US.[13] However, a 1904 Supreme Court case brought by Puerto Rican activist Isabel González declared Puerto Ricans to be US nationals, thereby paving the way for citizenship.[14] Despite this nominal progress, the US fought to maintain colonial power over Puerto Rico, and in 1909 passed the Olmsted Amendment to the Foraker Act, which took even more governance away from the people by establishing an external governing body appointed by the president.

THE JONES-SHAFROTH ACT
AND THE MERCHANT MARINE ACT

US citizenship was finally extended to Puerto Ricans in 1917 when President Woodrow Wilson signed the Jones-Shafroth Act. Approximately one month after this act was signed into law, the US entered World War I and 236,000 Puerto Ricans—newly made US citizens—signed up for selective service and another 104,550 registered for the draft. Almost eighteen thousand Puerto Ricans served in combat in the war.[15]

---

12. "Foraker Act (Organic Act of 1900)," Library of Congress, Hispanic Division, www.loc.gov/rr/hispanic/1898/foraker.html.

13. "Downes v. Bidwell, 182 U.S. 244 (1901)," US Supreme Court, https://supreme.justia.com/cases/federal/us/182/244/.

14. "Gonzales v. Williams, 192 U.S. 1 (1904)," JUSTIA U.S. Supreme Court, https://supreme.justia.com/cases/federal/us/192/1/. Immigration officials misspelled González's name.

15. Dr. Harry Franqui-Rivera and Monique Aviles, "World War I," CENTRO: Center for Puerto Rican Studies at Hunter, https://centropr.hunter.cuny.edu/digital

The Jones-Shafroth Act, however, does not supersede the colonial practices installed by the Foraker Act and the Olmsted Amendment. Therefore, the citizenship in which Puerto Ricans participate does not include a voting representative in Congress, the right to vote for president, or access to many services and benefits that are extended to other citizens. In 1970, the resident commissioner won the right to vote in committees but still cannot vote in general assemblies on the floor of the House.[16] The Jones-Shafroth Act also institutes triple-tax exemptions for the sale of bonds by the government of Puerto Rico, meaning that purchasers are not charged US federal, state, or local taxes, thereby denying Puerto Rico significant tax revenue while promoting the development of externally owned businesses.[17]

The Merchant Marine Act of 1920—commonly referred to as the Jones Act— furthermore includes articles that limit economic stability in Puerto Rico, including stipulations that all goods shipped to the archipelago must arrive on US-made, -owned, and -operated vessels—even if cheaper options exist—thereby raising the price of almost all imports.[18] Today, the estimated impact of this requirement on the Puerto Rican economy is a $1.5 billion loss annually.[19]

-humanities/pr-military/world-war-i.

16. Welcome to Puerto Rico, "Puerto Rico's History."

17. Ed Morales, *Fantasy Island: Colonialism, Exploitation, and the Betrayal of Puerto Rico* (New York: PublicAffairs, 2019), 34–35.

18. The Jones-Shafroth Act was introduced by Representative William Atkinson Jones of Virginia and the Merchant Marine Act was introduced by Senator Wesley Jones of Washington.

19. "Studies Peg Cost of Jones Act on Puerto Rico at $1.5 Billion," Caribbean Business, https://caribbeanbusiness.comstudies-peg-cost-of-jones-act-on-puerto-rico-at-1-5 -billion/.

THE GREAT DEPRESSION

The economic prosperity of Puerto Rico's plantation class was maintained after World War I, promoting extreme wealth disparity. The Great Depression had devastating effects on Puerto Rico both because of its extreme dependence upon the US and the decline of the agricultural industry. The Roosevelt administration's New Deal programs were extended to Puerto Rico and in 1933 the Puerto Rico Emergency Relief Act was signed, followed by the establishment of the Puerto Rico Reconstruction Administration in 1935. These programs were meant to address poverty, unemployment, public health, and food insecurity as well as to create infrastructure projects that would provide employment. The underlying issues facing Puerto Rico, however, were much more deeply rooted in its colonial status and could not be resolved by these temporary programs.

REFORM AND THE NATIONALIST MOVEMENT

Many reformists, including Luis Muñoz Marín and Carlos E. Chardón, called for deeper change to larger systems of inequity that kept Puerto Rico chained to its status as an unincorporated territory.[20] Chardón designed a plan for national restructuring that called for the redistribution of land from plantations into the hands of the populace, among other incentives to equalize wealth distribution.[21] Their affiliation with the US-appointed governor, Theodore Roosevelt Jr., and their attempts to work within the US legal system, however, caused widespread concern. Pedro Albizu Campos, president of the Puerto Rican Nationalist Party, decried their approach as an effort to "Americanize" Puerto Rico and advocated instead for independence. The Puerto Rican government responded to the independence

---

20. At the time, Muñoz Marín was serving in the Puerto Rican government as a senator for the Liberal Party and Chardón was the rector of the University of Puerto Rico.

21. Manuel Rodríguez, "Representing Development: New Perspectives about the New Deal in Puerto Rico, 1933–36," *CENTRO: Journal of the Center for Puerto Rican Studies* 14, no. 2 (2002): 149–79.

movement with force, killing four members of the Nationalist movement in a shooting in 1935 that became known as the Río Piedras
Massacre. The violence against the Nationalist movement continued, most notably in a police attack on a peaceful parade in Ponce in
1937. Nineteen people were killed and more than two hundred were
wounded, many shot in the back while trying to flee.[22]

OPERATION BOOTSTRAP

Muñoz Marín continued working for reform with the development
of the Industrial Incentives Act of 1947, better known as Manos a la
Obra or Operation Bootstrap. The stated intent of the law was to enact economic reform through industrialization by moving away from
a plantation economy in which landowners reaped wealth while the
remainder of the population lived in poverty. The law and its 1948
amendment, however, incentivized external investment through tax
breaks and the promise of a low-cost labor force, and these and other
elements of the law had long-reaching effects on economic stability.
After the purported success of this program, the US allowed Puerto
Rico to elect its own governor in 1948, and Muñoz Marín won. He
held the office from 1949 to 1965.

PUBLIC ACT 600

Under Muñoz Marín's leadership, the Puerto Rican Congress wrote
Public Act 600, and President Harry S. Truman signed it into law
in 1950. This law allowed Puerto Rico to write its own constitution,
which ultimately led to the change in status in 1952 from "unincorporated territory" to "commonwealth," thus making it the Estado Libre
Asociado de Puerto Rico (Commonwealth of Puerto Rico). Despite
the US government maintaining ultimate control of the archipelago,
this revision in status allowed for the removal of Puerto Rico from the
United Nations list of Non-Self-Governing Territories—colonies—in

---

22. "March 21, 1937: Ponce Massacre," Zinn Education Project, www.zinnedproj-
ect.org/news/tdih/ponce-massacre/.

1953. This change freed the US from having to make regular reports to the UN Special Committee on Decolonization.[23]

In reaction to Public Act 600 being signed into law, five activists in the Puerto Rican Nationalist Party attempted to assassinate Muñoz Marín in his office in Old San Juan. Muñoz Marín hid under his desk until rescued by the Puerto Rican National Guard. Four of the five nationalists were killed in the uprising. On November 1, two other nationalists attempted to assassinate President Truman in Washington, DC. One of the two nationalists and a White House police officer died in the assault.[24] This attack was followed by another, this time on the US House of Representatives in 1954, carried out by Lolita Lebrón, Rafael Cancel Miranda, Irvin Flores, and Andrés Figueroa Cordero. While the Independentista movement is still alive in Puerto Rico, armed insurrections petered out as Muñoz Marín and the US federal government responded to nationalists with military force.

CORPORATE TAX CODE, SECTION 936

Section 936 of the Internal Revenue Service tax code was adopted in 1976 in order to address the economic recession of the 1970s. It offered US corporations federal tax breaks on income generated on the island, encouraging large companies to move funds to Puerto Rican banks and to establish subsidiaries in the archipelago.[25] World Bank data on economic growth indicates that large sectors of Puerto Rico

---

23. "The International Place of Puerto Rico," *Harvard Law Review* 130, no. 6 (April 2017), https://harvardlawreview.org/2017/04/the-international-place-of-puerto-rico/.

24. Welcome to Puerto Rico, "Puerto Rico's History."

25. Scott Greenberg, "Tax Policy Helped Create Puerto Rico's Financial Crisis," Tax Foundation, June 30, 2015, https://taxfoundation.org/tax-policy-helped -create-puerto-rico-s-fiscal-crisis/; and Edwin Melendez and Charles R. Venator-Santiago, "Introduction to Puerto Rico Post-Maria: Origins and Consequences of a Crisis," *CENTRO: Journal of the Center for Puerto Rican Studies* 30, no. 3 (2018): 7–8.

prospered while these measures were in place, although significant wealth disparity remained.[26]

In the same year, Filiberto Ojeda Ríos, Juan Enrique Segarra-Palmer, and Orlando González Claudio organized the Ejército Popular Boricua or the Boricua People's Army, also known as Los Macheteros or the Machete Wielders.[27] Ojeda Ríos was also an organizer of the Fuerzas Armadas de Liberación Nacional (FALN), the Armed Forces of National Liberation, which claimed responsibility for more than seventy bombings in the US between 1974 and 1983. Ojeda Ríos attested that US attempts "to destroy the national identity of the Puerto Rican people, its culture, traditions, and language, while exercising total control over the national economy, the ideological superstructure, the communication media, the educational institutions, and all of the agencies responsible for establishing the norms for the nation's life" were at the heart of his revolutionary activities.[28] In 2005, on the anniversary of El Grito de Lares, Ojeda Ríos was shot and killed by FBI agents. A report from the Puerto Rico Commission on Civil Rights condemned these actions.

Ojeda Ríos's compatriot in the FALN, Oscar López Rivera, was imprisoned in the US in 1981 for "seditious conspiracy" to overthrow the government in response to the bombings. In 1999, President Bill Clinton offered to commute the sentences of some of the FALN members in jail, but López Rivera refused because not all members were included. His sentence was commuted in 2017 by President Barack Obama.

---

26. David Dayen, "How Hedge Funds Are Pillaging Puerto Rico," *American Prospect*, http://prospect.org/article/how-hedge-funds-are-pillaging-puerto-rico.

27. Ojeda Ríos was also a founder in 1967 of the Movimiento Independentista Revolucionario Armado (MIRA), the Armed Revolutionary Independence Movement.

28. Filberto Ojeda Ríos, "The Boricua-Macheteros Popular Army: Origins, Program, and Struggle," trans. Alicia Del Campo, *Latin American Perspectives* 29, no. 6 (2002): 104–16.

MILITARY BASES

After Puerto Rico's annexation from Spain, the US government continued to use it as a strategic military location and began buying up land for bases in the 1920s. In anticipation of entering World War II, Puerto Rico was situated as the primary line of defense against foreign attack and invasion and several army, navy, and air force bases were rapidly built.[29]

In the early twentieth century, the US Navy also took possession of large portions of Culebra and Vieques, island municipalities off the east coast of the main island, claiming that these were essential positions in its defense strategy. These locations, however, were instead used as missile test sites. In 1969, for example, Culebra sustained 228 days of direct missile bombings and 100 days of military exercises in which other types of live ammunition were used.[30] Large-scale peaceful protests organized by several groups—including the Nationalist Party and the Quaker Action Group—succeeded in expelling the navy from Culebra, but military operations on Vieques were heightened as a result. Grassroots efforts begun in 1999 were largely responsible for the cessation of weapons testing in 2003. Using these municipalities as military firing ranges has created lasting environmental damage, economic hardship, and health concerns for residents that are demonstrated by the significantly higher-than-average cancer rates.[31]

---

29. Dr. Harry Franqui-Rivera and Monique Aviles, "The Puerto Rican Experience in the U.S. Military: A Century of Unheralded Service," CENTRO: Center for Puerto Rican Studies at Hunter, https://centropr.hunter.cuny.edu/digital-humanities/pr-military/fortress-puerto-rico-and-hemespheric-defense.

30. "Puerto Ricans Expel United States Navy from Culebra Island, 1970–1974," Global Nonviolent Action Database, https://nvdatabase.swarthmore.edu/content/puerto-ricans-expel-united-states-navy-culebra-island-1970-1974.

31. Valeria Pelet, "Puerto Rico's Invisible Health Crisis," Atlantic, September 3, 2016, www.theatlantic.com/politics/archive/2016/09/vieques-invisible-health-crisis/498428/.

STERILIZATION AND BIRTH CONTROL

In 1937, at the same time that the Nationalist Party was calling for independence, Dr. Clarence Gamble, a known eugenicist and heir of the Proctor & Gamble fortune, opened twenty-two birth control clinics in Puerto Rico.[32] The Puerto Rican government—encouraged and supported by Gamble and the US government—passed Law 116, which legalized sterilization, made it free, and allowed it to be practiced without consent or notification at the discretion of a eugenics board. By 1946 many Puerto Rican hospitals performed postpartum sterilization, often without patient knowledge or consent. Beginning in the 1930s—over a forty-year span—about one-third of Puerto Rico's female population was sterilized, making it the highest rate in the world. The Nationalist Party joined with the Catholic Church to fight against sterilization in the 1950s and succeeded in repealing the law in 1960.[33]

In tandem with the sterilization program, unethical clinical trials for the first birth control pills were conducted by biologists from the US on Puerto Rican women in 1955. These women were often recruited for the trials through birth control clinics, some of which were funded by the US government and others by Gamble. Women

32. As abhorrent as it may seem in the twenty-first century, eugenics was an accepted scientific practice in the first decades of the twentieth century that promoted procreation of the "fittest" individuals. The determination of what "fittest" meant, however, excluded people of color and those in lower socioeconomic groups, leading to institutionalized sterilization. When eugenics was embraced by the Nazis, scientists in the US and Europe began to shun these practices. Steven A. Farber, "U.S. Scientists' Role in the Eugenics Movement (1907–1939): A Contemporary Biologist's Perspective," *Zebrafish* 5, no. 4 (January 2009), www.ncbi.nlm.nih.gov/pmc/articles/PMC2757926/.

33. Katherine Andrews, "The Dark History of Forced Sterilization of Latina Women," *Panoramas*, October 30, 2017, www.panoramas.pitt.edu/health-and-society/dark-history-forced-sterilization-latina-women; and Olivia Kinnear, "Sterilization: The Untold Story of Puerto Rico," Pasquines, September 1, 2015, https://pasquines.us/2015/09/01/sterilization-the-untold-story-of-puerto-rico/.

given the drug were not informed of the potential side effects or even that the drug was experimental.[34]

MIGRATION

Although migration from Puerto Rico to the US has been ongoing since citizenship was granted in 1917, there have been two main waves of mass migration from Puerto Rico to the US. The first was in the 1950s. When Muñoz Marín enacted Operation Bootstrap in 1947, dramatically changing the economy from agrarian to industrial, a sharp decline in the number of available jobs led many to seek employment elsewhere. This period also saw both a rise in air travel and the return home of thousands of Puerto Ricans who had served abroad in World War II and developed a more global outlook.[35] Between 1950 and 1960 an estimated 470,000 Puerto Ricans, almost a quarter of the population, moved to the continental US.[36] This mass migration created Puerto Rican diasporic communities throughout the US, with large concentrations in New York and Florida.

The second wave of migration is ongoing and appears to have two distinct stages. Phasing out incentives for businesses to invest in Puerto Rico in the early twenty-first century again led to dramatic job losses and the need for many to find employment elsewhere, triggering this second wave of mass migration. The Center for Puerto Rican Studies (CPRS) reports that between 2006 and 2016, Puerto Rico lost more than half a million people to migration, 14 percent of the total population. Again, a majority in this group moved to Florida and New York, but New Jersey, Massachusetts, Pennsylvania, Connecticut, and

---

34. Erin Blakemore, "The First Birth Control Pill Used Puerto Rican Women as Guinea Pigs," History.com, March 11, 2019, www.history.com/news/birth-control -pill-history-puerto-rico-enovid; and Andrews, "Dark History."

35. "Migrating to a New Land," Library of Congress, www.loc.gov/teachers /classroommaterials/presentationsandactivities/presentations/immigration/cuban3. html.

36. "Puerto Rican Emigration: Why the 1950s?" Lehman College, http://lcw.lehman .edu/lehman/depts/latinampuertorican/latinoweb/PuertoRico/1950s.htm.

Texas were also popular destinations. By 2016 there were more than 5.5 million Puerto Ricans living in the continental US and only 3.4 million in the archipelago. Hurricane María struck in the middle of this ongoing economic depression, resulting in extreme depopulation. CPRS estimates that almost 160,000 people left in 2018 as a result of the hurricane and that 470,335 residents may ultimately leave for hurricane-related reasons.[37] People who migrated because of Hurricane María have also been called "climate refugees" or "climate migrants" because these exoduses were spurred by climatological disasters.

Puerto Rican migratory patterns, however, are unique due to US citizenship, proximity to the continental United States, and access to air travel. Anthropologist Jorge Duany and others have noted circular migration patterns that are marked by "constant border crossings in both directions."[38] Many people from Puerto Rico move between the archipelago and the continental United States, sometimes moving back and forth more than once, thereby enacting circular patterns of migration. There are still others who move to Puerto Rico because that is where their parents or grandparents were born, and this move is a form of "return" migration.

III. Hurricane María: Contexts and Impacts

ECONOMIC CONTEXTS

Revisions to the US tax code in 1984 blocked Puerto Rico and Washington, DC, from declaring bankruptcy under Chapter 9, a

---

37. Jennifer Hinojosa and Edwin Meléndez, "Puerto Rican Exodus: One Year since Hurricane Maria," CENTRO: Center for Puerto Rican Studies at Hunter, September 2018, https://centropr.hunter.cuny.edu/research/data-center/research-briefs/puerto-rican-exodus-one-year-hurricane-maria.

38. Jorge Duany, *The Puerto Rican Nation on the Move: Identities on the Island and in the United States* (Chapel Hill and London: University of North Carolina Press, 2002), 209.

right previously extended to both. Although legislators provided no explanation for why they enacted this exclusion, Matthew D. Mc-Gill—lawyer for Puerto Rico's creditors in the current bankruptcy crisis—suggests that Congress may have wanted to protect investors.[39] A decade later, faced with a federal budget shortfall, President Clinton signed the Small Business Job Protection Act into law. This law enacts a phaseout of Section 936 of the tax code, which had incentivized US businesses to invest in Puerto Rico. These incentives were ended by 2006, and data shows a sharp decline in GDP growth rates after their removal.[40]

In response to this decline in revenue, the government of Puerto Rico created the Puerto Rico Urgent Interest Fund Corporation (also known as the Puerto Rico Sales Tax Financing Corporation), or the Corporación del Fondo de Interés Apremiante (COFINA) in 2006. Under COFINA, Puerto Rico was able to issue bonds that were backed by a 7 percent sales tax, allowing government debt to grow while asking consumers to shoulder the cost.[41] Just three years later, the legislature—led by then governor Luis Fortuño—passed Ley Siete, or Public Law 7, declaring a state of fiscal emergency. This declaration allowed the government to subvert labor protection laws and enact austerity measures that led to the firing of approximately twenty thousand government workers and significant cuts to social welfare programs, health care, and education.[42]

---

39. Mary Williams Walsh, "Puerto Rico Fights for Chapter 9 Bankruptcy in Supreme Court," *New York Times*, March 22, 2016, www.nytimes.com/2016/03/23/business/dealbook/puerto-rico-fights-for-chapter-9-bankruptcy-in-supreme-court.html.

40. Sean Holton, "Puerto Rico Loses Business Tax Break," *Orlando Sentinel*, August 3, 1996, http://articles.orlandosentinel.com/1996-08-03/news/9608021051_1_puerto-rico-ricans-section-936.

41. Morales, *Fantasy Island*, 91; Melendez and Venator-Santiago, "Puerto Rico Post-Maria," 11.

42. Yarimar Bonilla and Rafael A. Boglio Martínez, "Puerto Rico in Crisis: Government Workers Battle Neoliberal Reform," NACLA, January 5, 2010, https://

In 2014, the debt of Puerto Rico reached a record high of approximately $72 billion, and the following year the then governor Alejandro García Padilla announced that the debt was "unpayable." After this announcement, the Puerto Rican government defaulted on its monthly debt payment. It is important to note that during García Padilla's administration, US consulting firm AlixPartners was hired to cut costs at the Puerto Rico Electric Power Authority (PREPA)—in Spanish, the Autoridad de Energía Eléctrica Inicio.[43] While restructuring plans were ultimately denied because of their incompatibility with existing laws and procedures, the government did impose austerity measures that directly resulted in workers lacking the capacity and proper equipment to maintain the power grid. All of which contributed to the post-hurricane blackout in Puerto Rico, the largest in US history.

As severe as previous budget cuts had been, more recent cuts have been staggering. In June 2016, President Obama signed the Puerto Rico Oversight, Management, and Economic Stability Act (PROMESA) into law, which facilitated the restructuring of the commonwealth's debt and established the Financial Oversight and Management Board (FOMB), a body with final say on all economic decisions. Composed of seven members appointed by the president and one nonvoting member appointed by the governor of Puerto Rico, this board—as observers have widely noted—includes several FOMB members with strong ties to the financial sector, indicating an unchecked conflict of interest.[44] The austerity measures enacted by the FOMB under PROMESA have triggered a humanitarian crisis by cutting funds to health care, social services, utilities, and

---

nacla.org/article/puerto-rico-crisis-government-workers-battle-neoliberal-reform.

43. Nick Brown, Megan Davies, and Tom Hals, "Insight—Donahue May Bring Tough Love to Puerto Rico Power Agency," Reuters, September 9, 2014, www.reuters.com/article/puertorico-prepa-idCNL1N0R91U020140909.

44. Morales, *Fantasy Island*, 9, 169.

education as well as stunting the economy for residents. Puerto Rico was allowed to file for bankruptcy in May 2017.

Because of this crippling debt, the government of Puerto Rico cannot serve its people. In 2017 when Hurricane María made landfall, it was estimated that almost half the population of Puerto Rico was living below the poverty line, more than double the rate of any US state. The median income per household that year was approximately $19,000 and the unemployment rate was 10.1 percent. At that time, public schools began closing at an alarming rate and more than thirty thousand students were forced to relocate. Similar to the problems facing PREPA, the water utility habitually failed safe drinking water tests and claimed it lacked the resources to modernize infrastructure.[45]

BLOCK GRANTS

Several federal social welfare programs operating in Puerto Rico do so under block grants. A block grant is a single annual lump sum of funds that is then divided among those eligible for benefits. Block grants are also administered throughout the US, but in other regions they are based on a complex system of assessment that takes into account both how many people are in need of a particular service and what regional costs must be considered before providing the service. The limited form of block grants distributed in Puerto Rico shortchange the people, failing to provide adequate or equitable support.

For example, until 1982, Puerto Rico received full benefits under the largest federal nutrition program, the Food Stamp program. At that time, the program was reconfigured to create a single block grant for Puerto Rico to be shared by everyone, no matter how many people need benefits or how much the food costs. The reconfiguration was exclusive to Puerto Rico; everywhere else, the original funding formula remained in place. These changes created a substantial drop in the amount of assistance people receive in Puerto

---

45. "10 Facts about Poverty in Puerto Rico," Borgen Project, https://borgenproject.org/10-facts-poverty-puerto-rico/.

Rico. Furthermore, the version of the program available in Puerto Rico cannot be amended to accommodate certain circumstances, such as increased needs after a disaster, while the version implemented elsewhere can be revised as needed.[46]

This is also the case with Medicaid, a program that provides matching health coverage funds to states for people with lower incomes. Puerto Rico is awarded a single block grant each year, from which it draws to cover these health care costs. But this block grant is the extent of the matching funds that the federal government will pay toward these expenses—the Puerto Rican government is responsible for the rest of the costs. In the states, federal matching funds are not capped in this way. Also, unlike the policies for states, the block grant program for Puerto Rico does not incorporate per capita income in the funding formula. Further, the program in Puerto Rico requires a much lower income to qualify and includes far fewer benefits. This all helps to undermine the quality of and access to health care in Puerto Rico.[47]

AFTERMATHS

In early September 2017, Category 5 Hurricane Irma hit Puerto Rico, causing massive damage to the east coast and the island municipalities of Culebra and Vieques. Just two weeks later, on September 20, Hurricane María made landfall in the Puerto Rican archipelago as a "high end" Category 4 hurricane, with wind speeds of 155 mph. Its exit path to the west was blocked by Hurricane José, which stalled off the mid-Atlantic coast of the US where

---

46. "The Nutrition Assistance Program Helps over Half of Puerto Rico's Children," Center on Budget and Policy Priorities, www.cbpp.org/research/food-assistance/the-nutrition-assistance-program-helps-over-half-of-puerto-ricos-children.

47. An August 2020 ruling by a federal judge deemed this practice unconstitutional. However, the ruling has been contested and amendments regarding the distribution of funds have been delayed.

it was blocked by a low-pressure system, causing María to wreak havoc over Puerto Rico for approximately thirty hours. Among the destruction caused by the hurricane was the largest blackout in US history, the effects of which lasted well over a year in some regions. Most roads were blocked by fallen trees, downed power lines, electric cables, and other debris. Locals with chainsaws and machetes cleared narrow paths through the debris to allow for travel by car, but some roads remained blocked for weeks or even months after the hurricane.[48] No area of the island was left undamaged. And, as the cleanup began, huge trash piles began to appear across the landscape. According to NPR, the Puerto Rico Solid Waste Authority estimates that Hurricane María "created 6.2 million cubic yards of waste and debris." FEMA's guidelines for measuring refuse explains that this is "enough trash to fill about 43 football stadiums with piles of waste eight stories high."[49]

For weeks after the hurricane, access to cash, food, drinking water, and gasoline was severely limited. Banks remained closed or were only open for extremely limited hours and restricted the amount of money a person could withdraw to a nominal amount, typically between $50 and $100. ATMs were not working due to power outages. Most gas stations and stores were closed. If a business was open, only cash was accepted because point-of-sale systems that stores use to

48. In November 2017, *Axios*, sharing a FEMA update on the status of Puerto Rico's roads, reported that of the island's 5,073 miles of roads, 2,932 miles were open, most of which were located in the outer ring of the island, not the mountainous interior. Six months after the hurricane, Oxfam reported that roads were cleared. With very limited public transportation, Puerto Rico is almost completely car-dependent. Alyna Treene, "Puerto Rico after Maria, by the Numbers," *Axios*, November 6, 2017, https://www.axios.com/trump-tweets-puerto-rico-mayor-2495559018.html; and "Two Roads to Recovery in Puerto Rico," Oxfam, March 20, 2018, www.oxfamamerica.org/explore/stories/two-roads-to-recovery-in-puerto-rico/.

49. Merrit Kennedy and Lauren Migaki, "After Maria, Puerto Rico Struggles under the Weight of Its Own Garbage," NPR, December 14, 2017, www.npr.org/sections/thetwo-way/2017/12/14/570927809/after-maria-puerto-rico-struggles-under-the-weight-of-its-own-garbage.

process payments require a cell phone signal and after the hurricane, the majority of the island's cell phone towers and internet cables were destroyed.

The loss of lives and property from the hurricane is staggering. According to a report Governor Ricardo Rosselló presented to Congress, almost 90 percent of the households in Puerto Rico asked for some form of relief and housing assistance from FEMA. Out of those requesting immediate aid, 78 percent experienced significant damage to their home's structure.[50] The Associated Press reported that over 786,000 homes were damaged by the hurricane.[51] While the Puerto Rican government originally announced sixty-four deaths related to María, it later commissioned a study from George Washington University that raised the number to 2,975 deaths, which has been accepted as the official count.[52] A similar study by Harvard University, however, estimates that 4,645 people lost their lives as a result of the hurricane.[53]

On October 3, President Donald Trump visited Puerto Rico. In his press conference, he threw paper towels out into the crowd, congratulated himself on an excellent relief effort, joked that Hurricane María would "throw [the federal] budget out of whack," and suggested that María was not a "real catastrophe" in comparison to

50. Justin Agrelo, "30,000 Blue Tarps, 2.4 Million Downed Trees, Billions Short: 5 Ways Puerto Rico Is Still Struggling to Recover from Maria," *Mother Jones*, August 29, 2019, www.motherjones.com/environment/2019/08/blue-tarps-million-downed-trees-tens-of-billions-short-ways-puerto-rico-is-still-struggling-to-recover-from-maria.

51. Danica Coto, "Thousands in Puerto Rico Still without Housing since Maria," Associated Press, July 24, 2020, https://apnews.com/a2cf35e2f8893592ec4b59d90baae1ac.

52. "GW Report Delivers Recommendations Aimed at Preparing Puerto Rico for Hurricane Season," August 28, 2018, https://publichealth.gwu.edu/content/gw-report-delivers-recommendations-aimed-preparing-puerto-rico-hurricane-season.

53. Nishant Kishore et al., "Mortality in Puerto Rico after Hurricane Maria," July 12, 2018, https://www.nejm.org/doi/full/10.1056/NEJMsa1803972.

Hurricane Katrina.[54] On the same day, the US Navy hospital ship *Comfort* arrived in San Juan. The ship has 250 hospital beds, but nearly two weeks after its arrival, only thirty-three were occupied. The *Comfort* was docked in San Juan for fifty-three days but only saw an average of six patients per day. According to FEMA, patients had to go to local medical services first and then, if help was unavailable, that doctor had to contact the center in San Juan that was arranging admission. Someone there would decide if the patient should be sent to the *Comfort*. Local doctors reported that this bureaucratic process was unclear and made it difficult or impossible to access the aid provided by the ship.[55]

Almost one month after the hurricane, Whitefish Energy Holdings—a company with just two employees—signed a $300 million no-bid contract to fix the downed electricity grid in Puerto Rico.[56] Amid public and governmental outcry, Governor Rosselló canceled the contract. This fiasco significantly delayed essential work on the

54. David A. Graham, "Trump's Puerto Rico Visit Is a Political Disaster," *Atlantic*, October 3, 2017, www.theatlantic.com/politics/archive/2017/10/trump-puerto -rico-visit/541869/; and Mandalit del Barco, "In the Aftermath of Hurricane Maria, President Trump Visits Puerto Rico," NPR, October 3, 2017, www.npr.org/2017 /10/03/555425750/in-the-aftermath-of-hurricane-maria-president-trump-visits -puerto-rico.

55. Frances Robles and Sheri Fink, "Amid Puerto Rico Disaster, Hospital Ship Admitted Just 6 Patients a Day," *New York Times*, June 12, 2017, www.nytimes.com /2017/12/06/us/puerto-rico-hurricane-maria-hospital-ship.html; and Leyla Santiago and Mallory Simon, "There's a Hospital Ship Waiting for Sick Puerto Ricans— but No One Knows How to Get on It," CNN, October 16, 2017, https://edition. cnn.com/2017/10/16/health/puerto-rico-hospital-ship/index.html.

56. Investigations are pending; however, in June 2020, Andy Techmanski, the CEO of Whitefish Energy, was awarded another multimillion dollar no-bid contract to make personal protective equipment (PPE) for the Department of Veterans Affairs. Casey Tolan, "Montana Entrepreneur Who Sparked Controversy during Puerto Rico Hurricane Response Wins $4M No-Bid PPE Contract," July 14, 2020, CNN. com, https://edition.cnn.com/2020/07/14/politics/whitefish-montana-ppe-feder-al-contract-after-puerto-rico-invs/index.html.

power grid. Similarly, FEMA awarded a contract to produce thirty million meals to Tribute Contracting LLC, a company with only one employee—its owner—and that had no large-scale disaster relief experience before receiving the order. The company was only able to deliver fifty thousand meals—not one of which met the established guidelines—before its contract was terminated.[57] The emergency boxes that FEMA was able to deliver in the weeks after the hurricane were filled with foods that lacked nutrition, such as chocolate bars, Starburst candy, chips, and canned pasta.[58]

These contractual problems were paired with issues related to distribution. In September 2018, twenty thousand pallets—almost one and a half million *cases*—of bottled water were found at an abandoned airfield. They were brought in by FEMA in the aftermath of Hurricane María and left there, undistributed. By the time they were found, they were undrinkable.[59] It should be noted that after the hurricane there were numerous cases of leptospirosis—a deadly illness caused by water contamination—as the lack of running water and other sources of drinking water forced people to turn to unregulated freshwater springs.[60] The Puerto Rico Department of Health and the Environmental Protection Agency also estimated that 2.3

57. Patricia Mazzei and Agustin Armendariz, "FEMA Contract Called for 30 Million Meals for Puerto Ricans. 50,000 Were Delivered," *New York Times*, February 6, 2018, www.nytimes.com/2018/02/06/us/fema-contract-puerto-rico.html.

58. Laura Olivieri Robles and Reynaldo Leanos Jr., "Puerto Rico Food Aid Brought Too Much Salt and Sugar, Some Residents Say," *USA Today*, February 1, 2018, www.usatoday.com/story/news/nation/2018/02/01/puerto-rico-food-aid-brought-chocolate-bars-and-cookies-some-residents-say/1085800001/.

59. Bill Weir, "20,000 Pallets of Bottled Water Left Untouched in Storm-Ravaged Puerto Rico," CNN, September 12, 2018, https://edition.cnn.com/2018/09/12/us/puerto-rico-bottled-water-dump-weir/index.html.

60. McNelly Torres, "A Deadly Bacteria Has Killed People in Puerto Rico and Health Officials Didn't Detect It," Centro de Periodismo Investigativo, June 5, 2019, https://periodismoinvestigativo.com/2019/06/a-deadly-bacteria-has-killed-people-in-puerto-rico-and-health-officials-didnt-detect-it/.

million people were at risk for illnesses from E. coli and coliforms found in tap water, indicating the presence of high levels of fecal matter and bacteria.[61] In January 2020, a warehouse filled with undistributed goods intended for post–Hurricane María relief—including generators, batteries, emergency radios, cots, bottled water, food, and diapers—was also discovered in Ponce.[62]

These failures in distribution are more concerning in light of the obvious rise in basic needs. After Hurricane María, for example, requests for NAP benefits rose substantially. Congress provided additional temporary funding, and by 2019 almost half the population of Puerto Rico was receiving food assistance. In March 2019, though, benefits were cut by approximately 25 percent in an attempt to bring the spending back to pre-hurricane levels, leaving over one million residents struggling to feed themselves.[63]

Additional problems related to the hurricane stemmed from preexisting and systemic issues resulting from decades of budget cuts. The Institute of Forensic Sciences, which performs autopsies, is a prime example. A 2018 surprise inspection of the institute revealed 259 bodies in the morgue (some cases dated back to 2012) and another 76 bodies contained in trailers. In addition, there was also an extremely high number of cases waiting for resolution because evidence was not processed in a timely fashion; in 2014 there were 22,000 such backlogged cases. Much of this gross negligence could be attributed to over

61. Mekela Panditharatne, "New Data: 2 Million Puerto Ricans Risk Water Contamination," National Resources Defense Council, *Expert Blog*, December 11, 2017, www.nrdc. org/experts/mekela-panditharatne/over-2-million-puerto-ricans-risk-bacteria-water.

62. Associated Press, "Puerto Rico Residents Outraged after Discovering Warehouse of Unused Aid from Hurricane Maria," NBC News, January 19, 2019, www.nbcnews. com/news/latino/puerto-rico-residents-outraged-after-discovering-warehouse -full-unused-aid-n1118501.

63. Jeff Stein, "More Than 670,000 Puerto Rico Residents Have Received Cuts to Food Stamp Benefits amid Congressional Impasse," *Washington Post*, March 8, 2019, www.washingtonpost.com/us-policy/2019/03/08/puerto-rico-starts-cutting-food-stamp-benefits-used-by-more-than-million-people-amid-congressional-impasse/.

a decade of chronic understaffing, as many forensic scientists and other highly trained professionals leave Puerto Rico for higher salaries and better working conditions and are not replaced because of budget restrictions. Another factor, though, is the April 2017 consolidation of several interrelated emergency services offices that offered economic savings but eliminated the autonomy of the ICF. In 2018, the Puerto Rican legislature approved a budget that included the disbursal of an additional $1.5 million to the institute, but the FOMB vetoed this increase.[64] In August 2020, FEMA acknowledged the institute's need with a grant award of over $7.6 million.[65]

US FEDERAL AID

Estimates show the damages incurred from Hurricane María range between $90 and $120 billion. Congress allocated approximately $43 billion in relief funds; however, two years after the hurricane, only one third of the allocated funds had been disbursed.[66] In just one example of the failure to distribute funds, in October 2019 the Department of Housing and Urban Development (HUD) admitted at a US Congressional hearing that it purposefully failed to comply with the law by intentionally missing the deadline to initiate the process for Puerto Rico to access billions of dollars' worth of funds approved by Congress for hurricane recovery.[67] HUD's defiance was

64. Melanie Ortiz, "The Forensics of Death in Puerto Rico," *Metric*, July 13, 2018, www.themetric.org/articles/the-forensics-of-death-in-puerto-rico; and Danica Coto, "Puerto Rico Probes Forensics Institute as Bodies Pile Up," Associated Press, July 20, 2018, https://apnews.com/b5578b971a134ec5a13271216911b41d.

65. "FEMA Obligates Nearly $7.7 Million to the Puerto Rico Forensic Science Institute," FEMA, press release, August 13, 2020, www.fema.gov/news-release /20200813/fema-obligates-nearly-77-million-puerto-rico-forensic-science-institute.

66. Robert Farley, "Trump Misleads on Aid to Puerto Rico," FactCheck.org, April 2, 2019, www.factcheck.org/2019/04/trump-misleads-on-aid-to-puerto-rico/.

67. Nicole Acevedo, "HUD Officials Knowingly Failed 'to Comply with the Law,' Stalled Puerto Rico Hurricane Funds," NBC News, October 18, 2019, www

particularly problematic in light of the fact that heading into the 2020 hurricane season, upward of twenty-five thousand homes did not have their roofs replaced and their occupants were still living under temporary "blue roof" tarps.[68]

According to the US Army Corps of Engineers, Operation Blue Roof was designed to provide fiber-reinforced plastic sheeting that would protect property and allow residents to stay in damaged homes after a disaster. The US Army reported that the blue roofs it distributes in partnership with FEMA are good for up to thirty days.[69] It also stated that these tarps are not designed for flat or metal roofs and therefore the homes in Puerto Rico provided "less than ideal conditions" for the blue roofs, a problem that caused significant delays.[70] A 2018 story on PBS's *Frontline* documented that in the thirty days after Hurricane María, only 1 percent of qualified homes had blue roofs installed successfully. According to Alice Thomas, a disaster-response expert with Refugees International who was quoted in the story, "Homes that were salvageable are ruined now. They're beyond repair."[71]

As of May 2018, approximately 30 percent of the over 1.1 million households that had applied for FEMA grants were denied because they were deemed ineligible. The Puerto Rican Planning Society estimates that 260,000 homes in Puerto Rico don't have titles

---

.nbcnews.com/news/latino/hud-officials-knowingly-failed-comply-law-stalled -puerto-rico-hurricane-n1068761.

68. Coto, "Thousands in Puerto Rico."

69. Jacqueline Tate, "Corps Installs Last Blue Roof in Puerto Rico," US Army, March 22, 2018, www.army.mil/article/202599/corps_installs_last_blue_roof_in_puerto _rico.

70. Patrick Loch, "USACES Operation Blue Roof Hitting Its Stride," US Army, December 19, 2017, www.army.mil/article/198408/usaces_operation_blue_roof _hitting_its_stride.

71. Kate McCormick and Emma Schwartz, "After Maria, Thousands on Puerto Rico Waited Months for a Plastic Roof," *Frontline*, May 2, 2018, www.pbs.org /wgbh/frontline/article/after-maria-thousands-on-puerto-rico-waited-months-for-a -plastic-roof/.

or deeds.[72] Often property is passed down through generations or subdivided among family members according to a code of familial honor that does not seek or depend on official state documentation. FEMA follows strict guidelines for proof of ownership, which has prevented many claimants from receiving federal aid.

DISASTER CAPITALISM

Journalist Naomi Klein developed the term *disaster capitalism* to refer to the ways in which governments and investors utilize catastrophes for their economic advantage, often at the expense of people living below the poverty line. While Puerto Rico's history of incentivizing external investment has cyclically encouraged investors from the US, particularly onerous are Acts 20 and 22, passed in 2012 and then merged into Act 60 in 2019. The financial incentives—available only to people who move to Puerto Rico, not those already living there—include the extremely low 4 percent corporate tax rate, no capital gains taxes, and no US income taxes for revenue earned in Puerto Rico.[73] Klein observes that this deregulation, combined with the post-María disaster conditions, opened a door to cryptocurrency profiteers who were eagerly invited by the Roselló administration. "When it comes to taxing and regulating the wealthy," she affirms, Puerto Rico's "government has surrendered with unmatched enthusiasm."[74]

---

72. Nicole Acevedo and Istra Pacheco, "No Deeds, No Aid to Rebuild Homes: Puerto Rico's Reconstruction Challenge," NBC News, May 8, 2018, www .nbcnews.com/storyline/puerto-rico-crisis/no-deeds-no-aid-rebuild-homes-puerto -rico-s-reconstruction-n868396.

73. Vincenzo Villamena, "How Entrepreneurs Can Save on Taxes in Puerto Rico," *Forbes*, June 8, 2020, www.forbes.com/sites/theyec/2020/06/08/how-entrepreneurs -can-save-on-taxes-in-puerto-rico/#3ee4acd94cfc.

74. Naomi Klein, *The Battle for Paradise: Puerto Rico Takes on the Disaster Capitalists* (Chicago: Haymarket Books, 2018), 23.

One aspect of disaster capitalism that is perhaps more visible is the post-María housing market. In April 2018, the real estate website Point2 placed Puerto Rico third on its list of "Top 30 Home Buying Destinations in the Americas." A few months later, the same website published a study stating that property values were approximately half what they were a decade earlier. When Point2 surveyed visitors to the Puerto Rico section of their site, they found that 97 percent of those interested in purchasing property were from the continental US.[75]

Klein notes that disaster capitalism in Puerto Rico has been unique in the sense that the "infrastructure of crisis exploitation didn't need to be scrambled together . . . because the Fiscal Control Board [FOMB] . . . was already in place. . . . All they needed was the bloody-minded opportunism to push it through . . . harnessing trauma, the state of emergency, the fact that people are just struggling to stay alive, and using that dislocation to ram through a preexisting, totally articulated agenda."[76]

Anthropologist and Puerto Rican studies scholar Yarimar Bonilla extends Klein's analysis to suggest that "what we see in Puerto Rico is . . . a trauma doctrine." Bonilla explains that "the much-touted resilience of Puerto Ricans . . . needs to be . . . understood as a form of trauma: years of abandonment by local and federal governments have forced communities to take care of themselves. I think this is why people were able to move so quickly and to immediately begin thinking about alternatives at the community level. This is

75. Cristina Oprean, "Hot Spots: Top 30 Home Buying Destinations in the Americas," Point2, April 2, 2018, www.point2homes.com/news/us-real-estate-news/us-top-30-home-buying-destinations-americas.html; and Cristina Oprean, "More Americans Looking for Bargains in Puerto Rico as Home Prices Drop to an 8-Year Low," Point2, July 10, 2018, www.point2homes.com/news/us-real-estate-news/americans-bargains-puerto-rico-home-prices-drop.html.

76. "The Trauma Doctrine: A Conversation between Yarimar Bonilla and Naomi Klein," in *Aftershocks of Disaster: Puerto Rico before and after the Storm*, Yarimar Bonilla and Marisol LeBrón, eds. (Chicago: Haymarket Books, 2020), 23–24.

wonderful but also troubling, given the superhuman capacity for resilience that is now expected of residents."[77]

RICKY RENUNCIA

In the summer of 2019, hundreds of thousands of people assembled across Puerto Rico and the US to demand the resignation of Governor Ricardo "Ricky" Rosselló, chanting "Ricky Renuncia!" (Ricky Resign!). A report from the Puerto Rican Center for Investigative Journalism (in Spanish, El Centro de Periodismo Investigativo) sparked the protests by leaking 889 pages of a group chat the governor participated in that contained homophobic, misogynistic, and racist comments, as well as statements making light of the fatalities from Hurricane María.[78] "The Puerto Rican civil insurgency of July 2019," explains Christopher Powers Guimond, "was born with martyrs at hand: the thousands who died during the months of darkness and privatization after the twentieth of September." He continues, "The number 4,645—the tally popularly accepted as the death toll of Hurricane María—became a revolutionary image . . . [a] metaphor: written on signs, painted as graffiti on the colonial buildings of Old San Juan, stenciled onto the barricades at Fortaleza Street and circulated virtually. It manifested how the 'Ricky Renuncia' political movement . . . had become a generalized process of national mourning."[79] The governor left office on August 2.

---

77. Bonilla and Klein, "The Trauma Doctrine," in *Aftershocks of Disaster*, 26–27.

78. Alexia Fernández Campbell, "Puerto Rico Just Kicked Out Another Governor," *Vox*, August 7, 2019, www.vox.com/policy-and-politics/2019/8/7/20758998/puerto-rico-governor-supreme-court-pierluisi; and Rachel Bierly, "Ricky Renuncia: The Demand of Puerto Rican People," *Panoramas*, September 17, 2019, www.panoramas.pitt.edu/news-and-politics/ricky-renuncia-demand-puerto-rican-people.

79. Christopher Powers Guimond, *4645* (Cabo Rojo: Editora Educación Emergente, 2020), 14–15.

EARTHQUAKE SWARM

On December 28, 2019, the first of an ongoing swarm of earthquakes rocked Puerto Rico, causing significant material destruction, widespread blackouts, physical injuries, and at least one death. Thousands of people were relocated to tent cities in the southeastern portion of the main island, especially in Yauco, Guánica, and Guayanilla. In early January 2020, a 6.4-magnitude earthquake damaged the Costa Sur Power Plant in Guayanilla, the largest power plant in Puerto Rico, at that time producing 21 percent of its energy. The plant is now offline indefinitely.[80] In May 2020, PREPA announced that it was soliciting bids for two "emergency temporary" generators to replace Costa Sur, which they envisioned using for up to eighteen months at an estimated cost of $1.2 billion. Multiple citizens' groups and watchdog agencies have filed petitions against this proposal, objecting to both the cost and the lack of interest in renewable energy that may subvert the earthquakes and other environmental disasters.[81] Solar microgrids, for example, could sustain the energy needs of multiple individual barrios independently whereas an incapacitated central power source can leave all the surrounding communities in the dark. At the time of this writing, this swarm has included almost two thousand earthquakes.

---

80. "Puerto Rico's Electricity Generation Mix Changed Following Early 2020 Earthquakes," US Energy Information Administration, www.eia.gov /todayinenergy/detail.php?id=44216.

81. William Driscoll, "Puerto Rico Citizens' Groups Challenge Utility Plan for 500 MW of Temporary Generation," *PV Magazine*, May 26, 2020, https://pv -magazine-usa.com/2020/05/26/puerto-rico-citizens-groups-challenge-utility-plan -for-500-mw-of-temporary-generation/.

GLOSSARY

alcoholado: A salve made from bay rum and other herbs. Known as Bay Rum on other Caribbean islands, it is commonly used in Puerto Rico and the diaspora to treat cuts, abrasions, colds, asthma, muscular pain, and so on. Alcoholado is also integral to many religious ceremonies and expressions of faith that both supplement and stand in opposition to Christianity, the predominant religion of the archipelago.

archipelago: A group or cluster of islands. Puerto Rico is an archipelago, consisting of the main island, the island municipalities of Vieques and Culebra, and numerous other uninhabited islands and cays.

ayúdame: Help me.

barrio: A neighborhood or district of a municipality/*municipio* or town in a Spanish-speaking country. In the US, it can be used to refer to a diasporic and often Spanish-speaking neighborhood.

bolero: A music and dance style that dates back to eighteenth-century Spain; it has become a Latin American and Caribbean phenomenon.

bomba: A folkloric dance and music style that is unique to Puerto Rico. The percussion-driven music is part of Puerto Rico's African heritage, and the lyrics often have their roots in the songs of enslaved peoples laboring on plantations. The instruments used in bomba include maracas, sticks, and drums. At least two drummers are needed for bomba: a *buleador* who keeps the beat and a *subidor* or *primo* who interacts with the dancer. The dancer "converses with" or "challenges" the subidor in a call-and-response exchange.

Borinquén: Derived from "Borikén," the Indigenous Taíno name for Puerto Rico, which means Land of Great Lords. Puerto Ricans often refer to the archipelago as "Borinquén" and to the people of Puerto Rico as "Boricuas."

cabrón: The literal translation is "male goat." In Puerto Rican Spanish slang, depending on the context, it can be understood as "dude." The term was originally used as a chauvinist attack directed at a heterosexual man whose female partner cheated on him. However, since the 1980s the nouns *cabrón* and *cabrona* have been used to refer to "dudes" of all genders. The adjective *cabrón* or *cabrona*, depending on context, may mean outstanding, great, over the top, evil, hated, despised, or despicable.

diaspora: Large groups of people who have migrated from their home nations and reestablished communities with elements of shared cultural identity markers, including language, music, and food. For more on the Puerto Rican diaspora, see "Migration" in the "Contexts" essay.

el año de las guácaras: A phrase that refers to times of old. The origin of the term *guácara* has been traced back to some time between the late nineteenth and early twentieth centuries, when it was used to refer to a type of suit worn by wealthy landowners. Other scholars contend that the term derives from the Arawak word for caverns or caves. Either way, el año de las guácaras is a colloquial shorthand used to refer to immemorial times in the collective imaginary.

el viejo/a: A term of endearment that means "the old man/woman." This term is often used to refer to parents. The plural, los viejos, means parents or the elderly in general.

exclusive institutions: Can refer to institutions that are discriminatory or do not provide equal opportunity. It can also refer to a ruling party that favors itself instead of the needs of the nation. One of the major negative impacts of exclusive institutions is poverty.

Financial Oversight and Management Board of Puerto Rico (FOMB): Created by Congress under the Puerto Rico Oversight, Management, and Economic Stability Act (PROMESA) of 2016 in response to the Puerto Rican government-debt crisis of 2014. It was established to restructure the debt and combat the financial crisis, but the result has been austerity measures that have affected public works including health care, education, and utilities. Negotiations between the FOMB and Puerto Rico's government are ongoing and the fiscal plan continues to be amended. The board is also known as the Fiscal Control Board or (more commonly in Puerto Rico) as "la Junta," which is short for the board's Spanish title, Junta de Supervisión Fiscal y Administración Financiera para Puerto Rico. For more on the debt crisis, the FOMB, and austerity measures, see "Economic Contexts" in the "Contexts" essay.

finca: Farm.

la Junta: In general, this term means "the board," but in Puerto Rico it is now often used to refer to the Financial Oversight and Management Board of Puerto Rico.

leptospirosis: An illness caused by *Leptospira*, which are bacteria in the urine of rodents and other animals. Outbreaks occur after surface waters become contaminated following heavy rainfalls and floods resulting from storms and hurricanes. Leptospirosis can be contracted by wading through, washing in, or drinking contaminated water. After Hurricane María, many people relied on wells, rivers, and streams as sources of water.

mira: Look, or Look here.

MRE: Stands for Meal, Ready-to-Eat, a shelf-stable, individually portioned meal. Originally designed for the US military, MREs are now also sold as an emergency preparedness item or as survival food.

municipality/municipio: Municipalities in Puerto Rico are second-level administrative divisions (somewhat akin to counties in the US). The island is divided into seventy-eight municipalities, each with its own mayor. Most municipalities are then further divided into barrios. Every municipality has a town or city for which it is named. Many municipalities also have barrios that are more rural. For example, the municipality of Adjuntas has seventeen barrios, one of which is the town center (or the pueblo) that is also called Adjuntas, while the rest are mostly rural.

parrandas: A Puerto Rican holiday tradition in which a group of friends and family gather late at night to surprise others in their homes with music and song. Food and drink are shared, and often several homes are visited in one night, the group growing as the night progresses. Unlike the Christmas caroling tradition, parrandas are less focused on rehearsed or Christmas-themed songs and are more a collective expression of musical improvisation.

plaza: The center of a town or city. In Puerto Rico, plazas originate from Spanish colonization, as it was King Ferdinand who first commanded that they be built in the 1500s. Designed in the Spanish style, plazas are rectangular in shape with at least one prominently situated church. Municipal buildings and other businesses are often located around the plaza. They are popular meeting places and are also used as sites of markets, festivals, and other entertainment like live music and dancing.

plena: A type of Puerto Rican folk music. It is generally agreed that plena originated in the southern city of Ponce in the early 1900s, and that it is influenced by or developed from bomba. Like bomba, it reflects Puerto Rico's African heritage and is percussion driven, but plena has its own distinct style. For example, the lyrics of plena are often narrative and reflect current events. For this reason, it has been called "el periodico cantado," the sung newspaper.

PREPA: An acronym for the Puerto Rico Electric Power Authority, which is the English translation of Puerto Rico's Autoridad de Energía Eléctrica (AEE), the agency responsible for electricity generation, power distribution, and power transmission across the archipelago. It is also commonly referred to as AEE or Autoridad.

PROMESA: An acronym for the Puerto Rico Oversight, Management, and Economic Stability Act, a US federal law that was created in 2016 to address Puerto Rico's debt. The Financial Oversight and Management Board (FOMB) was established under PROMESA. For more on the debt crisis, PROMESA, and austerity measures, see "Economic Contexts" in the "Contexts" essay.

quinceañera: A celebration of a girl's fifteenth birthday, practiced throughout Latin America and in many diasporic Latinx families. It often involves large parties that include extended family and friends. The girl celebrating her fifteenth birthday is also referred to as the quinceañera.

tormenteras: Metal storm shutters.

tití or tía/tío: Auntie/uncle. In Puerto Rico these terms are not solely reserved for relatives. Children are generally taught to use them to refer to adults in extended circles of family and friends, whether they are related by blood or not.

urbanización: A planned community, generally located outside town centers. There are lower-, middle-, and high-income urbanizaciones across Puerto Rico. Most middle- and high-income urbanizaciones built since the mid-1980s are also gated communities, especially in the metropolitan area and adjacent municipalities.

válgame: An idiom commonly used in western Puerto Rico. The term is equivalent to "my goodness," "oh my God," or "geez."

vejigante: A demon from medieval Spanish folklore who has become intertwined with Taíno and West African mythologies in Puerto Rico. During the Carnival festivities in Ponce and Loíza leading up to Ash Wednesday, revelers often wear vejigante masks made of papier-mâché, coconut husks, or gourds. The masks are one of Puerto Rico's most cherished artistic expressions and have received prominent national and international attention in artistic circles and from museums and art historians.

Wepa!: In Puerto Rico, a common enthusiastic interjection akin to "Hooray!"

FURTHER RESOURCES

Aftershocks of Disaster: Puerto Rico before and after the Storm, edited by Yarimar Bonilla and Marisol LeBrón

The Battle for Paradise: Puerto Rico Takes on the Disaster Capitalists, by Naomi Klein

Candlelight: Life after the Storm, a short film by Verónica Ortiz-Calderón

The Diaspora Strikes Back: Caribeño Tales of Learning and Turning, by Juan Flores

The Future We Choose: Surviving the Climate Crisis, by Christiana Figueres and Tom Rivett-Carnac

Pa'lante, a music video by Hurray for the Riff Raff and Kristian Mercado Figueroa

The Puerto Rican Nation on the Move: Identities on the Island and in the United States, by Jorge Duany

Puerto Rico en mi corazón, edited by Carina del Valle Schorske, Ricardo Maldonado, Erica Mena, and Raquel Salas Rivera

"Puerto Rico Post-Hurricane Maria: Origins and Consequences of a Crisis," *CENTRO: Journal of the Center for Puerto Rican Studies* 30, no. 3 (2018), a special issue of the journal guest edited by Edwin Meléndez and Charles R. Venator-Santiago

Puerto Rico Strong: A Comics Anthology Supporting Puerto Rico Disaster Relief and Recovery, coedited by Marco Lopez, Desiree Rodriguez, Hazel Newlevant, Derek Ruiz, and Neil Schwartz

The Puerto Rico Syllabus, online at https://puertoricosyllabus.com/

Ricanstruction: Reminiscing & Rebuilding Puerto Rico, by Edgardo Miranda-Rodríguez

Voices from Puerto Rico: Post-Hurricane María/Voces desde Puerto Rico: pos-huracán María, edited by Iris Morales

ACKNOWLEDGMENTS

Our profound gratitude to our narrators for their patience, collaboration, and courage. The students at UPRM who worked with us on the Mi María project demonstrated exceptional commitment, especially those who helped to develop the stories included in this book. We appreciate their hard work and dedication. Thank you also to Voice of Witness and Haymarket Books for believing in this project and helping us to share these stories.

Many people supported us personally in the long aftermath of Hurricane María, and we appreciate each of them for their kindness and generosity. Ricia is especially grateful to her partner, Eric D. Lamore—two is always a team—and to her parents, Patricia and Howard Chansky, who continually listen with patience and encouragement. Additionally, she is thankful for the love and assistance from Maria Y. Chansky and Russ Swank, Ana Solares and Manuel Valentín, Peter Sancinito, Russ Lamore, Gerri Heim, Ingrid Goff-Maidoff, and Lynda and Michael Martone. Special thanks to the home team: Germaine, Gary, Martha, Mercedes, Marci, Missy, and Audrey. And endless gratitude to Charish, Noah, and Lily.

Marci and her family got through the hurricane and its immediate aftermath with help from Waleska Cotto Oyola, Alberto Guardiola, Marisa Hughes, Mike and Brooklyn Pastor, Manuel "Lito" de León, James Connelly, and Ricia and Eric. Marci is grateful to Marie Frankland and Sophie Trudeau for post-hurricane housing. Her deepest gratitude goes to her family and friends, who continue to support her in so many things, from living through hurricanes to writing about them—with special thanks to Lisa Denesiuk, Shirley Diachuk, Christine Marcinew, Nancy Liknes, Leah Weinberg, Tally Abecassis, Josée Blanchet, Shaughnessy Bishop-Stall, Catherine Bodmer, Benoît Chaput, Richard Deschênes, Colleen Dwyer Meloche, Ibi Kaslik, Penny Pattison, Patra Reiser, Eric Smith, Dean Turner, Kat Tzadik, and Leslie Wade. Many thanks go to the crew at Rincón Ride, who keep her moving, and to her son's school, Foresta Rincón. And finally, Marci is especially thankful for the love and support of her husband and son, Sean and Marlowe Locke.

Jocelyn Géliga Vargas made significant contributions to this book. In addition to teaching two of the courses affiliated with this project, she commented on drafts and helped arrange follow-up interviews. She and Yarelmi A. Iglesias Vázquez also participated in our initial meeting to conceptualize this book and it is a stronger volume for their insights and advice. We are also grateful to Laura Malischke—the eager adventurer—for acting as the project photographer. This project has received continual support from the University of Puerto Rico at Mayagüez. In the College of Arts and Sciences, Dean Fernando Gilbes Santaella, Associate Dean of Research Matías J. Cafaro, and Office Administrator Jamilette Acevedo González have given generously of their time and resources. The Mi María project has spanned the tenure of two directors of the Department of English, Leonardo Flores and Rosa I. Román Pérez, both of whom have offered their encouragement for our work.

Lester Jiménez at *Primera Hora*, Victoria and Mark Jury at Los Almendros, Cathy Mazak at UPRM, and Luz Rivera Cantwell at Fundación de Culebra—thank you for introducing us to five of the narrators included in this collection.

We are humbled by the awards that this project has received. We were awarded a generous grant for the development of this project from the National Endowment for the Arts. Marci was supported by a Research and Creation grant from the Canada Council for the

Arts. Ricia was recognized with two awards for the design of the courses affiliated with this project, a Humanities Innovation Grant from the Modern Language Association and the 2020 Postsecondary Teaching Award from the Oral History Association.

Finally, we are grateful to the people and establishments of our community. We recognize that surviving a disaster is a communal effort and acknowledge those who came together after the hurricane to share water, food, gas, phones, shelter, and other supplies. A special thank you to Café 413 and the Burger King in Rincón. When we were without electricity and internet for long months, both of these restaurants let us charge our phones and laptops, use their Wi-Fi, and turn their spaces into makeshift offices, which allowed us to get this project up off the ground.

UPRM Students Participating in the Mi María Project

Jonathan Acevedo Acevedo

Marco A. Acosta León

Abimael Acosta Marrero

Fernando Agosto Quiñones

Nicole Alayón Ruiz

Wildelia Alequín Otero

Adriana C. Almodóvar Zayas

Pierucci Aponte

Gabrielle M. Armstrong
  Velázquez

Daysel Marie Arroyo Morales

Pura Arroyo Morales

José F. Arroyo Vélez

Angélica M. Avilés Bosques

Rodniel Avilés Morales

Jashira Babilonia Banuchi

Roxana M. Baez Rodríguez

Wallace E. Barrios Abreu

Natalia M. Betancourt Malavé

Amanda Cabrera Santiago

Julianna M. Canabal Rodríguez

Belmaliz Cardona Rodríguez

Jorge E. Carlo Angleró

Emanuel Castro López

Joe A. Centeno Reyes

Guillermo Colón Bernardi

Alexandra Thaís Colón
  Rodríguez

Joseph F. Cortijo Tanco

Nathaniel Cruz Mundo

Luis Cruz Rosado

Lissette M. Dávila Carrión

Adriana De Persia Colón

Mara Y. Del Toro Rivera

Gabriela Díaz Almeida

Melanie Díaz Badillo

Jeredeth A. Díaz García

Yamilette Y. Domenech Gómez

Luis F. Domenech Ortiz

Aleyshka Estevez Quintana

William O. Figueroa Cardona

Julisa Figueroa Echevarría

Juan D. Flores García

Thairys N. Flores Ocasio

Brenda Y. Flores Santiago

Stephanie M. Fuentes Álvarez

José A. Fuentes Bonilla

Pedro González Figueroa

Troyane Harris

Hazel L. Hernández Hernández

Eddiel Hernández López

Jerry M. Hernández Merced

Ysabel S. Hightower González

Yarelmi A. Iglesias Vázquez

María Cecilia Iñigo Sánchez

Kevin López Matías

Angelic Lucca Feliciano

Grace A. Lucca Feliciano

Yarelis Marcial Acevedo

Daniela Marín Milián

Paula C. Mattei-Purcell

Kidanny J. Medina Droz

Emily Méndez Castro

Krystal Z. Mercado Morales

Jennifer Mojica Santana

Dennis Montalvo Pérez

Adriana Montes Pacheco

Francheska Morales García

Daniela Isabel Mulero Morales

Juliana B. Nazario Ortiz

Taína Nazario Zayas

Cyd Marie Negrón Ojeda

Sharon M. Nieves Ferrer

Tania C. Ocaña Cruz

Joel E. Ortiz Guerrero

Aníbal A. Ortiz Rivera

Leenahir Ortiz Rivera

Ana Patrón Fidalgo

Josué Pérez Del Valle

Juan M. Pérez González

Jesús J. Pérez Morales

Michael Pérez Rosa

Mitchell Pérez Vélez

Carol Quiles Colón

Valerie Quiñones Cordero

Omar J. Quiñones Mercado

Andrea Isabel Ramírez Figueroa

Aixamar Ramos Acevedo

Carolina M. Ramos López

Naylah M. Ramos Martínez

Ricardo L. Ramos Ríos

Bryan Ramos Romero

Janely R. Rentas Maldonado

Giselle Ríos Nieves

Arleemis Ríos Santiago

Orlando Rivera Russe

Gustavo Rivera Sanabria

Keila Rivera Santiago

Kiara M. Rivera Santiago

Isaac Rodríguez Aponte

Natalia Rodríguez Figueroa

Paola M. Rodríguez García

Heydi L. Rodríguez Morales
Emily M. Rodríguez Nuñez
Natalia Rodríguez Pérez
Andrea Rodríguez Quiñones
Andrea Rodríguez Santiago
Gabriel Rodríguez Sárraga
Fania Román Morales
Lourdes V. Rosado Rivera
Derling E. Sánchez Galloza
Dabnerys Sánchez Milián
Edwin J. Santos Rodríguez
José B. Segarra Santiago
Sebastián Serrano Pagán
José E. Soto Pérez
Iris A. Soto Ruiz
Joelys Tardy Vargas

Natalia Torres Negrón
Claudia Trogolo Franco
Javier Trujillo Dickson
Jaffet O. Tubens Bassat
Andrea Valdés Valderrama
Fabiola del Valle
Allyson Vargas Ortiz
Ángel Vázquez
Rafael Vázquez Correa
Miguel A. Velázquez Pagán
Rubén A. Vélez Baigés
Shecyann N. Vélez Tirado
Kiara M. Vélez Vélez
Jeremy A. Villafane Díaz
Astrid Zapata De Jesús

ABOUT THE EDITORS

Ricia Anne Chansky is a professor in the Department of English at the University of Puerto Rico at Mayagüez, where she teaches literature, oral history, and creative writing. She is the coeditor of the journal *a/b: Auto/Biography Studies* and editor of the Routledge Auto/Biography Studies book series. Her book publications include several coedited volumes: *The Routledge Auto/Biography Studies Reader, Life Writing outside the Lines: Gender and Genre in the Americas,* and *The Untied States: Unraveling National Identity in the Twenty-First Century.* She has also edited two books: *Auto/Biography across the Americas: Transnational Themes in Life Writing* and *Auto/Biography in the Americas: Relational Lives.* Her coauthored children's book, *Maxy Survives the Hurricane / Maxy sobrevive el huracán,* was published by Piñata Books, the children's imprint of Arte Público Press. She lives in western Puerto Rico with her partner, Eric, and their cat, Rafa.

Marci Denesiuk is a Canadian writer with a background in journalism and creative writing. Her award-winning fiction includes a book of short stories, *The Faraway Home,* which has also been published in French as *Le chez-nous perdu,* and stories in anthologies such as *Salut King Kong* and *In Other Words.* Marci's work has appeared in academic journals, magazines, and special projects, including a piece in the Unheard Voices of the Pandemic series with Voice of Witness. She teaches in the Department of English at the University of Puerto Rico at Mayagüez and also leads writing workshops in non-academic communities. She lives with her husband and son in Añasco, Puerto Rico.

ABOUT VOICE OF WITNESS

Voice of Witness (VOW) is an award-winning nonprofit that advances human rights by amplifying the voices of people impacted by—and fighting against—injustice. VOW's work is driven by the transformative power of the story, and by a strong belief that an understanding of systemic injustice is incomplete without deep listening and learning from people with firsthand experience. Through two key programs—our oral history book series and education program—we amplify these voices, teach ethics-driven storytelling, and partner with advocates to:

- support and build agency within marginalized communities;
- raise awareness and foster thoughtful, empathy-based critical inquiry and understanding of injustices;
- and inform long-term efforts to protect and advance human rights.

STAFF

EXECUTIVE DIRECTOR & EXECUTIVE EDITOR: Mimi Lok
MANAGING EDITOR: Dao X. Tran
EDITORIAL ASSISTANT: Rebecca McCarthy
EDUCATION PROGRAM DIRECTOR: Cliff Mayotte
EDUCATION SPECIALIST & PROGRAM COORDINATOR:
Erin Vong
COMMUNITY PARTNERSHIP COORDINATOR: Ela Banerjee
COMMUNICATIONS & OUTREACH MANAGER:
Annaick Miller
DIRECTOR OF INSTITUTIONAL PARTNERSHIPS
& STRATEGY: Kathleen Brennan
DONOR RELATIONSHIP MANAGER: Colleen Hammond
DEVELOPMENT ASSISTANT: Liz Duran

THE VOICE OF WITNESS BOOK SERIES

The VOW Book Series depicts human rights issues through the edited oral histories of people—VOW narrators—who are most deeply impacted and at the heart of solutions to address injustice. The VOW Education Program connects over 20,000 educators, students, and advocates each year with these stories and issues through oral history–based curricula, trainings, and holistic educational support. *Mi María: Surviving the Storm* is the twentieth book in the series. Other titles include:

HOW WE GO HOME
Voices of Indigenous North America
Edited by Sara Sinclair
"A chorus of love and belonging alongside the heat of resistance." —Leanne Betamosake Simpson

SOLITO, SOLITA
Crossing Borders with Youth Refugees from Central America
Edited by Steven Mayers and Jonathan Freedman
"Intense testimonies that leave one . . . astonished at the bravery of the human spirit." —Sandra Cisnero

SAY IT FORWARD
A Guide to Social Justice Storytelling
Edited by Cliff Mayotte and Claire Kiefer
"Reminds us the process through which we document a story is as important and powerful as the story itself." —Lauren Markham

SIX BY TEN
Stories from Solitary
Edited by Mateo Hoke and Taylor Pendergrass
"Deeply moving and profoundly unsettling." —Heather Ann Thompson

CHASING THE HARVEST
Migrant Workers in California Agriculture
Edited by Gabriel Thompson
"The voices are defiant and nuanced, aware of the human complexities that spill across bureaucratic categories and arbitrary borders." —*The Baffler*

LAVIL
Life, Love, and Death in Port-Au-Prince
Edited by Peter Orner and Evan Lyon
Foreword by Edwidge Danticat
"*Lavil* is a powerful collection of testimonies, which include tales of violence, poverty, and instability but also joy, hustle, and the indomitable will to survive." —*Vice*

THE POWER OF THE STORY
The Voice of Witness Teacher's Guide to Oral History
Compiled and edited by Cliff Mayotte
Foreword by William Ayers and Richard Ayers
"A rich source of provocations to engage with human dramas throughout the world." —*Rethinking Schools Magazine*

THE VOICE OF WITNESS READER
Ten Years of Amplifying Unheard Voices
Edited and with an introduction by Dave Eggers

PALESTINE SPEAKS
Narratives of Life under Occupation
Compiled and edited by Cate Malek and Mateo Hoke
"Heartrending stories." —*New York Review of Books*

INVISIBLE HANDS
Voices from the Global Economy
Compiled and edited by Corinne Goria
Foreword by Kalpona Akter
"Powerful and revealing testimony." —*Kirkus*

HIGH RISE STORIES
Voices from Chicago Public Housing
Compiled and edited by Audrey Petty
Foreword by Alex Kotlowitz
"Gripping, and nuanced and unexpectedly moving." —Roxane Gay

REFUGEE HOTEL
Photographed by Gabriele Stabile and edited by Juliet Linderman
"There is no other book like *Refugee Hotel* on your shelf." —*SF Weekly*

THROWING STONES AT THE MOON
Narratives from Colombians Displaced by Violence
Compiled and edited by Sibylla Brodzinsky and Max Schoening
Foreword by Íngrid Betancourt
"Both sad and inspiring." —*Publishers Weekly*

INSIDE THIS PLACE, NOT OF IT
Narratives from Women's Prisons
Compiled and edited by Ayelet Waldman and Robin Levi
Foreword by Michelle Alexander
"Essential reading." —Piper Kerman

PATRIOT ACTS
Narratives of Post-9/11 Injustice
Compiled and edited by Alia Malek
Foreword by Karen Korematsu
"Important and timely." —Reza Aslan

NOWHERE TO BE HOME
Narratives from Survivors of Burma's Military Regime
Compiled and edited by Maggie Lemere and Zoë West
Foreword by Mary Robinson
"Extraordinary." —Asia Society

HOPE DEFERRED
Narratives of Zimbabwean Lives
Compiled and edited by Peter Orner and Annie Holmes
Foreword by Brian Chikwava
"*Hope Deferred* might be the most important publication to have come out of Zimbabwe in the last thirty years." —*Harper's Magazine*

OUT OF EXILE
Narratives from the Abducted and Displaced People of Sudan
Compiled and edited by Craig Walzer
Additional interviews and an introduction by Dave Eggers and Valentino Achak Deng
"Riveting." —*School Library Journal*

UNDERGROUND AMERICA
Narratives of Undocumented Lives
Compiled and edited by Peter Orner
Foreword by Luis Alberto Urrea
"No less than revelatory." —*Publishers Weekly*

VOICES FROM THE STORM
The People of New Orleans on Hurricane Katrina and Its Aftermath
Compiled and edited by Chris Ying and Lola Vollen
"*Voices from the Storm* uses oral history to let those who survived the hurricane tell their (sometimes surprising) stories." —*Independent* UK

SURVIVING JUSTICE
America's Wrongfully Convicted and Exonerated
Compiled and edited by Lola Vollen and Dave Eggers
Foreword by Scott Turow
"Real, raw, terrifying tales of 'justice.'" —*Star Tribune*

ABOUT HAYMARKET BOOKS

Haymarket Books is a radical, independent, nonprofit book publisher based in Chicago.

Our mission is to publish books that contribute to struggles for social and economic justice. We strive to make our books a vibrant and organic part of social movements and the education and development of a critical, engaged, international left.

We take inspiration and courage from our namesakes, the Haymarket martyrs, who gave their lives fighting for a better world. Their 1886 struggle for the eight-hour day—which gave us May Day, the international workers' holiday—reminds workers around the world that ordinary people can organize and struggle for their own liberation. These struggles continue today across the globe—struggles against oppression, exploitation, poverty, and war.

Since our founding in 2001, Haymarket Books has published more than five hundred titles. Radically independent, we seek to drive a wedge into the risk-averse world of corporate book publishing. Our authors include Noam Chomsky, Arundhati Roy, Rebecca Solnit, Angela Y. Davis, Howard Zinn, Amy Goodman, Wallace Shawn, Mike Davis, Winona LaDuke, Ilan Pappé, Richard Wolff, Dave Zirin, Keeanga-Yamahtta Taylor, Nick Turse, Dahr Jamail, David Barsamian, Elizabeth Laird, Amira Hass, Mark Steel, Avi Lewis, Naomi Klein, and Neil Davidson. We are also the trade publishers of the acclaimed Historical Materialism Book Series, of Dispatch Books, and of the Voice of Witness Book Series.